CW00519246

MARY BATCHELOR'S

EVERYDAY

BOOK

To Bobbie
with love
from
Mary
Christmas 2000

BY THE SAME AUTHOR

ABOUT HIGHLAND BOOKS

Find out more by downloading our catalogue from www.highlandbks.com. Readers who spot any errors of fact or grammar may wish to email us at errata@highlandbks.com. From time to time we will publish corrections at www.highlandbks.com /errata.

MARY BATCHELOR'S

EVERYDAY

BOOK

Highland Books

GODALMING
SURREY

First published as hardback in 1983 by Lion Publishing

Second paperback edition in 1984 by Lion Publishing

This third edition published in 2000 by Highland Books,
Two High Pines, Knoll Road, Godalming, Surrey GU7 2EP.

Copyright © 1983, 2000 Mary Batchelor

The right of Mary Batchelor to be identified as author of this work has
been asserted by her in accordance with the Copyright, Designs and
Patents Act 1988.

All rights reserved. No part of this publication may be reproduced or
transmitted in any form by any means, electronic or mechanical,
including photocopying, recording or any information storage and
retrieval system, without either prior permission in writing from the
publisher or a licence permitting restricted copying. In the United
Kingdom, such licences are issued by the Copyright Licensing Agency,
90 Tottenham Court Road, London WIP 9HE.

Unless otherwise noted, Scripture quotations are taken from the Revised
English Bible, Copyright © 1989 by Oxford University Press and Cambridge
Univesity Press.

Cover design by Mike Pinkney.

ISBN: 1 897913 54 0

Printed in Great Britain by Omnia Books Limited, Glasgow.

Here is the GOOD news

Every day we hear bad news on television and radio or read sad stories of human distress in the papers. Sometimes natural disasters have struck; more often human greed and folly have brought about war, homelessness, drought and famine. Cruelty and cunning, lust for power and lust for money bring suffering, misery and even death to innocent children and helpless adults. A diet of such bad news can easily make us grow disillusioned and cynical. We begin to lose hope for our world; we also feel guilty and inadequate because it seems that we can do so little to help.

But to think this way is to focus on only one half of the human story. Over the course of the past two millennia into our own day, there have always been men and women who have championed the weak, brought about reform and given courage and happiness to others by their life and example. They are strong witnesses to the fact that God is alive and at work in our world. This book tells some of their stories. It aims to provide, for every day of the year, a story that will help to redress the bad news that day may bring. Many of the men and women whose stories are told are people of faith – faith in God and in Jesus Christ. Others, perhaps unconsciously, have been touched by God's grace to bring justice and freedom to those around them. All have changed the course of history, to some extent, for good.

'All that is true, all that is noble, all that is just and pure, all that is lovable and attractive, whatever is excellent and admirable – fill your thoughts with these things.'

That was good advice in the first century and it is in the twenty-first century too.

So read on …

The Open Churches Trust was set up at the inspiration of Lord Lloyd Webber. He wants to reverse the growing trend to lock churches up and to encourage those responsible to keep more churches open. The Trust pioneered Celebration 2000 and invited schoolchildren to write a prayer for the millennium.

Millennium Prayer

When Mrs Crompton fetched Anna from school after tennis one day, she handed her daughter the letter that had come for her. When Anna opened it she had the shock of her life – *her* prayer had been chosen out of thousands of others to be the millennium prayer. She first heard about the project when her class was given a prayer to write for RE homework. She was thirteen at the time and a pupil at Ipswich High School. Her prayer was chosen to be submitted to the Trust, along with thousands of others across the country. Now she learned that it was to be the official millennium prayer, used in churches throughout the country on 1 January 2000.

On 2 January, when the BBC *Songs of Praise* was held at Cardiff Arms Park, Anna's prayer was sung, set to music by Andrew Lloyd Webber, using variations from his *Whistle down the Wind*. Anna was there among the huge crowd of 66,000, celebrating the good news of Jesus' coming in a new year, a new century and a new millennium.

Prayer for the Third Millennium

Dear Lord our heavenly Father,
At the dawn of a new millennium,
In a world of darkness give us your light,
In lands of war and prejudice grant us peace,
In a world of despair give us hope,
In a world of sadness and tears show us your joy,
In a world of hatred show us your love,
In a world of arrogance give us humility,
In a world of disbelief give us faith.
Give us courage to face the challenge of feeding the hungry,
    clothing the naked, housing the homeless and healing the sick.
Give us the power to make a difference in your world, and to
    protect your creation.
Through Jesus Christ, our Lord. Amen.

2 January

Sabine Baring-Gould, clergyman and author, died on 2 January 1924.

Keeping the hymn-book politically correct?

The Reverend Baring-Gould had a strange childhood to match his strange name. His father was an officer in the Indian cavalry, who found it impossible to settle down to a life of retirement in Devon. So he spent the rest of his years touring the spas and cities of Europe. His son Sabine never went to school but entered Clare College Cambridge and was ordained in the Church of England. He married a Yorkshire mill-girl half his age, who gave him five sons and nine daughters. His uncle was a rector in Devon and when he died in 1872 he left the living to Sabine, who lived out his days there as squire and parson of the village.

Sabine Baring-Gould wrote a sixteen-volume *Lives of the Saints* as well as novels; he also collected old Devon folk songs and composed hymns. His best-known hymn, *Onward Christian Soldiers,* was written specially for the Sunday School Whit Walk which was a regular feature in the North of England where he was living at the time. The hymn has been criticised in recent years for glorifying war, but Baring-Gould is stirring up enthusiasm for spiritual battle, against the forces of evil. Even in his own time, Baring-Gould was persuaded to change some of the words. The claim of the church that 'We are not divided' was changed by request to 'Though divisions harass' – a sad but probably realistic comment on the state of the church at the time.

More recently another of his hymns has caused problems. *Through the night of doubt and sorrow* is actually a translation from a Danish original. The story is told that during a rehearsal for a BBC radio service in the eighties, a woman preacher objected to the line: 'Brother clasps the hand of brother'. She suggested substituting 'Person clasps the hand of person,' but fortunately the new words were not accepted and the verse was omitted instead. What would Baring-Gould's wife and nine daughters have made of the fuss?

(Source: *The Penguin Book of Hymns* by Ian Bradley)

John Ronald Reuel Tolkien, South African-born philologist
and novelist, was born on 3 January 1892. He died in 1973.
J R R Tolkien was Professor of English at Oxford University for
over thirty years. He began to 'create' Middle Earth, the world of
The Hobbit and *Lord of the Rings*, many years before, during
World War I, when he was recovering from trench fever in a
military hospital.

An Inkling

'In a hole in the ground there lived a hobbit. Not a nasty, wet
hole, filled with the ends of worms and an oozy smell, nor yet
a dry, sandy hole with nothing in it to sit down on or eat: it was
a hobbit-hole, and that means comfort.'

The little group of men who met on Thursday evenings
in the shabby sitting-room at Magdalen College, settled down
to listen as Professor Tolkien began to read from his hand-
written manuscript. There were four or five of them there:
C S Lewis, in whose room they met, his brother, Warnie, Tolkien
himself and one or two others. They called themselves 'The
Inklings', a good name for people with glimmerings of ideas
set down in ink. Any of the others who had written a new
poem or story would read it out to the rest.

They listened delightedly as Tolkien read on about Bilbo
Baggins, Gandalf the wizard and Gollum, in his strange
underground world. When, in due course, *The Hobbit* was
published, Lewis wrote a glowing review: 'No common recipe
for children's books will give you creatures so rooted in their
own soil and history as those of Prof. Tolkien – who obviously
knows much more about them than he needs for this book.'

Lewis spoke truly. Soon the Inklings were listening to
what they called 'the new Hobbit.' *Lord of the Rings* took eleven
years to write, because every detail of history, geography and
language was as carefully recorded as if it actually existed.
Tolkien created his own new world. 'It's more than good,' was
Lewis's verdict. 'The only word I can use is great.'

'But how the public will take it, I can't imagine,' his brother
added.

---

4 January

Louis Braille was born near Paris on 4 January 1809. Blind from the age of three, he became an educationist and invented a form of raised-point writing which could be read and written by blind people.

Tragedy at Coupvray

The saddler's sign had hung outside the workshop of the Braille family in the village of Coupvray for more than a century. Louis's grandfather had started the business. As a very small boy, Louis would watch his father cut and trim the leather for saddles and harnesses.

One day, the workshop was empty and the child went in. The curved blade of the saddler's knife gleamed temptingly and Louis grasped it with his small hands, trying to cut the leather as his father did. But the knife slipped and the blade pierced his eye. The doctor could not save the eye; but worse followed. The eye became infected and the infection spread to the other eye. Soon Louis was totally blind.

His father determined to help him to learn. The village priest – who had once been a Benedictine monk – taught him the Christian faith and the village schoolmaster did what he could to help. The story goes that his father took a piece of wood and drove in upholsterer's nails to form the letters of the alphabet, so that Louis could learn their shape by touch.

Some years before, in Paris, Valentin Hauy had been sickened by the sight of a group of ragged, blind musicians, exhibited at a fair for the amusement of the crowd. To be blind meant to be illiterate, the butt of others' ridicule. Hauy determined to educate them and eventually founded a school in Paris. When Louis Braille was ten years old, he won a scholarship to go and study there. He set off on the twenty-mile journey from Coupvray, determined to learn all he could.

5 January is the Feast Day of **St Simeon the Stylite**, who died in 459. Simeon, the son of a shepherd, lived at a time of luxury and self-indulgence. He set an example, by his simple, self-denying way of life and his love for others. He was nicknamed 'Stylites' – from the Greek word for pillar. The base of his pillar can still be seen amid ruins in Syria.

Climb to holiness

For many years Simeon was an anchorite, living in a remote place. But people flocked to see him, seeking his advice and asking for his prayers. The life of quiet and solitude that he desired seemed impossible. He had no time or privacy for his personal prayer and meditation. So he went to the desert to get away from the crowds and built a pillar on which to live, to lift him above human contact. At first the pillar was not very high but as time went by he found it necessary to keep adding to the pillar until he was sixty feet above the ground.

His attempts to rise above it all failed completely. Simeon became a talking point and more and more pilgrims – from the emperor down – flocked to gaze at the saint and ask his advice. But Simeon seems to have been kind and compassionate. Although he longed for solitude, he was sympathetic and ready to give help to all who came to him. Many became Christians through his loving words.

Fifth century collect

Bless all who worship thee,
From the rising of the sun
Unto the going down of the same
Of thy goodness, give us;
With thy love, inspire us;
By thy spirit, guide us;
By thy power, protect us;
In thy mercy, receive us;
Now and always.

6 January

Joan of Arc was born on 6 January 1412. She was born to well-off peasants in Donremy, on the borders of Lorraine and Champagne. At seventeen she ran away from home in obedience to her 'voices'. They told her to relieve the English siege of Rouen and to have the Dauphin of France crowned in Rheims Cathedral. For a while she was brilliantly successful.

'My Voices'

A saint? A witch? A patriot? A feminist? A martyr of conscience? Certainly 'one of the most remarkable women of all time' as one biographer claims.

In surviving witness statements Joan and the men and women who knew or encountered her tell their own story. Joan testified to the voices she first heard as a child of thirteen, and the bright light that accompanied them. She became certain that God was speaking to her, through St Michael, then through St Margaret and St Catherine.

Her voices told her to live a good life, then to leave home and go 'to the help of the King of France.' She still went regularly to Mass and lived the life of a good Catholic. She remained chaste and maintained that although she had led men into battle she herself had never killed anyone.

Witnesses described Joan as a simple country girl. One said:'Apart from the matter of war she was simple and ignorant ... But in the matter of warfare ... she behaved as if she had been the shrewdest captain in the world.'

Joan cleaned up the army. She forbade swearing, allowed no looting and sent the women camp followers packing. She also showed pity to prisoners. But she never considered herself specially holy. When admiring women brought her objects to touch, she laughed and told them that that their own touch would be just as effective. But others recognised her goodness. Even the secretary to the English king said, after her death, 'We are all lost, for we have burnt a good and holy person'.

(Source: *Joan of Arc* by Régine Pernoud)

Gladys Aylward died at the beginning of January 1970.
Once a Cockney parlourmaid, she was turned down by
missionary societies so saved enough money to travel to China
alone. In 1930, after an incredible journey through Siberia and
Japan, she joined Jeannie Lawson in remote Yangcheng.
Together they opened an inn, where they told Bible stories.

'Here's me!'

The bedroom was plainly furnished, with washstand, basin and
jug. Gladys, the new maid, sat on the edge of her bed and
surveyed her small store of belongings: a Bible, a *Daily Light*
book of devotional readings, and about three and a half old
pence. It seemed impossible to think of going to China, yet
she was absolutely certain that God had told her to go there
and tell the people there about him. She could not pass exams;
the missionary societies did not think she should go, but still
she knew that she must. She laid out her few possessions, put
her hand on them and prayed.

'O God. Here's me. Here's my Bible. Here's my money.
Use us, God. Use us!'

'Gladys!' a voice was calling. The mistress wanted her and
Gladys hurried downstairs.

'I want to pay your fare here,' the lady of the house
explained.

When Gladys returned to her room, she had ten times
more than when she had prayed a few minutes before. Of
course God could send her the money if he wanted her to go!
She would begin to save in earnest.

8 January

Galíleo Galílei, astronomer, died on 8 January 1642. Galileo, born in Pisa in 1564, was famous first for his invention of the thermometer, his experiments in physics and mechanics and his improvement of the telescope. Astronomy was to become his abiding passion.

The starry messenger

Unfriendly critics were surprised that Galileo could see anything through his new telescope, even though it magnified objects 1,000 times. But Galileo, peering determinedly through it to view the night sky, discovered amazing things. For the first time it was possible to see mountains and valleys on the moon and the shadow cast by sunlight. He discovered 'a myriad of stars planted together in clusters' – what we now know as the Milky Way.

One night in 1610, Galileo was looking at Jupiter and saw three tiny stars – two to the left and one to the right of the planet. Next night all three could be seen to the right. Since they moved, he knew that they could not be stars but must be satellites in orbit round Jupiter. He believed too that the Polish astronomer Copernicus was right and that the earth moved round the sun.

Galileo wrote a book – *The Starry Messenger* – telling of his findings. His first readers found his conclusions startling, and shocking too. The church considered herself to be the guardian of all knowledge and the church maintained that the earth stood still, at the very centre of God's universe. To think otherwise was blasphemy.

In vain Galileo protested that he was a staunch and true Christian. He was branded a heretic and sentenced to house arrest. His later years were dogged by opposition, personal tragedy and blindness. Although he was forced to recant and say that the earth did not move round the sun, Galileo's dying words were said to be, 'Yet it still moves.'

Postscript: It was not until the 1990s that a papal decree formally absolved Galileo of heresy and acknowledged the church's error.

On 9 January 1845 David Livingstone, missionary and explorer,
married **Mary Moffatt**, herself the daughter of pioneer
missionaries in the South African interior.

'The best spoke in the wheel'

Mary's third son was born on the banks of the Zouga river,
under the shade of a thorn tree. The father suggested
enthusiastically that the new baby be called Zouga, but, he
wrote reluctantly, 'the mother rebelled.'

Mary's mother thought it both dangerous and indelicate
for Livingstone to take his family with him on his explorations.
She wrote: 'O Livingstone, what do you mean?… A pregnant
woman with three little children trailing about with a company
of the other sex, through the wilds of Africa, among savage
men and beasts!' But Mary willingly went and she and her
small children waited by the wagons while Livingstone and
his companion pressed on further and heard for the first time
the far-off roar of 'The Smoke That Thunders,' – which he would
later rename the Victoria Falls, in honour of their queen.

At last, worn out with child-bearing and anxious over the
well-being of their small children, Mary agreed to go back to
Britain for a while, leaving her husband free to explore
unhindered.

Her time in Scotland and England was miserable in the
extreme. She had never lived in Britain before and struggled
to make ends meet. After her husband's return for a short
while – famous and lionised in society – she resolved that
when he returned to Africa she would join him there. But not
long after their reunion, at the age of forty-one, she died of
fever. Livingstone was devastated and remorseful. He had
described her as 'a little black-haired girl, sturdy and all I want
and always the best spoke in the wheel.'

*'Take me O Lord as I am and make me what thou wouldst have
me be.'* – Prayer found among Mary's papers.

(Source: *Wives of Fame* by Edna Healey)

10 January

In January 1881 *the Whitby crew of the Royal National Lifeboat Association* carried out an incredible rescue. The RNLI marked 175 years of saving life at sea in 2000. Lifeboats are manned by voluntary crews who set out in any weather and all conditions to rescue 'those in peril on the sea'. The RNLI is maintained entirely by voluntary contributions.

Overland to sea

It was January 1881 and bitterly cold on the North East coast of England. Snow had been falling and now lay deep. A blizzard was blowing. On that day, the *Life-boat* for 1882 records, an incredible rescue took place. The report states: Whitby 'A telegram was received at about 10.30am stating that a ship had sunk about six miles southward of this port, and that the crew had been compelled to take to their boat and come to anchor. A message was sent in reply to say that the life-boat *Robert Whitworth* should at once proceed there by road, and requesting that she might be met by men and horses, a gang of men being also despatched to cut the snow in front, which in places was six or seven feet deep. With the help jointly rendered by men and horses from both directions, the Life-boat was got to the scene of the disaster in little more than two hours, and was immediately launched.'

On August Bank Holiday Sunday morning in 1999, a sponsored re-enactment of this famous rescue took place. Coastguards, lifeboat crews and volunteers set off from Whitby using, as far as possible, the equipment available in 1881. Holding the boat back, on the final drop down to the sea, and manoeuvring the hair-pin bends was difficult and dangerous. In spite of good weather and the absence of bitter cold and blanketing snow, the operation took not two but nine hours!

All the publicity material for the RNLI's 175th celebrations bore a picture of **Henry Freeman**, the coxswain of the lifeboat *Robert Whitworth*, the man who led the rescue 'pull' in the raging blizzard in January 1881.

In peril on the sea

When the exhausted crew finally arrived at Robin Hood's Bay, and launched their boat, their efforts were only just beginning. The record runs: 'After pulling for an hour the steer oar and six other oars were broken, and she had to return to shore for a fresh supply. A double crew then manned the boat, and with a cheer she was again launched through terrific seas. After struggling for an hour and a half, the shipwrecked crew of six men was reached, and safely landed at four o'clock. The poor fellows were thoroughly exhausted and benumbed, and it was only with great difficulty that they were brought back to consciousness, with the help of the medical men who were at hand ready to receive them. The Life-boat crew also suffered severely; one of them was so exhausted that he could not for some time go home'.

The incredible understatement of the report increases admiration and respect for the courage and endurance as well as the teamwork of men ready to face death themselves in order to save the lives of others.

Lifeboat magazine 2000 'The RNLI exists to save lives at sea'. Lifeboats launch sixteen times a day on average. Every day, at least four people are saved.

> Oh Trinity of love and power
> Our brothers shield in danger's hour
> From rock and tempest, fire and foe
> Protect them whereso'er they go.
> Thus evermore shall rise to thee
> Glad hymns of praise from land and sea.
>
> William Whiting 1825-78

12 January

When Japan invaded China in 1940, **Gladys Aylward** led a hundred children to safety on an epic journey. A Hollywood film, *Inn of the Sixth Happiness,* told her story – with a little added glamour.

God is still God

Gladys Aylward sat on the bank of the Yellow River, in despair. She had trekked over the mountain from her home town of Yangcheng, in charge of more than a hundred children and teenagers, escaping from the fast-advancing Japanese armies. It had been unbelievably hard. The small children had grown tired and fretful, and they often had to beg to get enough food. Somehow Gladys had kept them going, carrying the little ones, singing to keep their spirits up, longing for the time when they would arrive at the river and cross over to greater safety.

Now they had been at the banks of the river for two nights. All the boats were safely moored on the other side, where no Japanese could commandeer them. There was no possible way to get her charges across.

'Why doesn't God open the Yellow River like he did the Red Sea for Moses?' one teenager asked Gladys.

'That was a long time ago,' she replied, 'and I'm not Moses.'

'But God is still God,' the girl persisted.

She was right, of course, and Gladys prayed again, imploring God to meet their need. Then she lay down exhausted. But she was soon stirred to action by the excited cries of the children. A Chinese Nationalist officer was approaching. He asked her some questions about the forlorn crowd of refugees, then promised, 'I'll get a boat for you.'

He went to the water's edge and whistled. In response, a boat pulled away from the opposite shore and made its way towards them. The children were rowed across in relays. Yes, God *was* still God!

13 January

George Fox, founder of the Society of Friends (the Quakers) died on 13 January, 1691. *'Justice Bennett of Derby was the first that called us Quakers, because I bid them tremble at the word of the Lord. That was in the year 1650.'* – George Fox

A faith to live by

Young George Fox would not be satisfied. He was disgusted by the empty, outward form of religion in his day. He determined to find a faith that he could live by. He went to London but none of the preachers there seemed to help him. The ministers around Fenny Drayton, in Warwickshire, where he lived, were no better. One advised him to cheer himself up with psalms and tobacco. Then he quoted George's private conversations with him in his sermons. Another one flew into a rage because George accidentally trod on his flower-bed.

Later George Fox wrote: 'When my hopes in them and in all men were gone, so that I had nothing outwardly to help me, nor could tell what to do, then, oh then, I heard a voice which said, "There is one, even Christ Jesus, who can speak to their condition", and when I heard it, my heart did leap for joy.'

One day, when Fox was travelling through Lancashire, preaching his new-found faith, he saw the strange hump of Pendle Hill. 'I was moved by God to go atop of it,' he recounted. 'There, atop of the hill… the Lord let me see in which places he had a great people to be gathered.'

True to the vision, Fox began to find a great band of followers, others who shared his dissatisfaction with the religion of the day. They, like him, were prepared to face persecution, imprisonment and the confiscation of their goods, in order to live by the faith they had found.

'Be patterns, be examples in all countries, places, islands, nations, wherever you come, that your carriage and life may preach among all sorts of people, and to them; then you will come to walk cheerfully over the world, answering that of God in everyone.' – George Fox

14 January

Albert Schweitzer, musician, theologian, philosopher and medical missionary from Alsace, was born on 14 January 1875. Schweitzer was a brilliant polymath. In 1896 he decided to live for science and art until he was thirty, then devote the rest of his life to serving humanity.

The debt we owe to others

Albert Schweitzer could have chosen any one of many professions in which to excel. Instead, he decided to set up a hospital in Lambarene, a deserted mission station in French Equatorial Africa, in order to fight the prevalent diseases of leprosy and sleeping sickness. He was awarded the Nobel peace prize in 1952 and many people regarded him as a saint and hero. His beliefs were based on 'reverence for life.'

In later years – he lived to be ninety – he was criticised for his paternalism and refusal to move with the times. Conditions on his station were a far cry from the sterile cleanliness of modern hospitals.

Schweitzer was keenly aware of how much he owed to many others who had passed on to him something of their own qualities and virtues. He wrote:

> 'One other thing stirs me when I look back on my youthful days, the fact that so many people gave me something or were something to me without knowing it. Such people entered into my life and became powers within me. We all live spiritually by what others have given us in the significant hours of our life. Much that has become our own in gentleness, modesty, kindness, willingness to forgive, in veracity, loyalty, resignation under suffering, we owe to people in whom we have seen these virtues at work.
>
> 'If we had before us those who have been thus a blessing to us and could tell them how it came about, they would be amazed to learn what had passed over from their life to ours.'

(Source: *Schweitzer, Hero of Africa* by Robert Payne)

Martin Luther King Jr was born on 15 January 1929.
He is remembered and honoured not only for championing the
cause of black Americans, but for refusing to use violence.

'My feet hurt!'

Mrs Rosa Parks had done a hard day's work at the sewing factory, as well as shopping for her family. She was thankful to sink down into the seat of the bus that would carry her home to Montgomery, Alabama. She had been careful to sit near the back, in the section reserved for black people, according to the rules laid down by the Montgomery City Bus Line.

At the next stop, more people climbed on and the driver ordered Mrs Parks to give up her seat to a white passenger. Rosa Parks usually did as she was told, but, as she later said, 'I was just plain tired and my feet hurt.' She sat tight. The driver called the police and Mrs Parks was arrested and taken to the courthouse.

It was the last straw for the black population of Montgomery. Not only were black people segregated and made to give up seats to whites, but they had to pay their fare at the front of the bus, then get off and enter by the back door. Often the bus would drive off while they made their way to the back, leaving passengers who had paid their fare stranded in the road. And this kind of treatment on the buses was only one example of the racial discrimination that they experienced in every part of life.

A bus boycott was suggested. No black person would travel by bus until the authorities changed their laws. Martin Luther King, the young black minister, led the protest – first with prayers, then with action. It was December 1955 and the great civil rights movement had been launched.

'He who passively accepts evil is as much involved in it as he who helps to perpetuate it.' – Martin Luther King Jr.

---

16 January

Martin Luther King Jr.

Innocent victim

Since Dr Martin Luther King had begun to lead the non-violent movement for black rights, he had frequently been arrested on trumped-up charges. The sentence was prison or a fine and eager friends had always paid the fine. But on one occasion Dr King decided to go to prison instead. This is part of his statement to the judge:

'Your Honour, you have no doubt rendered a decision which you believe to be just and right. Yet I must reiterate that I am innocent ... I have been the victim of police brutality for no reason ... In spite of this I hold no animosity or bitterness in my heart towards the officers ... These men, like all too many of our white brothers, are the victims of an environment blighted with more than three hundred years of man's inhumanity to man as expressed in slavery and segregation...

'Last night my wife and I talked and prayed over the course of action that I should take ... It was our conclusion that I could not in all good conscience pay a fine for an act that I did not commit and above all for brutal treatment that I did not deserve...

'I also make this decision because of my deep concern for the injustices and indignities that my people continue to experience ... Last month in Mississippi a sheriff, who was pointed out by four eyewitnesses as the man who beat a Negro to death with a blackjack, was freed in twenty-three minutes. At this very moment, in this State, James Wilson sits in the death house, condemned to death for stealing less than two dollars... The Negro can no longer silently endure ... because we are commanded to resist evil by God that created us all ... The time has come when perhaps only the willing and non-violent acts of suffering by the innocent can arouse this nation to wipe out the scourge of brutality and violence inflicted upon Negroes who seek only to walk with dignity before God and man.'

(Source: *My Life with Martin Luther King* by Coretta King)

Catherine Booth, wife of William Booth and joint founder of the Salvation Army, was born on 17 January 1829. Catherine Mumford grew up in a devout Methodist family. At 17 she wept and prayed night and day until she felt assured of her salvation. When she married William Booth, she brought her own ideals and gifts to the marriage and later to the founding of the Salvation Army. Her views on women's status had far-reaching results.

'My dear sir!...

In 1846, aged seventeen, Catherine Mumford wrote to her minister:

> 'Excuse me, my dear sir, ... in your discourse on Sunday morning ... your remarks appeared to imply the doctrine of women's intellectual and even moral inferiority to man ... Permit me, my dear sir, to ask whether you have ever made the subject of women's equality as a *being*, the matter of calm investigation and thought?'

Ten years later, when she was married with a family, she wrote a pamphlet entitled *Female Ministry*, in which she put forward the case for women preachers. At the time she had no desire to preach herself, but later felt compelled by God to do so. Accordingly she stood up one Sunday at the end of morning service in the Methodist Chapel where William was minister, and confessed that up to then she had been disobedient to God's call to preach. In spite of some personal misgivings, Booth recognised the validity of her call. He immediately followed her public confession by announcing her as the preacher for that very evening's service.

Owing, no doubt, to Catherine's courage and convictions – and her excellent preaching – the Salvation Army has always recognised God's call to women and men, equally, to preach and teach God's word.

'If God has given her the ability, why should not woman persuade the vacillating, instruct and console the penitent, and pour out her soul in prayer for sinners?' – Catherine Booth, writing to William in 1885

(Source: *Catherine Booth* by Catherine Bramwell-Booth)

---

18 January

On 18 January 1778 **Captain James Cook** first sighted the Hawaiian islands. James Cook was born in Yorkshire in 1728, became a shopkeeper's apprentice in the fishing village of Staithes, then was apprenticed to a master mariner in Whitby. In 1755 he joined the Royal Navy and quickly gained recognition as a first-class surveyor and captain.

A captain who cared

Everyone knew what caused the terrible disease that decimated crews but captains took no action. On his first long voyage Cook witnessed the death of twenty-six men – nearly all from scurvy – and when they docked, more had to be taken to hospital. A six week voyage was enough to cause the first signs of the disease. Teeth dropped out, skin became blotchy, then came a weakness ending in death. All for the lack of vitamin C.

When Cook set out on the *Resolution* in July 1772 the voyage lasted three years and eighteen days, 'In which I lost but four men and one only of them by sickness,' Cook was able to report. He insisted that his men ate fresh fruit and vegetables and when they were not obtainable, the sauerkraut they disliked. Wherever they landed, Cook aimed to take fruit and vegetables on board along with fresh water. His successful tactics were later followed world-wide.

Cleanliness was another of Cook's obsessions, absolutely necessary for the health of his reluctant crew. He insisted that clothes were washed frequently and decks kept scrupulously cleaned. The whole ship was aired and kept as fresh as possible. Some of the sailors had brought pet monkeys on board but when their droppings became offensive Cook ordered the monkeys overboard. 'The captain paid more attention to the health of his people than to the lives of a few monkies [sic].' They grumbled, but his men loved him and when Captain Cook met his death, his grief-stricken crew cried, 'We have lost our father! Our father is gone!'

(Source: *Captain James Cook* by Richard Hough)

19 January

On 19 January 1917 an explosion occurred in an East London munitions factory, causing 450 casualties, including 69 dead. *Cadets from the Salvation Army Training College* were some of the first on the scene to help in the aftermath of the explosion.

First on the scene

Many of those cadets – or students – were never to forget the harrowing experiences of that January night and of the days that followed. Catherine Bramwell-Booth, grand-daughter of William Booth, was a tutor at the college and wrote afterwards:

'Many things about our experiences on the scene of the disaster will never be forgotten. Danger, and death, and desolation, were seen in some of their most hideous forms ... Who could forget the flaming sky throwing into dark relief the ruined homes on all sides, the dumb despair of the people, the crushed and scorched bodies lying in the mortuaries...

'Ever since those days I have been asking myself: "What is the Salvation Army doing for those people and their like?..." But for the disaster that overtook them, the majority of those families would hardly have come in touch with a Salvationist.

'Surely no such disaster should be necessary to discover to us, as this one did, the old man of seventy-odd who lived alone with his two cats ... How he escaped with his life was a miracle ... He was the last to leave that street and sat in the midst of his ruined home three days and three nights after the people had left, a helpless heap of human misery ... But think if the [Salvation] Army could have found him *before* and made him understand that there was still someone in the world to care.'

Catherine was prepared to change her methods in any way so as to spur on her Salvation Army students to relieve distress and bring the good news of salvation to the inner cities of the land.

(Source: *Catherine Bramwell-Booth* by Mary Batchelor)

20 January

John Howard, prison reformer, died on 20 January 1790. The Howard League for Penal Reform, formed in 1907, was named after John Howard. The charity researches and works actively on a wide range of criminal justice issues such as suicides in custody, drugs in prison, mothers and babies in prison and children in the penal system. In the year 2000 it set up the country's first Centre for Penal Reform.

The state of the prisons

When John Howard paid his first visit to Bedford gaol he was horrified. He had not known that anything so degrading and inhumane existed.

Howard was born in 1726, in Hackney, London, the son of prosperous middle-class parents, so when he was apprenticed to a London wholesale grocery firm he could afford his own apartment, servants and two horses. But he was hardly fortunate in love and marriage. His first wife died two years after their marriage, and his second wife died in childbirth, leaving him to bring up their little son.

John Howard inherited considerable wealth and was able to live the life of a country gentleman in Bedfordshire. He was a model landlord and although he was a nonconformist he was made High Sheriff of Bedfordshire. As such he was responsible for the county gaol. He visited it and was appalled by what he saw.

He decided to travel around the other counties of England looking for a prison that would provide a model for Bedford to follow. He was allowed to visit cells, dungeons and torture chambers and to talk to the gaolers, turnkeys and even the prisoners themselves. He was deeply distressed to find in all the prisons conditions as dreadful as in Bedford. He reported that in Ely 'because of the insecurity of the old prison the gaoler chained the victims down on their backs on the floor, across which were placed several iron bars, with an iron collar with spikes about their necks and a heavy iron bar over their legs.' Howard was determined to take action.

On 21 January 1952, the Bethlehem Chief of Police, two archaeologists and two soldiers from the Arab Legion took possession of the Dead Sea caves and their rich hoard of documents. *The Dead Sea scrolls*, which document life in a Jewish religious community, also throw light on Bible records. Some contain the earliest known examples of Biblical texts.

Hidden treasure

Muhammed the Wolf was looking after goats down by the shores of the Dead Sea. The water was dull blue and the hills around yellow, brown and deep purple. The whole scene was lifeless and Muhammad, a teenage Bedouin, was bored. He climbed listlessly up the cliff to rescue a stray goat, and noticed a cave that he did not remember having seen before. Idly he picked up a stone and tossed it into the mouth of the cave.

A moment later he heard the sound of something shattering within the cave. Terrified, he took to his heels, returning later to explore the mystery with a friend for company. They clambered into the cave and there discovered some tall clay jars. It was one of these that had been broken by Muhammad's stone. When they took off the lids there was a nasty smell coming from some dark long lumps within the jars. They carried the oblong lumps outside to look at them in the daylight, and found that they were lengths of linen coated with pitch. Inside these wraps were manuscripts, sewn together and covered with strange writing. The boys decided to keep their finds and sell them on their next trip to Bethlehem.

Many months and many adventures later, the true value of these manuscripts was recognised. The Dead Sea Scrolls, as they are called, contain much of the Old Testament in copies dating from 1,000 years earlier than any manuscripts previously found. But many years of patient piecing together and deciphering have been necessary to yield their full treasure.

22 January

Lead kindly light

The year was 1833 and midsummer sun beat down on the stifling deck as the boat lay becalmed not far from the coast of Sicily where Newman had embarked. He sat on deck, pining for the breeze that would carry the cargo boat on its way to Marseilles and thence home to England. He had been travelling in southern Italy when he had fallen sick with a severe viral illness. He had survived, though he was still weak and longing to reach home.

But John Henry Newman had more than his physical health to concern him. He was anxious and disturbed by the direction that his thoughts and feelings were taking. He had been brought up in a wealthy evangelical Christian home and had done brilliantly at Oxford. When he was ordained, he had moved away from his roots to the Anglo-Catholic wing of the church. In June 1833 he was still struggling with his doubts. As he waited for the wind to set them on their way, he wrote the hymn *Lead kindly light*. It expresses his uncertainty of the way ahead but also confirms his trust that God *will* show him the way forward.

Newman did not write the verses as a hymn but they were set to music and became a Victorian top of the pops, appearing in Roman Catholic, Anglican and Nonconformist hymnbooks. It was a special favourite of Queen Victoria and the verses were read out to her as she lay dying at Osborne House in 1901.

> Lead kindly light, amid the encircling gloom,
>   Lead thou me on;
> The night is dark and I am far from home
>   Lead thou me on.
> Keep thou my feet, I do not ask to see
> The distant scene; one step enough for me.

23 January

On 23 January 1850, *the inhabitants of Pitcairn* celebrated the sixtieth anniversary of their landing on the island.

Thursday October Christian

In 1814, the British ship *Tagus* discovered an island not marked on the charts. To their amazement, a canoe from the island drew alongside their ship and they were hailed in English.

'Who are you?' the captain asked.

'Thursday October Christian,' the young man replied.

He and his companion were taken on board to breakfast with the captain. Before eating, 'they both rose and one of them pronounced in a pleasing tone, "For what we are going to receive, the Lord make us truly thankful."'

Explanations soon followed. In 1790, Fletcher Christian and his fellow mutineers had landed on this tiny island after setting their rightful captain, William Bligh, adrift with some of his crew in the ship's longboat. On Pitcairn they felt safe from the long arm of the law and hoped to spend happy and peaceful days in their new Eden.

Plenty went wrong. The record of the months that followed their landing tell of treachery, murder, drunkenness and conspiracy. After three years, only four white men survived and none of the coloured partners and helpers they took with them.

So how had these young men learned their courteous manners and Christian ways? Two Bibles had been brought ashore by the mutineers. They had caused the transformation.

Postscript: Fletcher Christian gave his son his unusual name because he had been born on a Thursday in October. Later, they realised that since they had crossed the international date-line to reach Pitcairn, he should have been Friday October. They tried to change his name but the old one stuck.

24 January

William Barclay died on 24 January 1978. William Barclay was a Scottish theologian and minister, a writer and broadcaster. He was a parish minister for thirteen years then returned to academic life. He became professor of Divinity and Biblical Criticism at Glasgow University.

'Plain truth for plain people'

William Barclay was an outstanding scholar but he is best known and loved for making the Bible come alive for his readers. The pages of his commentaries are packed with stories – from history, the classics or everyday life – which bring the meaning of the text alive.

One story, from his own experience, describes a train journey from England to Scotland. As William Barclay looked out of the window he noticed a whitewashed cottage, gleaming and spotless against the brown fields around. A week later he made the return journey and looked out for the little white house again. But now it looked very different. During the week heavy snow had fallen. The house that had looked so sparkling white now appeared dingy and drab against the pristine whiteness of the surrounding snow-covered fields. That, said William Barclay, is like us. We may seem good, clean-living people compared with others, but alongside the pure goodness of Jesus, we see ourselves as we truly are, sinners before God, needing *his* cleansing.

'Because I need simple things myself, I can talk simply to others,' – William Barclay

25 January marks the conversion of **St Paul** in the church calendar.
In his early days Paul was known as Saul, the Jewish form of his name.

Damascus road experience

The midday sun was burning down as Paul and his companions pressed wearily on towards Damascus. Once there, Paul's papers, signed by the religious authorities in Jerusalem, would give him licence to dispose of a few more troublesome followers of Jesus.

Suddenly, a light more brilliant and blinding than the noonday sun struck Paul full in the face. He dropped to the ground, blinded and overpowered in mind and body.

As he lay there, trembling and silent, he heard a voice say:

'Saul, why are you persecuting me?'

Memories of Christian men and women, young and old, carried off to prison by his orders, flashed through Paul's mind. They had not cursed or struggled but had gone to their death calmly and with courage. He felt sure that it was Jesus, their Lord, who was speaking to him now:

'Who are you, Lord?' he asked.

'I am Jesus,' the answer came, 'the one you are persecuting.'

The Christians Paul had tried to silence had been telling the truth. Jesus, their Master, really was alive. Humbly he asked,

'What do you want me to do, Lord?'

'First go into the city,' he was told.

Dazed and still blind, Paul got to his feet and his servants led him by the hand into Damascus. After three days Ananias, a Christian in the city sent to him by God, baptised Paul and restored his sight. His single-minded ambition was to serve and obey Jesus, his Lord. With many adventures and much hardship, he was to travel throughout the Roman Empire, to take the good news of Jesus far and wide.

(Source: *Acts 9; 22; 26*)

26 January

Edward Jenner, physician, discoverer of vaccination, died on 26 January 1823.

Cuckoo lore

For centuries country folk had known that cuckoos used other birds to hatch their eggs for them. But who sent the original fledglings packing? Jenner determined to find out. He could take all the time in the world, for life moved at a leisurely pace in his country practice. His wife was busy with her Sunday School – one of the first to be founded – but she provided a relaxed Christian home which was the ideal setting for his investigations into medicine and nature study.

Jenner wrote up his findings:

17 June – 'Saw a hedgesparrow's nest at Mr Bromedge's with two hedgesparrows in it just hatched, two eggs not hatched and a cuckoo just hatched.

18 June – 'In the morning early there were four hedge-sparrows and the young cuckoo in it. About noon it contained the cuckoo and one hedgesparrow only and at night the cuckoo was left alone in the nest.

'The nest was placed so near the extremity of the hedge that I could distinctly see what was going forward in it; to my astonishment saw the young cuckoo though so newly hatched in the act of turning out the young hedgesparrow.'

Jenner had observed that the cuckoo himself was the villain of the piece. But he was meticulous in checking his evidence. Only after repeated observations did he submit a paper to the Royal Society. He was elected a Fellow of the Royal Society later that year. The doctor who later was to begin to rid the world of smallpox also solved one of the tantalising puzzles of the bird world.

Frost Fairs were held on the frozen River Thames in January.
A Frost Fair began on the Thames on 14 January 1205 and
another in 1814. With global warming and the heat generated by
present-day traffic, the Thames could never freeze hard enough
to bear weight safely. The days of Frost Fairs are past.

Mixed blessings

John Evelyn, who lived from 1620 to 1706, was wealthy and
well-connected. He held many important posts, was often at
the court of Charles II and had much to do with the rebuilding
of St Paul's Cathedral. He is described as honest, intelligent
and God-fearing. He is best remembered for his *Diary*, covering
the years 1641-1706, which was discovered in 1817 in an old
clothes basket at the family home.

Frost Fair in January 1694
'The frost still continuing more and more severe,
the Thames before London was planted with
booths in formal streets, as in a city or continual
fair, all sorts of trades and shops furnished, and
full of commodities, even to a printing press,
where the people and ladies took a fancy to have
their name printed and the day and year set
down, when printed on the Thames. This
humour took so universally that 'twas estimated
the printer gained five pound a day, for printing
one line only, at sixpence a name.

'Coaches now plied from Westminster to the
Temple … as in the streets; also on sleds, sliding
with skates. There was bull-baiting, horse and
coach races, puppet plays and interludes … so as
it seemed to be a carnival upon the water, whilst
it was a severe judgement on the land; the trees
not only splitting as if lightning-struck, but men
and cattle perishing in divers places and the very
seas so locked up with ice, that no vessels could
stir out or come in.'

28 January

Henry Stanley, journalist and explorer, was born in Wales on 28 January 1841. Stanley, born illegitimate, sailed as a cabin boy to New Orleans and was adopted by a merchant named Stanley. He served in the Confederate army and US navy then became a journalist. He travelled widely as a correspondent for the *New York Herald*. In 1869 he received the instruction 'Find Livingstone.'

'How I found Livingstone'

David Livingstone was sick at heart. He was almost within reach of the lakes he hoped to find, when a terrible massacre in the town where he was staying put paid to his plans. Despairing, Livingstone moved back to Ujiji. He was skeleton-thin and without money or supplies.

'I felt as if I were the man going down from Jerusalem to Jericho, but no Good Samaritan would come my way,' he wrote.

But he was wrong. Henry Stanley (having first stopped to report on the opening of the Suez Canal) was on his way. He arrived at Ujiji on 10 November 1871, to the sound of gun salutes and beating drums. Livingstone came out of the house to see what the noise was about, then waited for Stanley under a large mango tree near the lake.

'Dr Livingstone, I presume,' Stanley said, as he alighted from his horse.

Livingstone replied gravely, 'Yes, that is my name.'

They talked endlessly but Livingstone was too polite to ask Stanley what had brought him to Ujiji. 'It was not my business,' he said. He waited patiently for a chance to open the long-delayed mail that Stanley had delivered. When at last he opened the letters he found that the government had voted £1,000 for his relief.

Stanley returned to give the world his story. He was captivated by Livingstone – 'a Christian gentleman,' he pronounced. He wrote about his experiences in his best-seller, *How I Found Livingstone*.

Viscount Tonypandy (George Thomas) was born on 29 January 1909. George Thomas grew up in a Welsh mining village and was able to stay on at school through the sacrifice of his brother and widowed mother. When he retired from the House of Commons in June 1983, members of all parties acknowledged his fine leadership and example and hailed him as one of the great Speakers in Parliament's history. George Thomas was never ashamed to confess that his Christian faith was the key to his actions in every part of his life.

A halfpenny bottle of milk

'What did you have for breakfast?' George Thomas asked anxiously as he bent over the boy who had fainted during class. The boy opened his eyes; 'Nothing,' he said, 'I never have breakfast, we can't afford it.' The year was 1932 and these were the days of the Depression. George Thomas, newly qualified school teacher, knew that pupils could get a bottle of milk for a halfpenny a day, but the week's money had to be paid in advance on a Monday. George asked a few more questions and discovered that George Edgebrook's family could not afford twopence-halfpenny on a Monday. Without hesitation George Thomas paid for the boy's milk every week.

He taught for thirteen years before being adopted as Labour candidate for Cardiff Central. At his first campaign meeting a young man stood up at question time and said: 'I want to say something.' Fearing trouble, the chairman tried to stop him speaking, but the young man persisted and was finally allowed to have his say. It was then that George Thomas recognised him – it was George Edgebrook. Very simply he told the story of his family's poverty and George's care and generosity in paying for his milk every day. It was powerful support for George Thomas's cause.

George really cared about people and was determined that the poverty of the thirties should not return. 'I will fight to see that no mother suffers as mine had to do,' he promised.

(Source: *George* by E H Robertson)

30 January

King Charles I was executed on 30 January 1649.

Nothing common, nothing mean

It was a freezing January morning. The king was wearing two shirts so that he should not shiver and be thought to be trembling as a coward. He stepped from a window of the palace at Whitehall onto the scaffold that had been made ready. It was two o'clock in the afternoon. Large ranks of soldiers separated him from the crowd of his subjects who stood watching their king. Only those nearest could hear his last words.

'I go from a corruptible crown to an incorruptible crown,' he told his chaplain, 'where no disturbance can be, no disturbance in the world.' He then handed Bishop Juxon a jewel made from a single onyx. He asked that it should be given to the Prince of Wales, then in hiding in Holland, with the message, 'Remember'.

The masked executioner raised his axe and, as Charles's head left his body, 'There was such a groan by the thousands then present,' wrote one spectator, 'as I never heard before and desire I may never hear again.'

After his death some counted Charles a martyr and saint; others believed that his death had secured democracy for England. But all recognised that Charles faced his death bravely.

'Nothing in his life became Charles like the leaving of it,' one person commented. The poet Andrew Marvell, who lived through the event, wrote:

> He nothing common did or mean
> Upon that memorable scene,
>   But with his keener eye
>   The axe's edge did try;
> Nor called the gods with vulgar spite
> To vindicate his helpless right;
>   But bowed his comely head
>   Down, as upon a bed.

Eleanor Strugnell, missionary in Chile, was born on 31 January 1887. Eleanor gained her nickname 'Struggles' partly because of her own name Strugnell and also because her favourite hymn was, 'Jesus knows all about our struggles'.

'Granny Struggles'

The doctor laid the new-born baby in a shoe-box near the wood stove. He did not expect her to live. But Eleanor Strugnell survived, and ninety years later was riding round the Chilean countryside on the back of a motor-bike. But that was her concession to age as she had covered the country alone on horseback until she was eighty.

From the age of eight Eleanor set her heart on going overseas as a missionary. But she was thirty-three before she set sail for Argentina, later moving to Chile, where she spent the rest of her long life among the Mapuche Indians.

The Mapuche are a tough people and Eleanor lived simply among them, taught in the schools, and in summer rode alone on horseback to the more remote areas, sometimes in deep mud up to her horse's belly. She lived with the Indians in their homes, taught them hygiene and explained the Gospel to them.

At fifty-four she married Dr. William Wilson, an older missionary who had helped the Mapuche to secure their land rights in the early days of the mission. He was supposedly retired, but the couple still travelled around in a converted bullock cart, like a Romany caravan. As they had no bullock, any community wanting their help had to send oxen to transport the Wilsons to their neighbourhood.

Eleanor suffered a stroke when she was ninety-eight but still sang hymns in Mapuche and English and would motion those around her to read the Bible to her; she chose verses that would help her reader to come to know Jesus Christ.

(Source: Obituary in *The Independent* of 15 June 1993, by Douglas Milmine and Rebecca de Saintonge)

1 February

1 February is the Feast Day of **St Ignatius**, bishop and martyr, who died in 107. Ignatius wrote a number of letters which throw light on Christian belief and practice less than a century after Jesus' ascension. They show Ignatius to have been a patient, gentle man concerned for Christians to be united.

God in his heart

Ignatius was also known as Theophoros, meaning 'God-bearer' or, more poetically, 'one who carries God in his heart.'

According to tradition, he was taken – chained – to Rome and sentenced to be thrown to wild beasts, probably in the Coliseum, because of his Christian faith. He wrote to the Roman Christians before he arrived, telling them not to try to get him reprieved. He wanted to 'follow the example of the suffering of my God.'

Legend identifies Ignatius with the child chosen by Jesus, in the incident which the Gospel writers record. Did Jesus know him well? Was it in his mother's house that Jesus and his disciples were sheltering – perhaps from the rain outside? Here is Mark's account:

'After going indoors, Jesus asked his disciples, "what were you arguing about on the road?"

'But they would not answer him, because on the road they had been arguing among themselves about who was the greatest. Jesus sat down, called the twelve disciples, and said to them, "Whoever wants to be first must place himself last of all and be the servant of all." Then he took a child and made him stand in front of them. He put his arms round him and said to them, "Whoever welcomes in my name one of these children, welcomes me; and whoever welcomes me, welcomes not only me but the one who sent me."

(From *Mark 9*, GNB)

2 February is celebrated in the church as **Candlemas**.
Six weeks after the birth of her baby, Mary and Joseph took Jesus to
the temple in Jerusalem, in accordance with Jewish regulations.

The light has come

When Joseph and Mary went to the temple with their new
baby, they were carrying out two Jewish rituals. Every mother
had to go through a purification ceremony after giving birth,
and bring an offering to the priests. Rich people offered a
lamb and a pigeon but there was special provision for those
who could not afford a lamb to bring two pigeons instead – it
was called 'the offering of the poor'. Jesus did not grow up in
a wealthy family.

As well as carrying out Mary's purification, Mary and
Joseph were observing the important ceremony of presenting
the new baby son to God. Like all Jewish parents, they were
acknowledging that a child is a gift, or loan, from God, to be
offered back to him.

From about 350, Christians held a feast in Jerusalem to
celebrate this early event in Jesus' life. It was known as
'Meeting', because it was on this visit that Simeon and Anna
met Jesus. The church in the East and West adopted this
custom, and in the seventh century it became known as
Candlemas. Before the service begins, candles are blessed and
given to the congregation. While Simeon's Song (the Nunc
Dimittis) is being sung, the candles are lighted and carried
round the church in procession. It is a celebration of the
coming of Jesus, the true Light, into the world.

Simeon's words as he held the baby Jesus in his arms: *'With
my own eyes I have seen your salvation which you have made
ready for every people – a light to show truth to the gentiles and
bring glory to your people Israel.'*

(From *Luke 2*, J B Phillips)

3 February

On 3 February 1998 **Karla Tucker**, aged 38, was executed by lethal injection. Karla had served fourteen years in prison on death row in a Texan prison. She was the first woman to be put to death by the state in Texas since 1863.

'Justice is blind to religion'

Outside the execution chamber there were emotional scenes. Christians and civil rights campaigners were keeping vigil but soon counter-demonstrators drove down from neighbouring towns and joined the crowd. They brandished banners saying: *Use a pickaxe on her not a lethal injection* and *Justice is blind to religion*. Police had to quell the disturbances that followed.

Karla served her sentence for murdering a woman with a pickaxe. Her victim's husband was present in Death House at Huntsville prison to see his wife's killer undergo the death penalty.

But Karla was a very different woman from the angry, violent woman who had been tried and sentenced for murder. During her fourteen years of imprisonment, she had become a Christian and experienced the forgiveness of God and new life in Jesus Christ. Her last words were of sorrow for the wrong she had done and of love for her family. One witness quoted her very last words: 'I am going to come face to face with Jesus.'

There had been worldwide support for a reprieve for Karla and last-ditch attempts by her lawyers. It was five minutes after the appointed time for the execution that the court gave its final ruling. George Bush Jnr, then Governor of Texas, refused to give a 30-day reprieve. He said he felt deeply pained and had prayed about his decision, but he had to respect the verdict of the legal system. He ended his statement: 'God bless Karla Faye Tucker and God bless Karla Faye Tucker's victims and their families.'

Dietrich Bonhoeffer was born in Germany on 4 February 1906. Bonhoeffer was exiled from Berlin for speaking out fearlessly against the Nazi regime. He was abroad on a lecture tour when World War II broke out, but insisted on returning to his own country in order to work for the church and against Hitler. He was arrested in 1943, imprisoned at Buchenwald and hanged. His last words – a message to a friend – were, 'This is the end – for me the beginning of life.'

God's guiding hand

'Please don't ever get anxious or worried about me, but don't forget to pray for me – I'm sure you don't! I am so sure of God's guiding hand and I hope I shall never lose that certainty. You must never doubt that I am travelling my appointed road with gratitude and cheerfulness. My past life is replete with God's goodness, and my sins are covered by the forgiving love of Christ crucified. I am thankful for all those who have crossed my path, and all I wish is never to cause them sorrow, and that they, like me, will always be thankful for the forgiveness and mercy of God and sure of it. Please don't for a moment get upset by all this, but let it rejoice your heart.'

(From *Letters and Papers from Prison* by Dietrich Bonhoeffer)

Holy Spirit, give me faith that will protect me from despair, from passions and from vice, give me such love for God as will blot out all hatred and bitterness, give me the hope that will deliver me from fear and faintheartedness. – Dietrich Bonhoeffer (1906-1945), from a prayer he used while awaiting trial in prison.

5 February

After nine months in prison, **Bonhoeffer** wrote to a friend about the way in which he dealt with painful separation from family and those dear to him.

Coping with separation

'I should like to say something to help you in the time of separation which lies immediately ahead ... I have learnt something about it myself during the last nine months, having been separated during that time from all those I love, [and] I should like to pass it on to you.

'In the first place nothing can fill the gap when we are away from those we love, and it would be wrong to try and find anything. We must simply hold out and win through. That sounds very hard at first, but at the same time it is a great consolation, since leaving the gap unfilled preserves the bonds between us. It is nonsense to say that God fills the gap: he does not fill it, but keeps it empty so that our communion with another may be kept alive, even at the cost of pain. In the second place, the dearer and richer our memories, the more difficult the separation. But gratitude converts the pangs of memory into a tranquil joy ... We must not wallow in our memories or surrender to them, just as we don't gaze all the time at a valuable present, but get it out from time to time, and for the rest hide it away as a treasure we know is there all the time...

'From the moment we awake until we fall asleep we must commend other people wholly and unreservedly to God and leave them in his hands, transforming our anxiety for them into prayers on their behalf'.

(From *Letters and Papers from Prison* by Dietrich Bonhoeffer)

6 February

Lancelot *'Capability' Brown*, landscape gardener, died on 6 February 1783.

'Nearer God's heart in a garden'

Sir William Loraine was sixty years old when he inherited the family estate at Kirkhale in Northumberland, but he was raring to make widespread changes and improvements to his newly-acquired property. In 1732 he took on local-born, sixteen-year-old Lancelot Brown as his gardener and soon discovered that his young employee had considerable talent for planning and designing buildings and landscapes. A century later Sir William's great-great-grandson wrote that the Kirkhale estate was 'the first landscape work ever entrusted to his [Sir William's] gardener, afterwards known throughout England as 'Capability Brown.'

Brown's reputation swiftly grew and his new, carefully planned 'natural' landscapes became the rage among landowners throughout the country. He gained his nickname, 'Capability', from his habit of assuring new clients that their grounds had capability. He was on familiar terms with many of the nation's great and good. One day he was chatting to Hannah More, well-known writer of religious books, as they strolled together in the grounds of Hampton Palace. He compared his art, she reported, to literary composition. "'Now *there*," said he, pointing his finger, "I make a comma, and there," pointing to another spot, "where a more decided turn is proper, I make a colon; at another part, where an interruption is desirable to break the view, a parenthesis; now a full stop, and then I begin another subject."'

More than two hundred years later we are still able to enjoy the fruits of Brown's genius for marrying art and nature. Horace Walpole of Strawberry Hill called him 'Lady nature's second husband' and wrote this epitaph when he died:

> With one Lost Paradise the name
> Of our first ancestor is stained
> Brown shall enjoy unsullied fame
> For many a Paradise he regained

(Source: *Capability Brown* by Dorothy Stroud)

7 February

John Pridmore was born on 7 February 1964.

'I'll take what I can get !'

The crunch point in John's life came when he was a boy of ten. His parents told him that they were splitting up and he could choose which one to go with. The two people he loved most had failed him, and he was determined not to risk giving – or receiving – love again.

Life with his father and his father's new wife was tough. His father showed more care for his new stepchildren than he did for John, so he tried to get attention in the only way he knew – by getting into trouble. At fifteen he was in a detention centre and once out he did not go home again. He gambled and stole to survive and took drugs to deaden the pain. Still he refused love. His philosophy was to take what you want from life – no one else will give you anything. At nineteen he was in prison; his role models were those who had money and everything that could bring, and organised crime seemed the route to get there.

He began 'bouncing' at several of London's most popular night-clubs, and earned plenty with the money that he gained from setting up drug deals. They could bring him in thousands in a few minutes. He had everything that money could buy – expensive flats, cars and women. Yet he had to take drugs to dull the pain he constantly felt. When he got home he could not bear the silence even for a few minutes. *Why* was he so unhappy, he asked himself? He had everything that anyone could ask for in life, but his life seemed empty.

It was then that God spoke to him.

John Pridmore.

'Now I want to give!'

John Pridmore had experienced a difficult couple of months. He had wounded a man seriously enough to put him in hospital and he did not yet know whether he might even be up on a murder charge.

He came back to his flat one night as usual but in the unbearable silence he heard a voice. It was the voice of conscience but more than that, it was the voice of God. And that voice told him all the wrong things that he had done. John felt terrified. Then for the first time he prayed – for God to give him another chance. 'All I've ever done is to take from you, God. Now I want to give.'

The first thing that John read in the Bible was the story of the Prodigal Son. He cried as he recognised in himself the wayward sinner. He knew that God had forgiven him, now he had to forgive himself. And that took longer. He heard the words of Jesus as he sat looking at a crucifix. He said: 'Go free – I love you.'

John gave up his job as a bouncer and gave away much of his money. He worked among young people in East London, as a postulant in a Franciscan order in the Bronx, but returned to the UK where he could work among young people with his own background and share the brokenness they experience and that he once knew. In schools he tells young people the truth about drugs, money and worldly success; best of all, he tells them about Jesus.

'Always, every day, give God permission to do what he wants with you.' – Mother Teresa's words to John Pridmore

9 February

Fyodor Dostoevsky, Russian writer, was born on 9 February 1881. Dostoevsky's life was marked by tragedy and suffering. His mother died when he was sixteen and two years later his father was murdered. He suffered from epilepsy and was dogged by debt. But he maintained a strong belief in the possibility of redemption for even the most depraved.

A convict meets Christ

Dostoevsky had no real interest in politics but a mild flirtation with socialists who wanted to overthrow the Tsar led to his arrest along with the ringleaders. They all received the death penalty but at the eleventh hour the sentence was commuted to eight years' hard labour in Siberia. It was Christmas Eve when he and his fellow convicts set out with their guards, dressed in convicts' clothes and with irons weighing more than four kilogrammes clamped to their legs. It was a long, bitterly cold journey; the bells rang out for Christmas Day as they made their way through the stark countryside. But when they stopped at a transit camp they were visited by some ladies who made it an act of mercy and compassion to visit convicts on their way to labour camp. They gave Fyodor a New Testament.

In the camp it was the only book that Dostoevsky had to read. And he read it avidly. In his desperate need he identified with the men and women in the Gospel stories who encountered Christ and recognised in him the one who could bring healing and life. In spite of times of great doubt and bitterness, he began to feel love and compassion for the men who shared his hard lot. He kept the new Testament to the end of his life and bequeathed it to his daughter on his death-bed.

Joyce Grenfell, entertainer, was born on 10 February 1910.
She made her debut in revue in 1939, but found fame through her
monologues, which she wrote and performed. She was a keen observer
of human nature and warmly and wittily reflected the foibles of her
characters. But she was never cruel or unkind and highlighted human
kindness and pathos as well as exposing petty snobbery and follies. She
had a strong religious faith and belief in goodness. Her autobiography,
Joyce Grenfell Requests the Pleasure was published in 1976. In the nineties,
her monologues were brilliantly revived on stage by Maureen Lipman.

Not afraid of sentiment

During the last year of World War II Joyce Grenfell travelled to
fourteen different countries, entertaining the troops.
Sometimes she would sing in the open air, competing with
wind or rain, encouraging men who were tense, awaiting
battle. But her more poignant memories were of army hospital
visits. One day she arrived at a hospital that had been an Italian
monastery and where serious casualties were arriving hourly
from the battle zone. The scene was horrific and Joyce
blanched at the thought of entertaining men in such
condition.

'You can't possibly want us here today. Shall we go away?'
she asked the nursing sister in charge. But instead the nurse
asked her to move the piano into a corner and sing for a few
soldiers at a time.

Before leaving England, Joyce had selected cheerful
dance songs and romantic numbers to bring with her, but she
discovered that it was the sad, gentle songs about home that
the men loved and asked for. On this occasion a young soldier
with fair hair and a Devon accent beckoned her over and asked
her if she would sing a song about a mother. For a moment
Joyce was at a loss. Then she remembered a lullaby and sang
that softly for him.

'You learn as you go,' was her comment, 'and you stop
being afraid of sentiment.'

11 February

11 February is the Feast Day of **Caedmon**, Anglo-Saxon poet. St Hilda was abbess at Whitby from 657. Five future bishops were among her monks, as well as Caedmon, whose story is told by the Venerable Bede in his *Ecclesiastical History*.

Singing the good news

When the evening meal was over in the monastery, the brothers would pass round the harp, so that each in turn could play and sing for the enjoyment of the whole company. Caedmon alone dreaded the ordeal of taking his turn. His job was to look after the cows and he had no skill in music or poetry.

One night, as he saw the harp getting nearer, he slipped quietly away and took refuge in his cow-shed, where he soon fell asleep. Suddenly he heard his name, called clearly, and the command,

'Caedmon, sing me something.'

In vain Caedmon protested that he could neither sing nor play, and that he had left the table for that very reason.

'Yet you must sing to me,' his unseen visitor insisted.

'What shall I sing about?' Caedmon asked.

'Sing me the story of Creation,' was the answer. Caedmon obeyed and this is the song he sang:

'O sing the praise of our Guardian King
The thoughts of the Lord who made everything!
(Eternal Lord, how great is your name!
Glorious Father, for ever the same!)
First he created for children of men
The heaven above as roof – and then,
Guardian King who does all things well –
He made the earth where folk can dwell.'

Next morning he was taken before the Abbess Hilda. She was sure that God had given Caedmon this gift. The monks must teach Caedmon all the stories and truths of the Bible. Then he could sing about the love of God, about heaven and hell. In this way, many people would learn the good news of Jesus and join in the singing too.

Abraham Lincoln, sixteenth president of the United States, was born on 12 February 1809. He was born in a Kentucky log cabin and never had a whole year's schooling in his life. He learned to read by spelling his way through the Bible. He was a giant of a man, strong, absolutely honest and upright. He worked for the emancipation of slaves and succeeded in his struggle to keep the States united. He had a deep religious faith.

Death of a president

The bitter Civil War between the northern and southern states was over. Abraham Lincoln was sitting with his wife in a box at Ford's Theatre in Washington, enjoying a comedy. He had already decided that he would treat the conquered rebel states with generosity and forgiveness. He would not listen to some senators' calls for hangings and confiscation of property.

'Enough lives have been sacrificed,' Lincoln insisted. 'We must extinguish our resentments if we expect harmony and union.'

During the interval he and his wife chatted happily and talked of travelling together when the duties of the White House were over.

'There is no place I should so much like to see as Jerusalem,' the president said. Then the curtain went up for the second half of the performance and the lights dimmed.

But an unobserved watcher had noted exactly where the president was sitting. As the second act began, he noiselessly opened the door of the box and fired point-blank at Lincoln. Lincoln rose in his chair, then sank back, head drooping and eyes closed.

The assassin, a handsome young actor called John Wilkes Booth, who bitterly opposed union, pushed past the rest of the party in the box, vaulted over the rail and made his escape. The president was carried across the street to the home of a tailor, who lived nearby. Next morning Abraham Lincoln, president of the United States, was dead.

13 February

On 13 February 1974 **Alexander Solzhenitsyn** was expelled from the USSR. Solzhenitsyn was born in Russia in 1918. He graduated in physics and mathematics then served in the Red Army in World War II. He was arrested in 1945 for criticising Joseph Stalin, and imprisoned for eight years. He was released on the day of Stalin's death in 1953, but forced to spend three years in exile.

The Gulag Archipelago

It was 1930 when the Gulag was founded. The word is an abbreviation for the body responsible for maintaining prisons and forced labour camps in the USSR. It was a new word for most people in the West when Solzhenitsyn's *Gulag Archipelago* burst on the scene. He used the word 'archipelago' to liken the deadly string of prison camps throughout the Soviet Union to an island chain.

Solzhenitsyn claims that between 1928 and 1953 'some forty to fifty million people served long sentences in the Archipelago'. Probably fifteen to thirty million people died in the camps, including dissident intellectuals and some innocent people swept up in Stalin's purges.

Statistics shock but human stories bring home the reality and horror of the camps. Solzhenitsyn's first book, *A Day in the Life of Ivan Denisovitch,* describes just one day spent by an inmate of a labour camp. *The First Circle* and *Cancer Ward* were published overseas and made their author famous. But in Russia his books were banned and when Solzhenitsyn was awarded the Nobel prize for literature in 1970, he was afraid to leave his country to receive it in case he was not allowed back. Exile came in 1974, and he made his home first in Switzerland, then in USA. But he was soon to denounce, with a prophet's courage, the godlessness and materialism of the West. When treason charges against him were finally dropped, he returned to his motherland.

'I am of course confident that I will fulfil my tasks as a writer in all circumstances … No one can bar the road to truth, and to advance its cause I am prepared to accept even death.' – Alexander Solzhenitsyn

14 February is **St Valentine's Day**. The earliest surviving
Valentine card – now in the British Museum – was sent by
Charles, Duke of Orleans, to his wife in 1415, while he was a
prisoner in the Tower of London. By the seventeenth century it
was possible to buy as well as to make Valentine cards. For
those who made their own, a book called The Young Man's
Valentine Writer helpfully provided sentimental rhymes and
messages. With the arrival of the penny post in 1840, Valentines
could be delivered anonymously as well as cheaply.

'From your Valentine'

Nobody really knows who St Valentine was, but one legend
links him with Valentinus, who lived during the reign of
Claudius II, a Roman emperor who persecuted Christians.
Valentinus was arrested for helping Christians, then he was
thrown into prison. After a year, he was summoned before
the emperor who tried to lure Valentinus back from his
Christian faith to worship the old gods. When the prisoner
denounced the Roman gods, he was sentenced to death. He
was beaten with clubs, stoned, then beheaded.

According to one legend, while he was in prison Valentine
befriended the jailer's blind daughter. He restored her sight
and the jailer and his family were converted to Christianity.
On the eve of St Valentine's death, it is said, he wrote a farewell
message to the jailer's daughter and signed it: 'From your
Valentine.'

Postscript: More cards are sent on St Valentine's Day in the
United States than at any other time of the year – except
Christmas.

15 February

On 15 February 1819, *Louis Braille* went as a pupil to the Royal Institute for Blind Children in Paris.

A system that works!

Louis Braille was a star pupil. He carried off every prize at the Royal Institute for Blind Children – whatever the subject. He was enthusiastic to test the newly-devised alphabet for the blind, introduced by Captain Barbier. Instead of the raised letters previously used, this so-called 'night writing' used dots punched onto cardboard to form the letters.

At twelve, Louis suggested improvements, and from that time began to produce a less cumbersome and more comprehensive system of reading for blind people. He was busy with his school-work during the daytime, so he persevered with his new alphabet at night and during the holidays. By the time he was fifteen, he had completed an entirely new and simplified system, which he continued to refine and improve. By using a combination of six dots, he was able to produce sixty-three permutations. Now it was possible to express mathematical symbols and musical notes too. No subject would be out of bounds for blind students.

The boys at the institute were delighted and all those who could not see recognised that a new age had dawned for them. But the authorities – and jealous rivals – tried to criticise and discourage Louis. It was twenty years before Braille's new system was officially recognised.

Louis Braille took setbacks and insults with gentleness and good will. His Christian faith sweetened all his circumstances. As he lay dying at the age of forty-three, he begged that the box containing debts owed to him should be burned. He did not want his debtors to be worried about repayment.

Postscript: One hundred years after Braille's death, his remains were taken from the village graveyard and buried with ceremony at the Pantheon in Paris. Braille's alphabet has been adapted to Chinese, African and Slavonic languages and is in use all over the world.

On 16 February 1977, **Archbishop Janani Luwum** of Uganda met his death. On 17 February Uganda radio announced the death of the archbishop in a car accident.

'He is not here – he is risen!'

There were many who did not believe the story of the accident. They knew that President Amin hated Christians, and they knew too how fearless the archbishop had been. The government promised that his body would be handed over for burial at the cathedral the following Sunday, so preparations were made for the service and huge crowds gathered. At the last minute it was announced that he had been buried in his home village instead. The radio also forbade any memorial service to be held at the cathedral.

But the order was ignored. Instead of being intimidated by this outburst of Amin's hatred and cruelty, all the Christians present determined to take their stand, as their leader had done, as loyal followers of Jesus Christ. It took an hour for the huge congregation to leave the cathedral. As they came out they were still singing. They gathered around the empty grave that had been prepared for Luwum's coffin. The retired archbishop stepped forward and spoke to the crowd.

'When we see an empty grave it reminds us of when the angels spoke to the women at the empty grave of Jesus, that first Easter.' Then he cried out, 'He is not dead, he is risen!' And the crowd knew that he spoke too of their beloved archbishop Luwum.

Postscript: Janani Luwum's coffin was left in the village church overnight. Christians opened it and saw bullet wounds, proof that he had been murdered. Almost certainly he was shot by Amin himself. He had died a martyr's death.

17 February

Graham Sutherland died on 17 February 1980. He was born in 1903. He studied at Goldsmith's College London, specialising in engraving. He later began to paint and was a war artist in World War II. From 1955-61 he painted portraits and was absorbed in the tapestry for Coventry Cathedral. He became a Roman Catholic in 1926.

The Crucifixion

Sutherland knocked together a few packing cases to act as a cross and slung himself up with cords under his armpits. Then, facing a mirror, he sketched himself. He was working on a commission for the vicar of St Matthew's church in Northampton. The Reverend Walter Hussey had big ideas for his church and had invited Henry Moore to sculpt a Madonna for the church and Benjamin Britten and Michael Tippett to write some music. He also wanted a painting and Moore strongly recommended Sutherland. The vicar had suggested a painting of Christ's agony in the Garden of Gethsemane, but Graham had already been thinking of a Crucifixion and that was agreed. His studio was too small for the canvas, so Sutherland went to work in a garage and it was here that he tried to draw himself in the posture of crucifixion. He wanted to know exactly what the arms would look like and how the stomach would be drawn in. Before the picture was unveiled and dedicated, Sutherland spent some time in the church where it was to hang, adjusting the tones to suit the light.

Sutherland said: 'The Crucifixion idea interested me because it has a duality which has always fascinated me. It is the most tragic of all themes yet inherent in it is the promise of salvation.'

Graham Sutherland.

Christ in Glory

In 1950 an architectural competition was held to find an architect to design the new cathedral at Coventry, to be built alongside the ruins of the old one destroyed by bombs ten years before. Sir Basil Spence was the chosen architect and Graham Sutherland was asked to design the huge tapestry that was a part of Spence's plan. It was an enormous project in every sense of the word. The subject was to be Christ in Glory, surrounded by the emblems of the four Evangelists, Matthew, Mark, Luke and John. It would be the largest tapestry in the world.

After Sutherland had accepted the commission he spent a whole year pondering the theme and researching how artists had treated it in the past. Then he tried many drafts before he decided how to make the final painting. He told a friend: 'The final head really derived from a hundred different things – photographs of cyclists, close-ups of people, photographs of eyes, Egyptian art, Rembrandt and many others.'

When the painting was finally to the artist's satisfaction, it had to be woven into a tapestry. A French firm of weavers was chosen for the task but there were problems. The painting was photographed in sections much smaller than the final tapestry was to be. After some false starts, when time was running out, Spence and Sutherland went over to France to look at a trial panel and were delighted.

Now, nearly fifty years later, the immense figure presides in glory and majesty but in real humanity too, over the splendour and beauty of the twentieth century cathedral.

19 February

Nicholaus Copernicus, Polish astronomer, was born on 19 February 1473. Copernicus was born in Poland and studied law and medicine in Italy. He was a distinguished churchman and also advised his government on currency reform and was asked by the Pope to help to revise the calendar.

At the centre of the universe?

Copernicus was sure that nature was simple. Why then were the paths of the planets so very complicated? Ptolemy – the Egyptian astronomer who lived around 90 to168, was the first to state the long-held belief that the earth is the centre of the universe and that the heavenly bodies revolve around it. In 1350 de Dondi in Padua had made a splendid clockwork machine of the heavens. It had seven faces, each representing the path of a planet as it revolved round the earth. The sun was included as one of those revolving bodies. At the centre of everything was the earth, immovable.

Copernicus decided that the planets' paths looked complicated because of the viewpoint from which they were observed – our earth. If it were possible to look at the sky from a different place ... why not put the sun at the centre? It was a revolutionary idea in every sense of the word, and it had far-reaching effects. It was Galileo who bore the full brunt of the church's wrath at this displacement of the earth from the centre of the universe.

Copernicus wrote a book explaining his theory. The first printed copy was rushed to his bed as he lay dying and placed in his hands. Copernicus never knew that someone had inserted a preface saying that his brilliant new findings were 'only theory'.

On 20 February 1779 the *Resolution* was anchored off Hawaii, awaiting the return of **Captain Cook**'s murdered body.

A sea captain's wife

It was December 1762 when Elizabeth Batts walked across the meadows in Barking on the arm of James Cook. They were going to the parish church to be married. Less than a week later a glowing letter to the Admiralty praised her new bridegroom's 'genius and capacity' and Elizabeth must have known that her handsome husband would soon be recommended for a further long and punishing voyage. In fact the couple would spend no more than a few weeks together at a time, interspersed by literally years apart. Yet they were extremely happy and when Cook set off on another voyage Elizabeth was usually pregnant.

Elizabeth was deeply distressed by her husband's death. Years before, she had coped alone with the deaths of two of their children. Before 1779 was out another son died at sea in a hurricane. A second son was lost at sea and her last child, up at Cambridge, died of scarlet fever.

But for much of her long widowhood she had the companionship of her nephew Isaac Smith, a retired admiral. He had sailed with Cook, who taught him kindly and well. Years before, when the coast of New South Wales was first sighted, Cook had generously said, 'Isaac, you shall land first.'

Elizabeth had a strong faith in God and on the anniversaries of her husband's and sons' deaths she would meditate, fast and read her Bible. She was inordinately proud of her famous husband and her strongest comment of disapproval was: 'Mr Cook would never have done so.'

(Source: *Captain James Cook* by Richard Hough)

21 February

John Henry Newman was born on 21 February 1801. Newman was ordained in the Church of England and served as a vicar in Oxford from 1828-43. He was received into the Roman Catholic church in 1845 and made a cardinal in 1879.

The Dream of Gerontius

His friends were badly shaken, especially those belonging to the high church wing. The man they had looked to as their leader, John Henry Newman, had left their ranks and been received into the Roman Catholic Church. Newman had long since moved from his Evangelical roots. When he was ordained and became vicar of St Mary's, the University church at Oxford, he had led the Tractarian, or Oxford, movement, which sought to bring back the Church of England to the way it had been before the split from Rome.

Newman himself had agonised before deciding to break with his own church and join Rome, but finally he followed the dictates of his conscience. He spent eighteen months in Rome and when he came back he founded a Roman Catholic brotherhood near Birmingham.

In 1865 Newman wrote a poem about an aged monk who was facing death and the progress of his soul to the life beyond. The story goes that Newman did not think much of the poem and threw it into the waste paper basket. But a friend rescued it and it was published in a Catholic magazine. At least two passages taken from the poem have been used as hymns, one of them – *Praise to the holiest in the height* – within the poet's own lifetime. It has remained a favourite hymn down to the present day.

> Praise to the holiest in the height
> And in the depth be praise;
> In all his words most wonderful
> Most sure in all his ways.

(Source: *The Penguin Book of Hymns* by Ian Bradley)

George Washington, the first President of the United States, was
born on 22 February 1732. He served his country with courage and
integrity both in war and peace. But he was never happier than on
his family farm at Mount Vernon.

'His High Mightiness'

The first President of America stood, acknowledging the cheers
of his people, dressed in a plain brown suit. He made his
promises and kissed the Bible as he solemnly took the oath.

No foreign country had thought it an important enough
occasion to warrant sending an envoy to attend the ceremony.
But George Washington was not interested in pomp and
circumstance. His aim was to build a sound foundation for
the new state of America.

But what title should he have and how should he be
addressed? No one was sure. Congress continued to discuss
what to call him. 'His High Mightiness' was one suggestion,
until some wit objected that the next president might not
reach Washington's six feet two. In the end it was decided
that he should simply be 'Mr President.'

Washington kept the promises he made at his
inauguration. He cared for the state but he cared for individual
citizens too. In his will he freed all his slaves, providing for
those too old or young to look after themselves. After his
death, one member of Congress described him as 'First in war,
first in peace and first in the hearts of his countrymen'. And
the federal capital of the USA still bears his name.

*Labour to keep alive in your breast that little spark of celestial
fire, called conscience.* – George Washington

---

23 February

Polycarp, bishop and martyr, died on 23 February c.155. Polycarp was Bishop of Smyrna (now Izmir in Turkey). He was put to death for his Christian faith.

'Eighty-six years have I served him'

'We want Polycarp! Get Polycarp!' the mob shouted.

Christians were the people that everyone loved to hate. But it was not only the ordinary people who were suspicious of them; the Roman rulers too were getting worried by this new religion. Wild tales circulated about what the Christians got up to when they met together. If they were to be left in peace the Romans must be sure that they were not plotting insurrection. There was one way of testing their loyalty to the State. Would Christians be willing to take the oath of allegiance to the Emperor? Everyone else did – just sprinkled a pinch of incense and repeated the formula 'Caesar is Lord'. That would be enough proof.

So the old man Polycarp, for many years a respected bishop in the city of Smyrna, was dragged before the captain of police and ordered to take the oath of allegiance. The captain felt sorry for him – he was an old man – and he wanted to save him from death. That was the penalty for anyone who refused the oath.

'What possible harm can there be in saying "Caesar is Lord" and offering incense to save your life?' he asked persuasively.

But Polycarp stood firm. He recognised that behind this ceremony was an acknowledgement that Caesar was divine. For him there could be only one Lord – his Master, Jesus Christ.

'Have some respect for your age,' the captain pleaded. 'Swear by the divinity of Caesar. If you take the oath I will let you go.'

Polycarp replied, 'Eighty-six years I have served him and he has done me no wrong; how then can I blaspheme my Saviour and King?' And he went to his death.

In February 2000 **Ramon Piaguaje** came to London to receive his
prize for winning the United Nations Millennium Art Competition.
Piaguaje was born in 1962 in the Ecuadorean rainforest, a member of
the Secoya tribe. His mother was a shaman and his father a chief, but
Piaguaje became a Christian and, in his own words, an evangelist.

Eternal Amazon

He came to England from his rainforest on foot, by car, by bus
and by planes, arriving at last in London. He had never heard
before of Europe or England. Heads turned when he walked
into a cosmopolitan London hotel in his green tunic with
headband of toucan feathers. Yet Piaguaje seemed unfazed.
When asked his feelings he invariably answered 'Tranquilo'.

The United Nations art competition was the largest ever
launched, and paintings were chosen for entry in fifty-one
countries. The theme was *Our World in the Year 2000* and
Piaguaje's was chosen from the selected two hundred and
fifty-five. He feels deeply about his world and the rainforests.
The tribe's reservation is safe but Piaguaje can hear the tree
cutters all around and knows that there are oil wells
dangerously near. He does not want his paintings to be the
only reminder in coming years of the forests he loves so much;
sometimes, he says, he cries as he paints.

His painting, called *Eternal Amazon,* was chosen for its
'clarity, integrity and sheer beauty'. It is a symphony in green,
in which every leaf is delineated and the mystery and awe of
the forest as well as its intricate beauty can be seen and felt.
He does not paint animals or people, only his beloved trees,
river and sky. When he was a child, Piaguaje used to draw in
the dust; there were no paints. When an anthropologist saw
his drawings and gave him some oil paints in 1993 Piaguaje
discovered with surprise and joy that it was possible to paint
in colours. All the twenty oil paintings he has since done he
has given away. But as for *Eternal Amazon* – 'I let this go with
tears', he says, 'it is one of my loved ones.'

25 February

On 25 February 1774 the rules of cricket were formulated in England, in the *'Star and Garter',* Pall Mall. Since then the game has spread to many other countries. ***Jonty Rhodes*** is one of South Africa's foremost cricketers. He had a disciplined, church-going upbringing, but his committed Christian faith came as a result of his wife, Kate. Together they put God, then one another, even before cricket.

JONTY RHODES – STATISTICAL SUMMARY
49 test matches, scoring 2,337 runs, with an average of 35.40 runs
169 one-day Internationals, scoring 3,856 runs; average of 31.34 runs

Rhodes revived

In the mid-nineties, it looked as though his cricket career might be over. He was still scoring a few runs, but he knew it was not good enough and younger players were overtaking him. And anyway, he had stopped enjoying the sporting world and the touring life. And in 1997 he did some serious thinking. He realized that as a lad he had been responding to pressure at home and at school to do well in his studies and in his cricket. It had not really been his own choice. Now he was facing the fact that he could break free and make his own choices.

Then he made the discovery that although he had been thrust into cricket, it was not just the decision of other people. He had a gift and he had not yet fulfilled that gift as he could do. Now he could make his own choice to play cricket and to do it with all his strength and might. So it was back to the nets and practice and Jonty did that too with all his heart. He put everything into correcting his mistakes and succeeded. He was chosen to tour Australia and played with confidence, both physically and mentally revitalised. For his own team, he is an inspiration, spreading the enjoyment and the confidence that every successful team needs.

'Being a Christian does not mean that you have to stand down from a conflict, or not be as competitive as the person next to you. God does not want me to have second best, so I am as determined as anybody on the field.' – Jonty Rhodes

26 February

Johnny Cash, American country and Western singer was born on
26 February 1932. Sometimes considered one of the greatest stars
of country music, Johnny Cash was at his height in the fifties and
was associated with Bob Dylan in the late sixties. He had a
childhood of poverty and hardship – picking cotton and hauling
five-gallon water jugs for work-gangs. He joined the USAF then
went to Memphis and found success as a Country and Western star.

Prisoners

One night Johnny Cash woke up in jail in Georgia and couldn't
remember how he got there. It gave him a severe jolt. The
pressures of touring, recording, working for radio and
television had become too much for him. He had taken to
stimulants and tranquillisers as the only way to survive. But
the habit brought its own train of disaster and Johnny ended
up that night in jail.

Life itself seemed something like a prison to Johnny. *Time*
magazine had summed up the message of his songs in a
similar way; they seemed to be saying, 'Life both in and out of
prison is a kind of sentence to be served.'

Johnny had great sympathy for those who were literally
inside. His compassion for convicts was expressed in many of
his songs. He had sung in many of the big prisons in the USA,
including San Quentin. He was strongly critical of the whole
prison system. 'You put them in like animals,' he said, 'and tear
the souls and guts out of them, then let them out worse than
when they went in.'

But after his own experience in prison Johnny found true
freedom – not only from the Georgia jail, but from his own
personal prison of drugs and despair. He found the freedom
that Jesus promised to give to those who trusted and followed
him.

27 February

The Roman Emperor **Constantine** was born 27 February 280. Constantine was the first Roman emperor to recognize the claims of Christianity. The changed relations between church and state had far-reaching results.

At the sign of the cross

'It was before the battle when I and my men were to march against Maxentius. At noonday I saw a vision – a cross high in the sky,' Constantine told the historian Eusebius. 'Then, the night before the battle I had a dream. I was told to mark my soldiers' shields with the sign of Christ and to carry my standard with that same sign and with the cross'

Whatever the exact truth of the matter, Constantine had certainly been fearful when he marched out against his rival. He had heard tales of Maxentius' mastery of magical arts, so he prayed to the Supreme God for help. The two forces met in 312 at Milvian Bridge outside Rome and Constantine was victorious. Although the emperor was not baptized until shortly before he died, he certainly embraced the Christian faith to some extent. Before, he had worshipped the 'Unconquered Sun' and he seems to have merged that belief with the Christian faith which he did not wholly understand.

After centuries of persecution Christianity now became the favoured religion; Christians had their confiscated goods returned and experienced a new spirit of tolerance. Sunday (also the day of the Sun) was the official holiday. But there was a price to pay. The church had mortgaged her independence. As one aged counsellor said to Constantine: 'Do not intrude yourself into church matters, nor give commands to us concerning them ... God has put into your hands the kingdom; to us he had entrusted the affairs of his church.' But the clock could not be put back.

Sir Wilfred Grenfell, medical doctor and missionary in Labrador, was born on 28 February 1865. The son of a clergyman, Grenfell made a personal commitment to Christian faith as a student. He was an Oxford rugby blue and a house surgeon at the Royal London Hospital. He took a master mariner's certificate and became a medical missionary in the North Sea fisheries. In 1892 he went to Labrador and founded hospitals, orphanages and trade co-operatives as well as fitting out hospital ships for the fishing grounds.

'To the memory of three noble dogs'

It was a calculated risk, but Dr Grenfell decided to take it. He must hope that the ice would hold.

It was Easter Day after church when the messenger arrived with the bad news that a patient he had operated on had a serious infection. No time must be lost in making the sixty-mile journey to the south. Grenfell set off with all speed on his dog-drawn sledge. Soon he was faced with a choice – should he take the long journey on land around the long arm of the bay, or cut across on the frozen sea and save valuable time? The first part of the crossing, to an island, was easily accomplished, but when Grenfell looked at the second stretch to the shore he noted that the ice had been badly smashed even though it was now packed together. There was nothing for it but to forge ahead and the dogs started off eagerly.

But a half a mile from the shore they paused as if sensing danger. The wind had dropped and the ice packs were beginning to drift apart. In between was loose ice that would not bear them. He urged the unwilling dogs forward but soon the sledge sank and Grenfell had barely time to cut the dogs free and with great difficulty get the dogs and himself onto a large block of ice. But he had lost his medical box and provisions as well as his cap, coat and gloves. And he was soaked to the skin. He took off his clothes and wrung them out, putting them back on one by one as the wind had dried them a little. The current was bearing his ice-pack gradually out to sea, where it would be pounded to smithereens. He must somehow keep warm and there was nothing for it but to kill three of his devoted dogs, use their skins for warmth and their bodies as some kind of wind-break. Then he prayed, and tried to get a little sleep while he waited for the day to come.

(Source: *Knight of the Snows* by R G Martin)

29 February

Sir Wilfred Grenfell.

'Not a single sensation of fear'

When Grenfell awoke from a light sleep, the wind had changed, the constant clash of ice-packs had quietened and he was no longer drifting out to sea. Although it seemed impossible that anyone would see him, Grenfell was determined to use some means of attracting attention. His matches were soaked and would not light but he made a flagstaff from the frozen legs of his dead dogs and tied his shirt to it. Then he began to wave his impromptu flag.

When first he caught sight of what seemed to be an oar he felt sure that he was hallucinating. But next he saw quite clearly the black hull of a boat. It came nearer and someone on board shouted to him to wait for them to fetch him. Grenfell was only too glad to do so and soon the rescuers had pulled him on board, wrapped him in blankets and revived him with hot tea. His remaining dogs were taken into the bows. The leader of his rescuers explained that the night before he had just been able to make out a strange object on the ice and felt certain that it was someone in distress. They had launched the boat with its volunteer crew as soon as it was possible to do so. Grenfell told a friend later: 'I could not help laughing at my position, standing hour after hour waving my flag at those barren and lonely cliffs; but I can honestly say that from first to last not a single sensation of fear crossed my mind.'

Grenfell did not forget the dogs who had been sacrificed in order that he might live. He had a bronze plaque fixed to the wall in the hospital. It said:

> To the Memory of
> Three Noble Dogs
> MOODY WATCH SPY
> whose lives were given
> for mine on the ice
> April 21st 1908

(Source: *Knight of the Snows* by R G Martin)

George Herbert, poet, died at Bemerton on 1 March, 1683.
Nobly born and gifted for high office, he became a clergyman in the
little village of Bemerton, where he died before he was forty.

'Musick at midnight'

Twice a week George Herbert would go to the cathedral at
Salisbury and on his way home he would call on some friends
for an informal session of music-making. One day, walking in
Salisbury, 'he saw a poor man with a poorer horse that was
fallen under his load; they were both in distress and needed
help; which Mr Herbert perceiving, put off his canonical coat
and helped the poor man to unload and after to load his horse:
the poor man blest him for it: and he blest the poor man: and
was so like the good Samaritan that he gave him money to
refresh both himself and the horse; and told him that as he
loved himself he should be merciful to his beast.

'Then he left the poor man and at his coming to his
musical friends at Salisbury they began to wonder that Mr
George Herbert, which used to be so trim and clean came into
that company so soiled and discomposed; but he told them
the occasion: and when one of the company told him he had
disparaged himself with so dirty an employment, his answer
was, that the thought of what he had done would prove
musick to him at midnight – "and though I do not wish for the
like occasion every day, yet let me tell you, I would not pass
one day of my life without comforting a sad soul or showing
mercy; and I praise God for this occasion: and now let's tune
our instruments."'

(Adapted from *Life of Mr George Herbert* by Isaak Walton)

2 March

Cardinal Basil Hume, Roman Catholic Archbishop of Westminster, 1976-1999, was born in Newcastle upon Tyne on 2 March, 1923. He was educated at Ampleforth College, entered the monastery there as a novice and in 1963 was elected Abbot of Ampleforth. His appointment as Cardinal and Archbishop of Westminster, was accepted by Basil Hume only 'out of a monk's obedience'.

A much-loved leader

In 1993 when the Duchess of Kent met Cardinal Hume she was surprised to see a teddy bear, dressed in the strip of Newcastle Football club, propped up on the mantelpiece in his study, beside his Cardinal's hat. He was a fan of his home team to the end of his life. He loved sport and was rugby coach at Ampleforth School until his appointment as Abbot.

Basil Hume was attuned and sensitive to others' feelings. One friend said that when he came into a room he knew instinctively who was suffering the most. He was always warm and approachable. However brief a meeting might be, his secretary noted, 'there was a real eye-to-eye contact that was a special quality of his. An impressive memory and a ready sense of humour were other ice-breaking gifts that helped considerably.'

If he thought a visitor was nervous, he would purposely leave a button of his cassock undone or his skull cap askew. 'That way,' he explained, 'they can rest assured that I am not perfect.'

But sympathy and concern for others never led him to compromise his beliefs. He combined gentleness with moral strength. His close walk with God made him the man and leader that he was and he drew others to God by his own gentleness, strength and love.

'What unites people has to be very deep. It is the life of prayer. Get that right and much else falls into place.' – Cardinal Basil Hume

George Herbert, clergyman and poet, was buried in Bemerton churchyard on 3 March 1633. The scientists of George Herbert's time were experimenting in order to find the philosopher's stone, which they believed would turn all base metals to gold. Another name for this so-called 'tincture' was the 'elixir'. In his poem with that title, Herbert claims to have found the secret of turning the basest and dullest task into an act of golden worth and value.

The Elixir

Teach me, my God and King,
In all things thee to see,
And what I do in anything
To do it as for thee ...
All may of thee partake;
Nothing can be so mean,
Which with this tincture, 'for thy sake',
Will not grow bright and clean.
A servant with this clause
Makes drudgery divine;
Who sweeps a room, as for thy laws,
Makes that and the action fine.
This is the famous stone
That turneth all to gold;
For that which God doth touch and own
Cannot for less be told.

George Herbert 1593-1633

4 March

Irina Ratushinskaya, Soviet poet and dissident, was born on 4 March 1954 in Odessa and brought up according to Soviet beliefs. In 1979 she married human rights activist Igor Geraschenko. Both were arrested and Irina sent to labour camp where she was brutally treated. Her release followed intense pressure from the West headed by *Keston Institute*, the churches and *Amnesty International*.

'How the road to find him?'

The teacher droned on, while the children glanced furtively and longingly out of the window, where snow had begun to fall. Would it last till school was over? The lesson was 'atheist instruction' – a compulsory subject. For the past hour the teacher had drummed into the children the fact that God did not exist.

'Then why,' ten-year-old Irina asked herself, 'do they spend so much time talking about something that doesn't exist?'

Irina began to feel sorry for God. How lonely he must be! He was all alone, with everyone against him!

Secretly, she began to talk to God. She asked him questions about what kind of God he is. Is he kind? Did he *really* love her? Was he the kind of God she could worship and love? In reply she received no blinding vision but she *did* get answers – sometimes through something she read, sometimes through a strong inward certainty. She had never held a Bible and dared not go into a church and risk danger to her family. One night, she crept down to the communal kitchen and wrote:

> How the road to him to find?
> With what hope and pain to measure?
> People seek a God who's kind.
> God grant they find, and trust, and treasure.

(Source: *In the Beginning* by Irina Ratushinskaya)

Gerhard Kremer, better known by his Latin name of **Geradus Mercator**, was born in Flanders on 5 March 1512. Mercator was a man of many talents – mathematician, engraver, instrument-maker and geographer. He is most famous for his map-making. Mercator had a strong religious faith which led at one time to his arrest and imprisonment. When he was freed he settled in Germany, where many of his family had lived. He died in 1594.

'You will certainly get there!'

A map of the world in a school-type atlas gives the impression that Greenland is bigger than South America. But on a globe of the world the relative sizes seem to be reversed. The globe, of course, is correct. South America is nine times larger than Greenland. The atlas is based on what is known as Mercator's projection.

Mercator was a skilled and painstaking map-maker and the apparent discrepancies are not the result of his ignorance or mistakes. He had already made fine globes of the world in which he had corrected long-standing errors in cartography. But he recognised the need for a map to help sailors. So in 1569 Mercator produced his Great World Map.

To make this map he 'stretched' the earth in both directions and 'flattened' the globe, in order to produce a map from which mariners could easily chart a course. To help them further, he invented an easy-to-read italic writing to take the place of the illegible script usually used for maps.

He explained the characteristics of his new map for the benefit of the sailors who were to use it: 'If you wish to sail from one part to another here is a chart, and a straight line on it, and if you follow this line carefully, you will certainly arrive at your destination. But the length of the line may not be correct. You may get there sooner or may not get there as soon as you expected, but you will certainly get there.'

Four hundred years later, sea-charts were still being prepared on Mercator's projection.

6 March

Louisa May Alcott, author, died on 6 March, 1888. Louisa Alcott enjoyed a happy, if frugal upbringing in Massachusetts and was deeply attached to her family. Her philosophical and unpractical father brought his daughters up on the Bible and *Pilgrim's Progress* and introduced Louisa to such literary luminaries and friends as Emerson, Hawthorne and Thoreau.

'You can't write!'

Louisa walked slowly away from the publisher's office, carrying her rejected manuscript in her hand. His words rang in her ears: 'Stick to teaching, Miss Alcott. You can't write.' But not for the first time in literary history, the publisher was wrong. And Miss Alcott was sure he was. She not only determined to go on writing but to have a story accepted by the very firm that had rejected her.

Everything was grist for her mill. People, places and events were all the raw stuff from which she created her stories. Louisa found that she could turn her hand to colourful melodrama as well as sober moral tales and the short story seemed to suit her talents best. Increasingly she found a market for her work.

With the coming of the American Civil War Louisa felt strongly drawn to help the Union cause. She learned all she could about nursing from Florence Nightingale's *Notes on Nursing*, then went to Washington to nurse in conditions almost as bad as any that the Lady with the Lamp had encountered. The wounded poured into the inadequate Union Hotel Hospital in Georgetown, especially after the bloody battles at Petersburg, and Louisa's skill and compassion were strained to the limit. She finally became very ill herself and was at death's door when she was taken home to Concord.

The writing flourished and when she was thirty-six she was asked – by the very editor who had first turned down her work – to write a girls' story, a 'domestic novel'. *Little Women*, the story that resulted, was based largely on Louisa's own family – with herself as the tomboy Jo. It was an immediate success and riches and fame came at last to its surprised and modest author.

On 7 March 1804 the **British and Foreign Bible Society** was formed in the London Tavern at Bishopsgate. The often told story of Mary Jones, who walked many miles to obtain a Bible, may be no more than legend but it is typical of many other true happenings. A widespread hunger for Bibles led to the founding of the Bible Society.

'God speaks my language'

The Revd Joseph Hughes had heard about a scheme to provide Welsh Bibles at a low cost and he asked, 'If for Wales, why not for the kingdom and if for the kingdom, why not for the world?' It was an ambitious plan but the Bible Society was formed in 1804 in order to put it into action. At first, depots were set up in different places and travelling salesmen – known as colporteurs – sold Bibles from door to door. In some countries the colporteur faced great hardships. In Siberia a colporteur and his son endured frostbite, bandits and dense fog during a four-day drive by reindeer sledge.

People-groups who receive a Bible for the first time in their mother tongue often exclaim, 'Now God speaks my language!' But languages change over the years and English-speaking people need contemporary versions, which the Bible Society has also provided. As well as distributing new language versions of the Bible, the Bible Society is constantly finding new ways of making the Bible better known. Now, more than ever perhaps, people love to hear a story and the Bible Society is organising story-telling workshops to teach people how best to tell the Bible stories in order to capture the imagination and convey the good news about Jesus Christ. It may be nearly two hundred years old, but the Bible Society is right up-to-the-minute in communicating the Bible far and wide.

8 March

Dr Jonathan Sacks was born on 8 March 1948. He is Chief Rabbi of the United Hebrew Congregations of the Commonwealth. During the Six Days War in Israel in 1967, Jonathan Sacks was reading philosophy at Cambridge. He realised, with a sudden shock, the threat to Israel's survival: 'I just got the feeling that what was at stake was more than military. It wasn't a voice: it was more like hearing the beginning of a sentence and wanting to hear the end.' He travelled the United States in a Greyhound bus, looking for a teacher and found one in Lubavitcher Rebbe, who laid the mantle of leadership on the young Jonathan Sacks.

The bad news – and the good news!

Rabbi Jonathan Sacks describes an experiment that he once carried out on an audience. He showed them a sheet of plain white paper; at its centre was a black dot. Then he asked his listeners to tell him what they saw. All except one answered: 'A black dot.' But the black dot took up less than one per cent of what they were looking at. Almost every one ignored or discounted the large sheet of white paper. In the same way, he believes, one little speck of evil or misery can so easily discount an expanse of goodness and kindness.

Newspapers and television encourage us to concentrate on the evil and suffering in our world, to the exclusion of the good things we need to feed our minds on if we are to be spiritually healthy. Seeing the good encourages us to be thankful and Jonathan Sacks believes in the importance of 'saying thank you to God.' Gratitude, and the acknowledgement that what we have is a gift from God, he affirms, is to the mind what serotonin is to the brain. It lifts depression. It could be called the oldest known method of cognitive therapy.

The psalm writer said: *It is good to give thanks to the Lord, for his love endures for ever.*

Gilbert White was born in 1720 in the Hampshire village of Selborne, where he lived most of his life. His grandfather was vicar there and he in turn became curate. He was a keen naturalist in an age when such study was considered eccentric. His *Natural History of Selborne* fully and delightfully documents the birds, animals and plants of the area. Here is an entry for March 1773:

Parent love

'A willow-wren had built in a bank in my fields. This bird a friend and myself had observed as she sat in her nest; but were particularly careful not to disturb her, though we saw she eyed us with some degree of jealousy. Some days after as we passed that way we were desirous of remarking how this brood went on; but no nest could be found, till I happened to take up a large bundle of green moss, as it were, carelessly thrown over the nest, in order to dodge the eye of any impertinent intruder.

'The flycatcher ... builds every year in the vines that grow on the walls of my house. A pair of these little birds had one year ... placed their nest on a naked bough, perhaps in a shady time, not being aware of the inconvenience that followed. But a hot, sunny season coming on before the brood had half fledged, the reflection of the wall became insupportable, and must inevitably have destroyed the tender young, had not affection ... prompted the parent-birds to hover over the nest all the hotter hours, while with wings expanded, and mouths gasping for breath, they screened off the heat from their suffering offspring.'

10 March

Harriet Tubman died on 10 March 1913, at the age of 93. There is no exact date of birth, but Harriet was born into slavery in Maryland, in about 1820. She escaped to freedom, then returned many times, to rescue at least 300 slaves and guide them to freedom.

Crossing the line

'There were good masters and mistresses, as I've heard tell. But I didn't happen to come across any of them,' Harriet remarked sharply. As a little girl of seven, Harriet was hired out to work. Her masters soon discovered that she was best at outdoor work and in spite of injuries from ill-treatment, she grew up tough and wiry.

Harriet – one of eleven children born to two slaves brought from Africa in chains – had her parents' strong faith in God. In a dreamlike trance she saw 'a line, and on the other side of that line were green fields, and lovely flowers, and beautiful white ladies who stretched out their arms to me over the line, but I couldn't reach them no how, I always fell before I got to the line.'

Once wide awake, Harriet was convinced that God was telling her that the time had come to escape. She was tough, practised in moving quietly and moving around in the dark. She set off, travelling by night, finding her way by the stars, and slept in caves or treetops, blazing a trail through forests and swamps, until at last she reached the safety of the free state of Pennsylvania. She could scarcely believe that she was free. She looked at her hands, she said, to see if she was the same person. 'There was a glory over everything,' as she described it later; 'I had crossed the line!'

Harriet Tubman.

The underground railroad

Instead of relishing her own freedom, Harriet Tubman determined to go back to the south and retrace the perilous journey. 'I was free,' she said, 'but I was alone ... *They* should be free. I would make a home in the north and bring them there, God helping me.' She prayed, lying all alone on the cold damp ground. '"Oh, dear Lord," I said, "I ain't got no friend but you. Come to my help, Lord, for I'm in trouble!"'

In 1850, the Fugitive Slave Act made it compulsory to return any escaped slave and there were heavy penalties for those who helped slaves to escape. But Harriet took her life in her hands and returned again and again, rescuing her own family, her old parents and hundreds of others. Travelling alone was one matter, but to take elderly people and children on the dangerous route was far more risky. But by this time 'safe houses' had been set up – places where sympathisers hid the fugitives before helping them on their way. Harriet became known as 'Moses' – the rescuer of her people from slavery. On all her many sorties into 'enemy' territory and her dangerous treks to safety, Harriet never lost a single one of her charges.

'The midnight sky and the silent stars have been the witnesses of your devotion to freedom and to your heroism. Excepting John Brown – of sacred memory – I know of no one who has willingly encountered more perils and hardships to serve our enslaved people than you have.' – Letter from Frederick Douglass, freed slave and leading abolitionist

(Sources: *Harriet Tubman* by M W Taylor, Chelsea House Publishers, New York; *All Saints,* Robert Ellsberg Crossroad Publishing Company, New York)

12 March

12 March is the Feast Day of **Gregory the Great**. Gregory was born in about 540 into an aristocratic Roman family and entered the civil service rising to high office. When his father died, he gave away his money and went into a monastery (one of seven he had established) and enjoyed a few happy years of seclusion. He was recalled to public life by the church and in 590 appointed Pope.

'Servant of the servants of God'

'Not angles but angels' are probably the best known reported words of St Gregory the Great. The Venerable Bede, in his *Ecclesiastical History of England*, tells the story of Gregory catching sight of a group of fair-haired English slaves in the market-place at Rome. He asked who they were and when told that they were Angles he replied, 'They are well-named, for they have angelic faces and it becomes such to be companions with the angels in heaven.'

Gregory was determined to bring the Gospel to these fair-haired Angles and set out himself but was called back for duties in Rome. Instead he despatched forty monks, led by Augustine, to England. The party stopped in Gaul, alarmed by stories of English fierceness and savagery. But according to Bede, Gregory urged them on, writing, 'My very dear sons, it is better never to undertake any high enterprise than to abandon it when once begun. So with the help of God you must carry out this holy task.'

Once in England and shepherding a newly-converted flock, Augustine was plagued with uncertainty as to how to cope with the situations that arose with these one-time pagans. He repeatedly turned to Gregory for help and received advice that was wise, practical and Christian. In fact, Gregory's great skill was in administration; he completely systematized the affairs of the church. But unlike many efficient and well-organized people, he was also tolerant and loving. He did his best to prevent slavery and was gentle towards those of other faiths. Loving humility marked a man who never wanted to be head of the church but called himself 'the servant of the servants of God.'

'And did those feet?'

Joseph of Arimathaea is mentioned in the account of Jesus' crucifixion in all four Gospels. He seems to have been rich and influential. Luke tells us that he was a member of the Sanhedrin, the Jewish ruling body who tried, condemned and handed Jesus over to Pilate, the Roman Governor. Luke also says that Joseph did not agree with the Jewish rulers' decision to have Jesus executed and describes Joseph as 'a good and upright man ... who looked forward to the kingdom of God.'

After Jesus' crucifixion, Joseph asked Pilate for permission to give Jesus' body decent burial. He and another Jewish leader, Nicodemus, prepared the body for burial and laid it in Joseph's own garden tomb.

A fourth century legend says that Joseph was sent from Gaul with twelve others to be a missionary in England. When they arrived at Glastonbury they rested on Weary-all Hill and Joseph stuck his staff into the ground; it miraculously took root and blossomed. A shoot from the original thorn tree, now in the grounds of Glastonbury Abbey, is said still to blossom during the time of Christ's nativity.

There is another legend that places Joseph's visits to England earlier still. Joseph, it is said, was Jesus' uncle and he used to come to Cornwall to trade for tin. On one voyage he brought the boy Jesus with him. William Blake adopts this legend when he pictures the 'holy Lamb of God' walking the hills and vales of England.

> And did those feet in ancient time
> Walk upon England's mountains green?
> And was the holy Lamb of God
> On England's pleasant pastures seen?
>
> William Blake 1757-1827

For Blake, the legend was the impetus to create a just and compassionate England worthy to be Christ's dwelling.

14 March

Global Care was founded by **Ron Newby** whose birthday is tomorrow, 15 March. Today's is the first of a two-part story. Global Care is an international Christian charity working for needy children through relief, development, education and child-care programmes.

'One child at a time'

Eight-year-old Indira lives with her mother in the former Soviet Republic of Kazakhstan. One day when she was playing she had an accident and banged her head. The injury was so severe that it left her blind. Local doctors acted quickly to relieve the pressure and managed to restore her sight. But they did so by making a large hole in her skull. They knew that if Indira's skull was left like that for long she would die, but there were no surgeons in Kazakhstan with the skills to perform the further necessary surgery.

Steve Craggs, now in Britain, but who had known Indira when he was working in Kazakhstan, set to work to find some way of saving the little girl's life. He found a surgeon and an anaesthetist in Dallas, USA, who were willing to give their services free. The hospital offered to have Indira without charge and an airline agreed to provide a free flight, but £1,000 was still needed to cover all costs if Indira and her mother were to accept these kind offers.

Steve contacted every charity he could think of through the Internet, but without success. Then he discovered the Global Care website, previously unknown to him, and he e-mailed Ron Newby to ask for help. Ron agreed without hesitation and because Global Care is not a large charity, with lots of red tape, he was able to respond immediately and draft £1,000 to Steve. Indira and her mother were able to set off at once for the United States.

Ron Newby.

Making a world of difference

Steve was overjoyed when Ron responded so quickly. It restored his faith, he said, in Christian charity and compassion. The operation was incredibly delicate. Instead of using a bone graft, the surgeon cut a second hole in Indira's skull, exactly the size of the first one. The piece removed was then sliced in two and the two thinner pieces used to plug both holes. Soon after the operation Ron had a phone call direct from the hospital to say that it had been successful. Indira recovered rapidly and she and her mother were soon able to return to Kazakhstan.

Ron and his colleagues sent the money without stopping to think if they could afford it. Provided they had enough in hand they felt impelled to save Indira's life. As Ron often says: 'We can't change the whole world, but we can make the world of difference to one child at a time.'

Postscript: *The very day they had drafted the money to Steve, a cheque for £400 arrived at the Global Care office from a church in Jersey, to be used as they saw fit. Later that day a gentleman walked into their charity shop. He had been a widower and he and his new wife asked for gifts to Global Care instead of wedding presents. He handed over a cheque for £600. That day £1,000 – the exact money that Global Care had given to Indira – had been given to them. Indira's mother learned to trust God too. She said, 'I know there is a God who cares for us – we can trust him in the future as we have done in the past'.*

(Source: *All God's Children – Stories of Children at Risk in a World of Need*, Global Care Publishing, Coventry)

16 March

16 March is the Feast Day of **Abraham**, Old Testament patriarch. The Jews regard Abraham as the father of their nation. St Paul says that Abraham is the spiritual father of all Christians, because he showed the way to be right with God through trust and obedience.

Unknown destination

'Look up at the sky – can you count how many stars there are? Look down at the ground – can you count the specks of dust? The number of your descendants will be just as countless. I will give you a son and I will give you a country where your descendants will live.'

Many years before he made these promises God had made himself known to Abraham, while he was living in the city of Ur, where the people were moon-worshippers. Abraham had learned instead to worship the One who *made* the moon, and to believe that what he said was true.

He was seventy-five years old when God first told him about the great future ahead of him and his descendants. Although he and his wife Sarah were both very old and had never been able to have children, Abraham got ready to do as God told him. He left the comfortable city home in Haran, where they were then living, and set off to travel as a desert nomad, nor knowing where he was going or how it would be possible for them to have a son, but trusting God to keep his promise.

A New Testament writer put it this way:

'It was faith that made Abraham obey when God called him to go out to a country which God had promised to give him. He left his own country without knowing where he was going … He trusted God to keep his promise.'

(From *Hebrews 11*)

In 1912 **Captain Scott** and his four companions reached the South Pole, only to find that the Norwegian explorer, Amundsen, had arrived there a month before them. Their journey home was dogged by bad weather and hampered by frostbite and shortages of food and fuel. Oates, particularly, was badly affected by frostbite in his feet. Scott's diary tells the story.

'The end is not far'

Friday 16 March or Saturday 17

'Lost track of dates but think the last correct. At lunch, the day before yesterday, poor Titus Oates said he couldn't go on; he proposed we should leave him in his sleeping-bag. That we could not do, and we induced him to come on, on the afternoon march. He struggled on and we made a few miles. At night he was worse and we knew the end had come. We can testify to his bravery. He had borne intense suffering for weeks without complaining. He did not – would not – give up hope till the very end. He slept through the night before last, hoping not to wake; but he woke in the morning – yesterday. It was blowing a blizzard. He said, "I am going outside and may be some time." He went out into the blizzard and we have not seen him since. It was the act of a very brave man and an English gentleman. We all hope to meet the end with similar spirit, and assuredly the end is not far.'

Postscript: The bodies of Scott and his two remaining companions were found eight months later inside their tent which was pitched only eleven miles from the depot – and certain relief. Under Scott's shoulders was the wallet containing his notebooks and charting the course of the disastrous expedition. Oates's body was never found.

18 March

William Tuke was born in March 1732. He was a tea and coffee merchant in York and a member of the Quakers, or Society of Friends.

The Retreat

One of William Tuke's fellow Quakers had been admitted to a local lunatic asylum and her relatives asked Tuke to visit her. But all his attempts to do so failed. The authorities would not allow him near the place. Soon after, he learned that the patient had died.

But Tuke was not prepared to let the matter rest. He had heard too much about the cruelty meted out to so-called 'mad' patients. He found a way of finding out for himself. He and one or two other Quakers managed to become governors of the asylum. As a Governor he had every right to make a thorough examination. And what he saw horrified him. He made up his mind to set up a hospital where proper treatment would be given. Many years ahead of his time, Tuke realised that mental disorder was an illness that called for compassion and medical treatment, like any other sickness.

In 1792 he founded *The Retreat*, a hospital for the mentally sick, in York. His son and grandson followed in his footsteps and brought medical training and skills to the treatment of mental illness. As well as compassionate nursing, patients received – and still do receive – medical care and the possibility of cure.

Postscript: William Tuke's grandson, Samuel, took an early interest in The Retreat. His family would not let him study medicine and insisted he went into the family business, but his main concern was still in psychiatry and the work that his grandfather had begun. His son, Daniel, who lived from 1827-95, did become a leading psychiatrist.

19 March

Bishop Ken died on 19 March 1711. Thomas Ken lived through the reigns of many different monarchs. Sometimes he suffered persecution for his beliefs. But he refused to trim his sails to the wind. He combined moral courage with mercy and kindness to others.

'Be sure to sing'

'Be sure to sing the Morning and Evening hymns in your chamber devoutly, remembering that the Psalmist assures you that it is a good thing to tell of the loving kindness of the Lord early in the morning and of his truth in the night season.'

Bishop Ken compiled a book of prayers specially for the scholars of Winchester School, and he added his advice to them to sing God's praises regularly. The tunes he sang – accompanied on the viol or spinet – are unknown to us now, but the *words* of the hymns he wrote have been sung ever since.

An evening hymn 1695

Glory to thee, my God, this night
For all the blessings of the light;
Keep me, O keep me, King of kings,
Under thy own almighty wings.

Forgive me, Lord, for thy dear Son,
The ill that I this day have done,
That with the world, myself, and thee,
I, e'er I sleep, at peace may be.

Teach me to live that I may dread
The grave as little as my bed;
Teach me to die, that so I may
Triumphing rise at the last day.

Thomas Ken 1631-1711

20 March

David Livingstone, missionary, doctor and explorer was born in March 1813.

Call of the unknown

When David Livingstone went to Africa, he expected the life of a missionary to be one of constant advance – leaving new converts behind in their own communities and pressing forward to break fresh ground. He was horrified to find that his fellow missionaries were settled in mission stations which were made to be permanent and as like 'home' (in England) as possible. He had no intention of settling down with them. The unknown called to him. Besides that, he seemed to be unsuccessful at winning converts. Altogether he felt a failure as a missionary, and his missionary society seemed inclined to agree.

But Livingstone had skills and vision that other missionaries lacked. 'I shall open up a path into the interior or perish,' he declared, and through his exploration he made a whole continent accessible for others to preach the gospel.

Livingstone took a keen delight in everything he saw on his famous journeys into the interior of Africa. He noted birds, insects and plant-life. When at last he saw the Zambezi river he could only exclaim, 'How magnificent! How glorious! How beautiful!' It reminded him so much of his native Scotland. 'The long-lost scenes came back so vividly I might have cried,' he wrote. But he added that he kept back his tears lest his African guide thought they were caused by fear of the basking crocodiles.

Within ten years of his death, the region Livingstone had explored was dotted with Christian missions, and a cathedral stood on the site of the great slave-market in Zanzibar.

Johann Sebastian Bach was born on 21 March 1685. J S Bach, one of the greatest musicians of all time, belonged to a family of musicians. He wrote to a friend: 'All my children are born musicians'.

Making do with the second-best?

Every night Johann stealthily extracted the precious manuscript from the lattice-fronted cabinet and copied out some more bars of music by the light of the moon. The manuscript belonged to his brother, Johann Christoph, who had locked it away, out of reach. But Johann was impatient to get on more quickly than his brother's slow lessons on the keyboard would allow. So he spent six months, night after night, laboriously copying out music by the world's greatest composers. He completed his task only for his brother to find and confiscate the treasured score he had spent so many hours copying.

Bach's father had taught him to play the violin when he was very young and he joined in the family music-making. Then his mother died, when he was only nine, and his father soon after, so Johann and his brother were sent to live with their eldest brother, Johann Christoph, who was himself an organist. But Johann Christoph had a family of his own to provide for so Johann Sebastian was sent off to choir school at Luneberg. It was here that he was inspired by his teacher's playing to become an organist himself. He began to write music and to listen to other fine organists, and by the age of eighteen he was appointed choir master and organist in Arnstadt.

After many ups and downs Johann Sebastian took the post of choirmaster at Leipzig. Surprisingly the authorities were disappointed – he was not their first choice. The council commented: 'Since we cannot get the best man, we must make do with the second best.'

Bach was in his element. There were skilled players at the university and among the citizens and Bach became conductor of a musical society, meeting in a garden in summer and a coffee-house in winter. It was at Leipzig that he composed his great religious works.

(Source: *Bach and his World* by Cynthia Millar)

22 March

The Lord Lloyd Webber was born on 22 March 1948. Andrew Lloyd Webber comes from a musical family. His brother Julian is a cellist and his father was a brilliant organist, choirmaster and Director of the London College of Music. Recent purchases by his company *The Really Useful Group* mean that Lord Lloyd Webber has a controlling interest in over half of theatreland in London's West End.

Open churches

Joseph and the Amazing Technicolor Dreamcoat, Jesus Christ Superstar, Evita, Cats, Phantom of the Opera – musicals and films known by name to thousands who have never even seen them on stage. Their composer, Andrew Lloyd Webber, is described as 'critic-proof' after so many successes.

But music is not the only absorbing love of Andrew's life. 'When I was a boy I developed two passions,' he says,' one was for music and the other was for art and architecture.' Brought up in London, he fostered and fed his love of buildings by browsing around churches. At one time it was possible to walk into any church in town or country but, increasingly, fear of vandalism and theft have led to churches being locked up except at service times.

Andrew was still finding time to slip into a favourite church for five minutes, only to discover more and more that he was locked out. He was very frustrated and talked about it to Betty Boothroyd, Speaker of the House of Commons, who persuaded him that he should do something about it. So in 1994 Andrew contacted Brigadier Adam Gurden and asked him to set up a Trust to encourage churches to remain open. As a result the Open Churches Trust was formed. There are about 1,500 Grade 1 listed churches in England alone and every year the Open Churches Trust encourages some twenty of the finest churches in three new areas to stay open. Often the churches appoint volunteers to welcome visitors and point out features of special interest. There must be many who come to admire, to enjoy the history, the art and the architecture, who feel God's presence, mediated through the continuing prayers of men and women over many centuries of worship and service to the present day.

Anna Sewell, who wrote the book *Black Beauty*, was born in March 1820. Anna was brought up a Quaker. She lived with her strong-minded mother, who wrote improving stories and verses. Anna's foot was injured following an accident, and she spent her last seven years as an invalid, confined to a couch. When she was twenty-five, she heard a 'powerful sermon' which changed her life. 'As I listened, I truly felt Christ precious,' she wrote. 'I believed I was justified from all things. I do now trust in none but Jesus.'

Black Beauty

'I am writing the life of a horse,' Anna confided to her diary in November 1871.

Scenes and events came clearly into her mind as she lay on her couch. She sadly missed her own little pony, which she had driven, like so many before him, with skill and kindness. When she could no longer go out, she had given the pony and chaise away. She still listened with pleasure for her brother Philip's black mare, Bessie, when he came to visit.

Anna talked horses with Philip. She also learned from the passers-by beneath her window. She wrote: 'I have for six years been confined to the house and my sofa and have been writing what I think will turn out a little book, its special aim being to induce kindness, sympathy and an understanding treatment of horses. Some weeks ago I had a conversation at my open window with a cabman who was waiting at our door, which has deeply impressed me.'

At last the book was finished and sent to a publisher. Anna received £20 payment. It was only after her death that *Black Beauty* became a best-seller, topping two million copies in two years in the United States – a record in publishing history at that time.

24 March

On 24 March 1980 **Oscar Romero** was shot dead. He was a Salvadorean, ordained a priest in the Roman Catholic church in 1942, made bishop in 1970 and archbishop of San Salvador in 1977.

'Give us courage!'

The right-wing military government in El Salvador approved the appointment of Oscar Romero as archbishop. He had a reputation for being gentle and shy and they were sure that he would give them no trouble. As far as they were concerned, he would be a satisfactory puppet leader of the church. But they were soon to be proved wrong. Only a few weeks after his appointment the police fired upon a crowd of peaceful demonstrators, killing many of them. Romero protested to the leaders of the country.

Not long after, a Jesuit priest was murdered. Romero was concerned that there was no official inquiry and that power was in the hands of violent men who murdered with impunity. He took up the cause of the poor and persecuted and preached boldly about right and wrong. His church began to document the abuses of human rights and the disappearance of people without trace. He was attacked by the newspapers and increasingly isolated within his church. More priests were murdered and Romero refused to keep quiet. In 1979 he presented the Pope with seven dossiers on the atrocities that had been committed.

On 24 March 1980 Romero was celebrating Mass in a hospital chapel in San Salvador. As he lifted the cup he spoke the words: 'May Christ's sacrifice give us the courage to offer our own bodies for justice and peace.' At that moment a shot rang out and Romero fell dead at the altar, gunned down by an assassin.

In 1998, statues of ten modern-day martyrs were unveiled, sited in niches on the west front of Westminster Abbey. One of them is of Oscar Romero. He said himself that murdered priests were 'testimony of a church incarnated in the problems of its people.'

25 March

25 March is **Lady Day**. Lady Day, also called Annunciation Day, is nine months before Christmas Day and therefore observed as the day on which the angel Gabriel told the Virgin Mary that she was to be the mother of Jesus, God's Son. Lady Day is also one of the four quarter days in England, Wales and Ireland. The other quarter days are Midsummer Day, Michaelmas and Christmas Day. These are the days when payments of rent must be paid by tenant farmers and others.

'Let it happen!'

It is difficult to imagine just what Mary's feelings were when Gabriel appeared to her. Did he come trailing clouds of glory that were his from standing in God's presence? Or did he cloak his angelic brightness so that Mary would not be frightened? However he may have looked, what he had to say was enough to stop the heart of a teenage village girl, quietly awaiting her marriage to the local builder and joiner.

Many girls longed and dreamed of giving birth to the promised Messiah. Now that she knew that she was the chosen one, the how of it all baffled Mary more than anything else. She was a virgin – how could she have a baby? Gently Gabriel makes it clear that this birth was to be no ordinary one. Her child was to be 'the holy Son of God.' He was to be King over a never-ending kingdom. Therefore his birth was to be unique. God's power and his Spirit would come down and rest upon her.

Mary must have been unable to take in all that Gabriel said. Perhaps something of the heartache and the weight of God's calling for her overshadowed the privilege and joy of bearing the Messiah. But Mary did not stop to balance probabilities or consider what the cost would be for her. Simply, humbly and obediently she answered the angel: 'I am the Lord's servant! Let it happen as you have said.'

(Source: *Luke 1*)

26 March

Oliver Goldsmith's only novel, *The Vicar of Wakefield*, was published in March 1776. Dr Johnson sold the manuscript of *The Vicar of Wakefield* in 1772 for sixty pounds, in order to save Oliver Goldsmith from being arrested for debt.

Dr Primrose

The fortunes of the vicar, Dr Primrose, and his family, go from bad to worse. Theft, deception, fire, arrest and imprisonment follow one another rapidly and the good, but gullible man finds it hard to practise what he preaches and to show 'fortitude'. After many turns and twists of fortune, everything ends well. Is Goldsmith writing from experience when he describes the Primrose family as innocent victims of fraud and deception? In one chapter Moses, the eldest son, is returning from the fair where he went to sell their colt and buy a better horse in its place.

> 'Moses came slowly on foot ... "Welcome, welcome, Moses; well, my boy, what have you brought us from the fair?" – "I have brought you myself," cried Moses with a sly look... – "Ay, Moses," cried my wife, "that we know, but where is the horse?" – "I have sold him," cried Moses, "for three pounds, five shillings and twopence." – "Well done, my good boy," returned she,... "Come, let us have it then." – "I have brought back no money," cried Moses again. "I have laid it all out in a bargain, and here it is," pulling out a bundle from his breast: "a gross of green spectacles, with silver rims and shagreen cases." – "A gross of green spectacles!" repeated my wife in a faint voice. "And you have parted with the colt, and brought us back nothing but a gross of green paltry spectacles!" – "Dear mother," cried the boy, "why won't you listen to reason? I had them a dead bargain, or I should not have bought them. The silver rims alone will sell for double the money." – "A fig for the silver rims," cried my wife in a passion.'

The silver rims are not silver and the spectacles are worthless. Moses has been the victim of a confidence trick.

(From *The Vicar of Wakefield* by Oliver Goldsmith)

On 27 March 1766, **Oliver Goldsmith**'s *Vicar of Wakefield* was published. Oliver Goldsmith was born in Ireland in 1728. He wrote poetry, essays and plays, which included the highly successful *She Stoops to Conquer*. He died of a fever in 1774.

'A very worthy man?'

'When do you intend to grow handsome?' a rakish relative asked Oliver. 'When you grow good,' he replied.

Oliver Goldsmith was the fifth child in a family of eight born in Ireland to an Irish curate. He certainly was not handsome and severe smallpox left him badly scarred. His career was a series of stops and starts as he was refused for the church, and gave up the study of medicine. He was good at spending whatever money he managed to lay hands on, often at the gambling table. Nothing daunted, he decided to make the 'grand tour' on foot, living on his wits and his takings as a busker. Finally he found his vocation and once recognised as a writer of wit and charm, he saw better days. Dr Johnson became a firm friend. In his poem *The Deserted Village* he describes the village parson as a gentle, kind and thoroughly good man. Was he remembering his own father? In spite of his faults and failures, he seems to have retained some of that simple goodness himself.

The Village Parson

At church, with meek and unaffected grace,
His looks adorned the venerable place;
Truth from his lips prevailed with double sway,
And fools, who came to scoff, remained to pray.

'Dr Goldsmith is one of the first men we now have as an author, and he is a very worthy man too. He has been loose in his principles, but he is coming right.' – Dr Johnson

28 March

Teresa of Avila was born on 28 March 1515 into a large and wealthy Spanish family. At the age of twenty she ran away to become a nun. After twenty years of discovering herself and discovering God, she set about reforming the Carmelite Order of nuns, to make them more disciplined and with a simpler life-style. She possessed extraordinary practical and administrative skills but was a mystic who knew – and wrote – much about prayer.

Seeing the Lord

In Teresa's young days life did not offer women many options – marriage or the veil were the only real choices. When she was twenty, Teresa ran away to become a nun. But convents were comfortable places for those who had money. Novices could take a maid with them, have an apartment or suite, and entertain friends. Teresa loved company, enjoyed dancing and excelled at chess. But when she was thirty-nine she had an experience that transformed her life. She was looking at a picture of Christ on the Cross when a wave of revulsion swept over her at the thought of her own shallow way of life. She determined to devote herself to God and to a life of prayer. Immediately she was filled with an overwhelming sense of God's love. Her life of love and obedience to God began.

Teresa took time to be still and experience the presence of Christ. She called it 'the prayer of quiet.' One day, as she was praying this way, she knew Christ with her in a special way. Then she saw his hands as she prayed and later 'the divine face'. At last she saw the whole figure of Christ. She wrote about 'the Divine beauty'. 'It is not a radiance that dazzles, but a soft whiteness and an infused radiance which, without wearying the eyes, causes them the greatest delight.'

Teresa not only experienced the difficulties and joys of prayer, she taught her 'daughters' – the Carmelite nuns – how to pray too. Using the example of different ways of watering a garden, Teresa explained that the best method of watering is to do nothing but let the rain fall. Strenuous human effort does not always point the way. Waiting quietly for God to come to us and refresh us is the surest way to enjoy prayer.

John Keble died on 29 *March* 1866. Keble was a clergyman, a poetry professor and a religious poet and, with Newman and Pusey, a prime mover in the high church Tractarian Movement.

Red Letter Days

Saints' days were holy days and holy days were holidays! In the Middle Ages people looked forward to them eagerly, as the only time off work. Fairs and processions and all kinds of celebrations took place on these special days. When *The Book of Common Prayer* was published in 1662, it was decided that the number of official saints' days should be whittled down to thirty-two. These were marked in red in the prayer book and became known as 'red letter days', while all the others were printed in black.

The Puritans under Cromwell went much further. No day, they maintained, was to be observed as holy, except Sunday – The Lord's Day.

It was John Keble who helped to bring the events of the Christian calendar to everyone's notice again. He wrote a volume of poems, called *The Christian Year*, which included a poem to celebrate every saint and commemorate every special festival in the year.

'New truths, in the proper sense of the word, we neither can nor wish to arrive at. But the monuments of antiquity may disclose to our devout perusal much that will be to this age new, because it has been mislaid or forgotten; and we may attain to a light and clearness, which we now dream not of, in our comprehension of the faith and discipline of Christ.' – John Keble 1792-1866

30 March

'Love one another'

It was early in 1923 when Elizaveta Skobtsova and her family finally arrived in France. Like many other Russians, she had escaped during the revolution and civil war. She was pregnant when the family set off and gave birth to her baby in Georgia. It was some time before she was reunited with her husband, and they could settle with her mother and children in France.

It was hard to make ends meet, but real suffering came when little Nastia, the youngest child, wasted away and died. Elizaveta later recognized this tragedy as the spiritual turning-point in her life. It led to deep repentance and the longing to live a new kind of life, based on the Bible command: 'Love one another.'

She began to care for Russian émigrés, many of whom were not only poor but despairing and desperate. She was certain that they could be reclaimed from their wretchedness and debauchery. She was finally accepted into a Russian Orthodox monastic order and given the new name of Maria.

Mother Maria did not settle down as a cloistered religious. She believed that the true Christian should go out to others, showing them Christ's love. She urged the church, 'Open your gates to homeless thieves, let the outside world sweep in to abolish your magnificent liturgical system, abase yourself, empty yourself, make yourself of no account.'

She leased a house where she welcomed and cared for the kind of people others would describe as riffraff. In her dusty cassock and her men's shoes, she regularly foraged for food that was sold off cheaply in order to feed her 'guests'. As well as working hard in the kitchen, she listened to their troubles, sometimes comforting and counselling forty people a day.

When the Germans occupied France during World War II Maria refused to countenance the Nazi treatment of Jews. Finally she was arrested and after she was taken off, her old mother was told by the German guard, 'You will never see your daughter again.'

(Source: *Pearl of Great Price* by Sergei Hackel)

John Donne, poet and divine, died on 31 March 1631.
He was the leading light of a group of poets now known as
the Metaphysicals. They were scholarly and witty, strongly
influenced by the science of their time. Donne later regretted
the excesses of his earlier erotic poems; human love had
been transmuted into an all-absorbing love for God.

Death vanquished

Only one effigy in St Paul's Cathedral in London survived the
Great Fire of London. It is of John Donne, one time Dean of St
Paul's.

In an age of mass entertainment we find it strange to
think of people packing the churches to listen to famous
preachers whose sermons lasted several hours. Crowds, which
included the king himself, flocked to hear John Donne.
Reading his sermons now, it's still possible to feel a tingle of
excitement as he declaims: 'Any man's death diminishes me,
because I am involved in mankind. And therefore never send
to know for whom the bell tolls; it tolls for thee.'

Death was a favourite theme of contemporary poems and
sermons. War, plague and disease made it a common
happening for young as well as old. Like others of the time,
Donne thought much about death, sleeping with his coffin in
his room, to remind him of its close approach.

But for Donne, death was not a final disaster. Jesus Christ
had conquered death.

> Death, be not proud, though some have called thee
> Mighty and dreadful, for thou art not so;
> For those whom thou thinkest thou dost overthrow,
> Die not, poor death, nor yet canst thou kill me...
> For thou art slave to fate, chance, kings and desperate men,
> And dost with poison, war, and sickness dwell,
> And poppies or charms can make us sleep as well
> And better than thy stroke; why swell'st thou then?
> One short sleep past, we wake eternally,
> And death shall be no more; death, thou shalt die.

(From *Holy Sonnets* by John Donne)

1 April

Wisdom in folly

The first of April, some do say,

Is set apart for All Fools' Day.

But why people call it so

Nor I nor they themselves do know

That jingle appeared in *Poor Robin's Almanack* of 1760. If the origin of April Fools' Day had been forgotten then, there doesn't seem much chance of our discovering it now. But the first mention of this day for tricks and practical jokes goes back to 1698, so the custom is at least 300 years old.

Some people are prepared to be fools all the year round. An organisation called *Holy Fools* has about one hundred and fifty members in the UK. They visit churches in clown's dress and make-up using their own clown names. They perform sketches or meet and greet the congregation as they arrive. They believe that: 'A clown reflects human nature with all its strengths and weaknesses; the "holy fool" takes this further and performs with faith, hope and love.'

Fools risk being rejected – they are open and vulnerable to their public. It requires faith to take that risk. They demonstrate hope too – clowns are always willing to try to do the impossible, even though they risk failure – and the laughter of the onlookers. Fools show love by giving themselves entirely to their audience. We, the onlookers, can choose to take them to our heart, to laugh and cry with them – or else to reject them. Above all, fools bring us laughter and joy. *Holy Fools* demonstrate the joy and laughter that the Christian faith can bring to a sad world.

The Holy Fools are inspired by :
'We are fools for Christ' *I Corinthians 4:10*
'God chose the foolish things of the world to shame the wise' *I Corinthians 1:27*
(Richard James is Chairfool of Holy Fools Ltd)

Carlo Carretto was born on 2 April 1910. When he was forty-four Carlo gave up a powerful position in the Roman Catholic Church to join the Little Brothers, a religious community living and working near the Sahara desert.

Faith in the darkness

Temperatures in the desert range from burning heat by day to cold at night. When the cool night breeze replaced the searing daytime wind, Carlo Carretto would walk out in the desert night to pray among the sand dunes. The stars shone with more than usual brilliance. At first he wanted to learn their names but soon he came to enjoy them for their own sake. He discovered after a while that he could find his way in the desert more easily by night than by day, guided by the position of the stars.

Carlo Carretto found another way of valuing the stars, not for their usefulness to him but for the spiritual lessons that they taught him. He saw them as witnesses to God's faithfulness and truth, while the darkness all around reminded him of faith – faith that can trust God when much around is dark. He knew that if he were to see God fully the glory and brightness would be blinding. As a mortal, he could not bear more than the bright pin-points of light from God, like the stars in the night sky. The darkness protected him from the full brilliance of God's glory and the pinpoints of starlight were reassurances of God's faithfulness and love.

> As long as I have known God I have never known him to let me down.
> Knowledge of him has led me to trust in him.
> I trust in him even when my faith is put to the test and I understand nothing.
> I trust in him even when my horizon is dark, arid and painful.
> Yes, he is faithful.
> I trust him
>
> (Source: *Why O Lord?* by Carlo Carretto)

3 April

'When the sweet showers of April fall ... then people long to go on pilgrimages.' – From the Prologue to *The Canterbury Tales* by **Geoffrey Chaucer**. Chaucer was a busy civil servant. He looked after customs and excise and the upkeep of walls, ditches and sewers for the king of England in the fourteenth century. He was also a great poet, best known for *The Canterbury Tales*.

Going on pilgrimage

Then

Pilgrimages were popular in the Middle Ages and 'package tours' were arranged to faraway places. In England, the tomb of the martyr Thomas a Becket was a favourite shrine. As Chaucer's imaginary band of pilgrims rode to Canterbury together, they took it in turns to tell stories to pass the time. In his *Prologue* Chaucer describes his pilgrims, satirising the rogues and hypocrites among the church dignitaries. But for the parson and his ploughman brother, Chaucer has only kind words. Their goodness shines out.

Now

'"Mind your head," said the guide as we entered the Church of the Holy Nativity in Bethlehem.' Bishop Nigel McCulloch wrote of his own experience of a present-day pilgrimage to Israel. It was Helena, mother of the fourth century Emperor Constantine, who first set the trend but there were also those who frowned on the practice. Gregory of Nyssa wrote: 'When the Lord invites the blessed to the kingdom of heaven, he does not include a pilgrimage to Jerusalem among the good things to do.'

The low door through which pilgrims enter the Church of the Nativity is a parable, Bishop Nigel suggests, symbolising the need to stoop, in humility as well as worship, when we come into the presence of Jesus Christ. But, he concludes, Jesus is not confined to far off places or a faraway time. He is present now – where we are.

On 4 April 1968, **Martin Luther King** was assassinated. He was
the leader of the black civil rights movement in the United States.
In August 1963, about 250,000 people, black and white, marched in
Washington to demonstrate the need for legislation to integrate
blacks with whites. Dr King made one of his most memorable
speeches to the thousands packed in the capital. The last words,
from the Negro Spiritual, 'Free at last!' were used as the inscription
carved on his grave.

'I have a dream'

'I have a dream that one day on the red hills of
Georgia the sons of former slaves and the sons of
former slave-owners will be able to sit down
together at the table of brotherhood.

'I have a dream that one day every valley
shall be exalted and every hill and mountain shall
be made low. The rough places will be made
plain and the crooked places will be made
straight ... With this faith we will be able to hew
out of the mountains of despair the stone of
hope. With this faith we will be able to work
together, to pray together, to struggle together, to
go to jail together, to stand up for freedom
together, knowing we will be free one day...

'When we allow freedom to ring from every
town and every hamlet, from every state and
every city, we will be able to speed up that day
when all of God's children, black and white men,
Jews and Gentiles, Protestants and Catholics, will
be able to join hands and sing in the words of the
old Negro spiritual, "Free at last ! Free at last!
Great God Almighty. We are free at last."'

(Source: *My Life with Martin Luther King* by Coretta King)

A man who won't die for something is not fit to live – Martin
Luther King.

5 April

Robert Raikes, pioneer of Sunday schools, died on 5 April 1811.

Sooty Alley

It was Sunday – the day for the rich and respectable citizens of Gloucester to go to church. But as Robert Raikes, wealthy owner and editor of *The Gloucester Journal,* walked quietly through the city, he stopped in concern. There, in front of him was a bunch of children, shrieking and fighting with one another. He asked a bystander for the reason. She explained that the children lived in the houses around and had nothing better to do on Sundays than to fight and gamble. Every other day of the week they were working hard at the local pin factory. On Sundays, not surprisingly, they ran wild.

Raikes, who was a Christian, was deeply concerned for these savage, swearing scraps of humanity. The first thing to be done, he decided, was to try to give the children some kind of education. That could be the first step to reforming them.

He talked over his plan with others and in 1780 he opened the first Sunday School in Sooty Alley – the home of the chimney sweeps. The Bible was taught and also used as a reading book to help them to learn to read.

Raikes used another kind of publicity. As the owner and editor of a newspaper, he was able to run a long and stirring campaign on behalf of these children. His new school began to be widely talked about not only in Gloucester but further afield. As a result people in other parts of the country set up similar schemes.

The Sunday School movement was launched.

Sadhu Sundar Singh disappeared in April 1929, on a journey to Tibet. The exact date of his death is unknown. Sundar Singh was born to wealthy Sikh parents in Northern India. His mother was a deeply pious woman who influenced him greatly, but died when he was fourteen.

A *change of direction*

He would *not* accept the teachings of Jesus – and to prove it, the young Sundar Singh set fire to a copy of the New Testament and burned it to ashes. But he could not destroy the turmoil in his mind and he grew more and more confused about the right way in life.

One night, he was so unhappy and desperate that he prayed: 'Please, God, reveal yourself to me tonight.' He had made up his mind that if nothing happened he would commit suicide the next morning. But that night he had a vision of Jesus, who spoke to him in Hindustani and said, 'Why are you persecuting me? I gave my life for you on the cross.' Sundar embraced the Christian faith as wholeheartedly as he had at first rejected it. But he did not agree with the Indian practice of adopting European clothes and customs along with Christianity. He determined to live his Christian faith Indian-style, and within an Indian culture. So he put on the saffron robe and turban of Indian sadhus, or holy men. Like them, he lived as a pilgrim, with no fixed home and no money. He travelled around, praying, preaching and sharing the good news of Jesus with his own people and those in Tibet and Nepal.

'I am not worthy to follow in the steps of my Lord, but, like him, I want no home, no possessions. Like him I will belong to the road, sharing the suffering of my people, eating with those who will give me shelter, and telling all men of the love of God.' – Sundar Singh

7 April

Sundar Singh felt impelled to take the gospel to Nepal and Tibet, to the north of the Punjab, where he grew up. He met with bitter opposition especially in Tibet. Once he was arrested and flung into a dry well to die among the remains of earlier victims. During the night, a rope was lowered and he climbed out. But when he reached the top there was no one to be seen.

The warmth of love

Snow was beginning to fall as Sundar Singh strode across the bleak mountain-pass on his return from a preaching mission in Tibet. He was joined by another traveller and as the snow turned to a blizzard, they were buffeted by icy winds and blinding sleet.

Suddenly they heard a cry. Someone had fallen from the narrow pass and was lying on the ledge below. Sundar stopped at once to help him, but his companion argued that they would both die themselves if they tried. They parted – Sundar picking his way carefully down the mountainside, while the other man pressed on to the next village.

The injured man was unable to walk, so Sundar gently picked him up and with great difficulty dragged him up the steep incline. Once back on the path, he slung him on his back and continued his journey. The going was hard, with the weight of the injured man as well as the snow and the wind to contend with. Then, as they rounded one bend, Sundar saw beside the path the still figure of the traveller who had pressed on alone. Sundar called to him, then touched him, but he was dead.

At last, Sundar struggled into the village with his burden. Both were safe. The man who tried to save his own life had lost it. Sundar Singh, who risked his life out of love for another, had saved his. The warmth of the two bodies, in close contact, had kept them both alive.

In April 1769 **John Newton**'s prayer meeting moved premises. After his conversion, John Newton was ordained and in 1764 became curate-in-charge of Olney in Buckinghamshire.

Write a hymn by Tuesday!

Four prayer meetings a week was the general rule, when the Reverend John Newton came to Olney. More people came to the Tuesday evening meeting than to any other and soon there was not enough room for them all. In 1769 Newton wrote: 'We are going to remove our prayer meeting to the great room in the Great House. It is a noble place, with a parlour behind it, and holds one hundred and thirty people conveniently. Pray for us, that the Lord may be in the midst of us there.'

One highlight of the Tuesday prayer meeting was a new hymn, composed by John Newton himself or by his friend, the poet William Cowper, who was living in Olney at the time. Most of the hymns they wrote were originally composed specially for the Tuesday prayer meetings. When the move to the Great House took place, *two* new hymns were written for the occasion, one by each of them. There was special significance in the words that Cowper composed, for a congregation that had been uprooted. They must have found the words reassuring:

Jesus, where'er thy people meet,
There they behold thy mercy seat:
Where'er they seek thee, thou art found,
And every place is hallowed ground.

Here may we prove the power of prayer,
To strengthen faith and sweeten care;
To teach our faint desires to rise,
And bring all heaven before our eyes.

9 April

William Law was born in 1686 and died on 9 April 1761. He was a teacher and churchman. He spent ten years as 'the much honoured friend and spiritual director of the whole family' of Edward Gibbon, whose son was the historian and author of *The Rise and Fall of the Roman Empire*. His influence was great even in his own lifetime. Many people came to visit and consult him, including John Wesley. His best-known book, written in 1729 is his *Serious Call to a Devout and Holy Life*.

Be thankful!

'Would you know him who is the greatest saint in the world? It is not he who prays most or fasts most; it is not he who gives most alms, but it is he who is always thankful to God, who receives everything as an instance of God's goodness and has a heart always ready to praise God for it.

'If anyone would tell you the shortest, surest way to all happiness and perfection, he must tell you to make a rule to thank and praise God for everything that happens to you. Whatever seeming calamity happens to you, if you thank and praise God for it, you turn it into a blessing. Could you therefore work miracles you could not do more for yourself than by this thankful spirit; it turns all that it touches into happiness.'

(From *Serious Call to a Devout and Holy Life* by William Law)

10 April

William Booth, founder of the Salvation Army, was born on 10 April 1829. The Salvation Army was founded in 1865. Fifteen years later a sixteen-year-old Salvation Army girl emigrated from England to the United States, where she and her parents began evangelistic meetings in an old shed. Soon after, the Salvation Army sent a group to New York, to begin the work there.

'Ash-barrel Jimmy'

New York did not know quite what to make of these newcomers. The little group of Salvation Army members – most of them young women – would stand at street corners, singing their newfangled hymns. The tunes were familiar – *My Old Kentucky Home* and *The Old Folks at Home* – but the words were strange. The preaching was different too – not at all what they were used to in church.

The Salvation Army tried a different way to attract crowds. They appealed to the theatres in the city to give up their Sunday performance in favour of a Salvation Army meeting. The only one to agree was Harry Hill, who ran a 'disreputable den' of a music-hall. But even he was not prepared to stand down himself but merely billed the Salvation Army as part of his performance – a gimmick to draw the crowds. The crowds turned up all right, but the Salvation Army contribution was a complete flop. Most of the audience thought it was only good for a laugh.

The little group left the theatre feeling that their attempt had been in vain. But there was a man waiting for them at the stage door. 'It's Ash-barrel Jimmy,' they were told.

They chatted to the down-and-out and found out how he came by his name. He had once been discovered dead drunk, upside down in a barrel. But every human being was of value to the Salvation Army. They invited Jimmy to come to the meeting arranged for the next night. He came, and the message of the gospel changed his whole life. Ash-barrel Jimmy was the first Salvation Army convert in the United States.

11 April

Since his death in April 1761, **William Law**'s *Serious Call to a Devout and Holy Life* has continued to influence many people. In spite of strong differences of opinion, John Wesley said of Law's writings: 'The light flowed in so mightily upon my soul that everything appeared in a new view.' Dr Samuel Johnson is reported by Boswell as saying that reading Law was 'the first occasion of my thinking in earnest of religion, after I became capable of rational enquiry.'

'Slugabeds'

William Law believed in getting up early. He was in the habit of rising at five for prayers, before going to milk the cows. Then he cooked gruel, or porridge, for the beggars who came to the Gibbon great house for breakfast. But he did not wake the rest of the sleeping 'slugabeds' in the household until nine o'clock.

Early to rise

'I take it for granted that every Christian, that is in health, is up early in the morning; for it is much more reasonable to suppose a person up early because he is a Christian than because … he has business that wants him. If he is to be blamed as a slothful drone that chooses the lazy indulgence of sleep to worldly business, how much more is he to be reproached that would rather lie folded up in a bed than raising his heart to God in praise and adoration!

'Receive … every day as a resurrection from death, as a new enjoyment of life … meet every rising sun with such sentiments of God's goodness as if you had seen all things new created on your account; and under the sense of so great a blessing, let your joyful heart praise and magnify so good and glorious a Creator.'

(From *Serious Call to a Devout and Holy Life* by William Law)

Law's character was a blend of great gentleness and strict personal discipline. In those days, larks and linnets were sold in cages. He would buy them so that he could set them free.

Alan Paton died on 12 April 1988. He was a South African
Christian and strongly anti-apartheid. During the difficult time
of his first wife's terminal illness, he wrote a book of meditations
called *Instrument of thy Peace*.

Breaking down barriers

Although in the years since Alan Paton died, new laws and
attitudes have emerged in South Africa, his words about
prejudice and discrimination are still needed in our world
today. Class, gender, lifestyle, religious belief and many other
differences still divide humankind and some groups are still
rejected or despised by others:

> 'In my own country there are many races, and
> where race difference is established and
> maintained by law, it is difficult for many
> members of the so-called superior group to
> serve those of the so-called inferior group. For
> every white person who would help an old
> black woman across a busy street, there would
> be some who would not; though perhaps some
> of those would wish that they *could* do so. But
> once the barrier is crossed, the whole
> personality becomes richer and gentler. There is
> only one way in which man's inhumanity to
> man can be made endurable to us, and that is
> when we in our own lives try to exemplify man's
> humanity to man.'

My plan be in thy mind O God
My work be in thy hands
My ears be ever swift to hear
The words of thy commands

Instrument of thy Peace by Alan Paton

13 April

On 13 April 1742 the first performance of Handel's *Messiah* was given in Dublin. **George Frederick Handel** (1685-1749) was a German-born composer who settled in England in 1712. He wrote operas, orchestral works and oratorios, the most famous of which is *Messiah*.

'All heaven before me'

On 13 April 1742, a notice appeared in the Dublin papers heralding the first performance of Handel's oratorio *Messiah*.

'The doors will open at eleven and the Oratorio will begin at twelve. The favour of the ladies is requested not to come with hoops this day to the Musick Hall in Fishamble Street. The gentlemen are desired to come without their swords.'

A full house was expected and the fashionable hooped petticoats would take up valuable space. Swords could be dangerous in a crush. Sure enough, a capacity audience of 700 packed the hall and hundreds more waited outside in the street.

Seven months earlier, Handel had sat alone in the little front room of a house in Brook Street, London. His health was broken and many thought that his career had ended. He looked at some words sent to him by a writer called Jennens. The words were not Jennens' own but were taken from the Bible and all referred to Jesus the Messiah.

Handel began to compose music to fit the words. For twenty four days he did not leave the house. His servant brought him food but he often left it untouched. One day the servant came in to find Handel composing the 'Hallelujah Chorus'. He sat at the table with tears streaming down his face. 'I did think I did see all heaven before me and the great God himself,' he exclaimed.

In Dublin, *Messiah* was an immediate success. One critic wrote: 'Mr Handel's new grand sacred oratorio ... was performed so well, that it gave universal satisfaction to all present; and was allowed by the greatest Judges to be the finest composition of music that ever was heard.'

George Frederick Handel died on 14 April 1759. Handel, German-born, settled in England. He wrote a great number of Italian style operas, but is best remembered for his Biblical oratorios. At his request he was buried in Westminster Abbey.

'All standing'

When *Messiah* was first to be performed in London there were those who strongly objected to 'sacred' words being performed for 'diversion and amusement' in playhouses and sung by 'a Set of people very unfit to perform so solemn a service.' So Handel simply advertised it as 'A New Sacred Oratorio'.

The custom of everyone standing for the *Hallelujah Chorus* is explained in a letter of 1780: 'When Handel's *Messiah* was first performed, the audience was exceedingly struck and affected by the music in general; but when that chorus struck up, "For the Lord God Omnipotent reigneth", they were so transported, that they all, together with the king (who happened to be present), started up, and remained standing till the chorus ended: and hence it became the fashion in England for the audience to stand while that part of the music is performing.' The same letter quotes Handel's words when he was complimented on the 'noble entertainment' he had given. '"My lord," said Handel, "I should be sorry if I only entertained them. I wish to make them better."'

Handel gave to various charities and was sympathetic to the work of Thomas Coram, a retired sea-captain, to help the plight of the thousands of new-born illegitimate babies, who were abandoned. Coram appealed for subscriptions and in 1745 was able to open the foundling Hospital. All but the chapel was finished by 1749 and Handel held a concert to raise money for its completion. For a time, annual performances of the oratorio were performed at the Foundling Hospital; later the comment was made that *Messiah* had 'fed the hungry, clothed the naked, fostered the orphan, and enriched succeeding managers of Oratorios more than any single musical production in this or any other country.'

(Source: *Handel* by Wendy Thompson, from *The Illustrated Lives of the Great composers* series)

15 April

Malta – Now – 2000

'Malta is a mere 17 miles long by nine miles wide, so you can easily plan your holiday programme to take in sightseeing of the magnificent churches, ancient villages and prehistoric sites, or to enjoy the bays and beaches, water sports and boat trips, or the shopping in the town and village markets… And of course there is the sunshine!' (Holiday brochure for Malta)

Malta – Then – 1940s

The sirens wailed in Valetta, on the besieged island of Malta, but the governor-general, Sir William Dobbie, went on writing at his desk. Two young army officers approached him apologetically: 'There's a raid on, sir.'

'Yes, I know,' the general replied and went on writing. 'I just want to finish this page.' It never occurred to General Dobbie to be frightened, and the people of the island followed his lead. His courage and faith in God won their trust and affection.

Dobbie determined that the beleaguered island would not only defend itself from attack by air or sea, but also use its prime position to take the offensive against the enemy who threatened the freedom of the world.

In recognition of that contribution King George VI wrote, on 15 April 1942,

'The Governor, Malta,

To honour her brave people I award the George Cross to the island fortress of Malta to bear witness to a heroism and devotion that will long be famous in history.'

It was the first time that a community rather than an individual had been given this highest British civil award.

Postscript: It was another 57 years before the George Cross was awarded to a group of people. In November 1999 Queen Elizabeth II awarded it to the Ulster Constabulary.

16 April is the Feast Day of **St Bernadette**. Bernadette Soubirous was the eldest daughter of a poor miller; she was small and undernourished and many local people despised her family and thought her slow and backward.

Pilgrimage to Lourdes

Bernadette crawled on hands and knees up and down the cave, then, watched by a curious crowd, stopped and scraped the ground near a muddy puddle. Everyone had heard that this unpromising fourteen-year-old girl claimed to have seen a lady in white many times, near the grotto. Now they had come to see what was happening:

'Why ever are you doing that, Bernadette?' they called out;

'Because the Lady told me to,' she replied. Most of the onlookers smiled and walked away. A few stayed and witnessed what happened next. Where a muddy puddle had been, a clear spring bubbled up. Soon local people came to believe that the lady that Bernadette had repeatedly seen was none other than the Virgin Mary and that it was she who had directed the girl to the hidden spring, whose waters could heal.

In the wake of Bernadette's experiences a flurry of religious and superstitious stories began to circulate and for a long time the church authorities were sceptical of Bernadette's visions. Bernadette herself remained unspoiled by fuss or fame. She entered a convent and lived a gentle and self-effacing life, dying in 1879 at the age of thirty-five. Her experiences made Lourdes a place of pilgrimage and healing, which it is to the present day. But Bernadette was canonised not for her visions but for her life of quiet goodness and simple humility.

HCPT – The Pilgrimage Trust, takes about two thousand disabled or neglected children to Lourdes every year, including groups from Slovakia. Elena, who leads those groups describes one boy who was severely depressed and suicidal: 'The effect on him was dramatic. "I really felt the love of God in my heart", he said and he has undergone a complete conversion experience. He never tires of telling people about it.'

17 April

Daniel Defoe, writer, died in April 1731. Defoe, born in 1660, worked as a merchant, economist, journalist and spy. He was too young to remember much about the Plague and the Great Fire of London in 1666, but his vivid *Journal of the Plague Year* reads like an eyewitness account. *Robinson Crusoe*, his first novel, written at 60, is based on the adventures of Alexander Selkirk, a Scottish sailor, but although it is fiction, Defoe's skills and powerful imagination make it ring true.

'Why God no kill the Devil?'

After years of solitude Robinson Crusoe is delighted to have the companionship of Friday, as he names him. Crusoe helped him escape from cannibals and won his lifelong allegiance. Friday soon picks up numerous skills and learns some English. Crusoe confides: 'This was the pleasantest year of all the life I led in this place; Friday began to talk pretty well ... and besides the pleasure of talking to him, ... I began really to love the creature ... I began to instruct him in the knowledge of the true God ... He listened with great attention, and received with pleasure the notion of Jesus Christ being sent to redeem us ... I found it was not easy to imprint right notions in his mind about the Devil ... "Well," says Friday, "but you say God is so strong, so great; is he not much strong, much might than the Devil?" "Yes, yes," says I, "Friday, God is stronger than the Devil, God is above the Devil." ... "But," says he again, "if God much strong, much might as the Devil, why God no kill the Devil, so make him no more wicked?"

'I was strangely surprised at his question. And at first I could not tell what to say; so I pretended not to hear him and asked him what he said. But he was too earnest for an answer to forget his question.' (Crusoe then explained that the Devil was 'reserved' for judgement as all are who do not repent and receive pardon.) '" Well, well," says he mighty affectionately, "that well; so you, I, Devil, all wicked, all preserve, repent, God pardon all."'

Crusoe wisely 'diverted the present discourse', sent Friday on an errand, then 'seriously prayed' for wisdom to instruct Friday 'savingly'.

(From *Robinson Crusoe* by Daniel Defoe 1660-1731)

On 18 April, 1521 **Martin Luther** made his defence at the Diet of Worms.

'Here I stand'

The religious authorities decided that something had to be done about Martin Luther. His preaching was bad enough – but his books were worse. And they were rolling off the newly-invented printing presses and selling like hot cakes. So Luther was summoned to appear before a court presided over by the new Holy Roman Emperor, Charles V.

A big, imposing man, Dr Ecken, solemnly asked Luther if he was ready to renounce his writings. Luther replied that he would do so on one condition only. If anyone, even a child, could prove him wrong *from Scripture,* then he would retract. His accusers insisted that all heretics claimed to base their beliefs on the Bible. But in vain. Luther was too sure of his ground. He maintained his reliance on:

Faith alone – Men and women are freely forgiven by God not by good works or penance, but by putting faith in Jesus Christ.

Grace alone – Salvation comes through God's undeserved love and goodness.

The Bible alone – No church rules, decrees or traditions have any weight if they contradict the teaching of the Bible.

Dr Ecken pleaded: 'For the last time I ask you, Martin. Do you or do you not repudiate your books or the errors they contain?' 'I cannot and will not recant,' Luther replied, 'for to go against my conscience is neither right nor healthy. Here I stand, I cannot do otherwise.'

Luther summarised the ordeal in a letter to a friend: 'All they said was: "Are these books yours?" – "Yes." – "Will you recant?" – "No!" – "Then get out."'

Prayer

Ah, dearest Jesus, holy Child
Make thee a bed, soft, undefiled,
Within my heart, that it may be
A quiet chamber kept for thee.

Martin Luther 1483-1546

19 April

'Dickie' Bird, the cricket umpire, was born on 19 April 1933. Harold Dennis Bird, known from schooldays onwards as Dickie – was born in Barnsley, Yorkshire, the son of a coal miner. After playing county cricket he trained to be a first class umpire and became the third youngest Test umpire. He was awarded the MBE and has received many honours for his umpiring achievements.

Married to cricket

It was a Sunday morning and Dickie Bird was in Barbados for umpire duty. Just before morning service began, he slipped into a Methodist church, jam-packed with local people in their Sunday best. The preacher announced: 'Brothers and sisters, we have in our midst Mr Dickie Bird, the Test umpire from England.' The church erupted in a burst of applause and Dickie had a job to escape afterwards, surrounded by so many welcoming people. 'It was a great feeling,' he writes, 'all those thousands of miles away from home, yet among so many friends. That is what belonging to a Church family means, and I believe my faith has helped me through many dark times.'

When he was due to umpire his first Test match at the Oval, he was so afraid that the London traffic would make him late that he insisted on being called in his hotel at 4.30 am, to set off in time for 11.30 start of play. Not surprisingly, he arrived very early – at 6am – and found the ground still locked up. He threw his bag over the gate and was just climbing over himself when he was stopped midway by a London bobby, demanding to know just what he was doing. It was hard to convince him that he was the official umpire, due for a match that would not begin for another five and a half hours.

Dickie Bird's story (*Dickie Bird – My Autobiography*) is packed with fascinating and amusing anecdotes. 'A good umpire must have five qualities,' he writes, 'honesty, concentration, application, dedication, and the calm confidence to inspire and retain the respect of the players. If I could help in that way I would feel that I was putting something back into a game that has given me so much.'

On 20 April 1781 **Boswell** recorded the events of 'one of the
happiest days that I remember to have enjoyed in the whole course
of my life'. In the evening of the happy day, Boswell and Johnson
dined with Mrs Garrick in the company of Miss Hannah More (who
lived with her), Sir Joshua Reynolds and others.

Ordinary people matter

'In the evening we had a large company in the drawing-
room.

'Talking of a very respectable author, [Dr Johnson]
told us of a curious circumstance in [the man's] life, which
was, that he had married a printer's devil.
Reynolds: "A printer's devil, Sir! Why, I thought a printer's
devil was a creature with a black face and in rags."
Johnson: "Yes, Sir. But I suppose, he had her face washed,
and put clean clothes on her." (Then, looking very
serious, and very earnest.) "And she did not disgrace him;
the woman had a bottom of good sense." The word
"bottom" thus introduced, was so ludicrous when
contrasted with his gravity, that most of us could not
forbear tittering and laughing; though I recollect that
the Bishop of Killaloe kept his countenance with perfect
steadiness, while Miss Hannah More slyly hid her face
behind a lady's back who sat on the same settee with her.
His pride could not bear that any expression of his
should excite ridicule when he did not intend it; he
therefore resolved to assume and exercise despotick
power, glanced sternly around, and calling out in a strong
voice, "Where's the merriment?" Then collecting himself,
and looking aweful [sic], to make us feel how he could
impose restraint, and as it were searching his mind for a
still more ludicrous word, he slowly pronounced, "I say
the *woman* was *fundamentally* sensible"; as if he had
said, hear this now, and laugh if you dare. We all sat as
composed as at a funeral.'

(*A printer's devil was an apprentice or errand boy in a printing
firm*)

(From *The Life of Samuel Johnson* by James Boswell)

21 April

The Bluestockings

In the eighteenth century intelligent and serious-minded women craved something more stimulating than playing cards and began to arrange cultural evenings. This new kind of 'evening assembly' was being held at about the time that Boswell enjoyed his evening at Mrs Garrick's. At these events, as he explained, 'the fair sex might participate in conversation with literary and ingenious men ... These societies were denominated *Bluestocking Clubs.*'

According to one story the Bluestockings came by their name when a learned man called Benjamin Stillfleet was invited to one of their parties. He refused because he said that he had no suitable clothes to wear, so his hostess told him to come as he was, 'in his blue stockings' – the ordinary everyday worsted stockings he was wearing at the time. He did, and the name caught on as a nickname for the group. Horace Walpole, contemporary writer and man of letters, dubbed the Bluestocking groups 'petticoteries'.

When Hannah More visited London in 1773 to 1774, she was welcomed into the circle. She hoped to be a successful writer and David Garrick, the actor and theatre manager, took her under his wing and produced two of her plays. When Garrick died in 1779 Hannah More gave up writing for the stage. Her Christian faith became more important to her, especially when she became friendly with Wilberforce and his evangelical friends. In her Somerset cottage she wrote Christian tracts and set up schools and clubs to give education to children and adults – much to the disapproval of clergy and landowners. 'We shan't have a boy to plough or a wench to dress a shoulder of mutton,' they complained. But Hannah More was undeterred.

Glen Campbell, country singer, was born on 22 April 1938.

Rhinestone cowboy

'There have been two anchors in my life,' Glen Campbell told his interviewer, Steve Chalke, 'they are my faith and my guitar.' But he acknowledged that he had not had a life free from turmoil and suffering.

Glen was the seventh son in a family of twelve children. His father taught him to play the guitar and he first used his skills in a Baptist church.

When he left home to be a musician he entered a highly competitive world, but by 1968 he had his own TV show and fame began to come his way. He performed with Frank Sinatra and did a movie with John Wayne. But his closest friend was Elvis Presley. 'We were like brothers,' he says. He vividly remembers their last meeting, how they spent the night talking about the mess they had both made of their private lives and the hopelessness of trying to change. Elvis never did find a way but Glen found help.

He was drinking hard by this time and also had a cocaine habit. One day he touched bottom. He remembers lying shaking, hot one minute then freezing cold the next. In desperation he prayed: 'God, get me out of this and I'll never do it again!' And when he recovered he kept his word; he never took drugs again. He began to think about the things that really matter in life. He sang 'Try a little kindness,' as he felt compassion for others and the need to 'shine your light for everyone to see.'

He had experienced unhappiness and pain in three broken marriages. But, he says, when he asked God back into his life things began to change. His fourth wife Kim, to whom he has been married for seventeen years, is a Christian too and sees the secret of their success in the fact that God is in charge of their relationship.

He reached the depths in a way that perhaps only the rich and famous can, but now he has made harmony in his singing and his relationships. He is in tune with God and with life.

(Glen Campbell was talking on the BBC *Songs of Praise* programme)

23 April

Man of the millennium

How much do we know about William Shakespeare? No fascinating anecdotes, only a few bare facts emerge but perhaps that is all we need. In Shakespeare's poetry and through the characters in his plays we have all the human situations and emotions – love, hate, jealousy, lust, ambition, power, rage, tenderness, grief, humour and wit. He shows us our own hearts more perfectly than we knew them ourselves.

William Shakespeare was the eldest son of a glove and wool dealer, probably educated at Stratford's excellent grammar school. At eighteen he married twenty-six year old Anne Hathaway, who was already pregnant. When he was still young he went to London and won fame – and money – as poet, playwright, actor, joint-manager of an acting company and part-owner of one of the theatres. In 1612 he quitted London and returned to Stratford, where he died four years later.

In one of his sonnets Shakespeare testifies to the nature of lasting love between two people. It is the kind of love that also reflects God's unchanging love for us.

Let me not to the marriage of true minds
Admit impediments. Love is not love
Which alters when it alteration finds
Or bends with the remover to remove: –
Oh no! It is an ever-fixed mark
That looks on tempests, and is never shaken;
It is the star to every wandering bark,
Whose worth's unknown, although his height be taken.
Love's not Time's fool, though rosy lips and cheeks
Within his bending sickle's compass come;
Love alters not with his brief hours and weeks
But bears it out e'vn to the edge of doom.
If this be error, and upon me proved,
I never writ, nor no man ever loved.

William Shakespeare

Anthony Trollope, writer, was born on 24 April 1815. Trollope's *Chronicles of Barsetshire* centre on life in a cathedral close, where good and bad clerics are skilfully portrayed. Mr Harding, once warden of a charity hospital for old men, was wrongfully sacked then tricked out of reappointment. In this extract he introduces the new warden to the inmates with Christian kindness and lack of malice.

'All for the best'

'It was a clear bright morning, though in November, that Mr Harding and Mr Quiverful, arm in arm, walked through the hospital gate ... Now that he re-entered, with another warden under his wing, he did so with ... quiet step and calm demeanour ... one might have said that he was merely returning with a friend...'

'Arm in arm they walked into the inner quadrangle of the building and there the five old men met them...

'"I am very glad to know that at last you have a new warden," said Mr Harding in a very cheery voice.

'"We be very old for any change," said one of them, "but we do suppose it be all for the best."

'"Certainly – certainly it is for the best ... It is a great satisfaction to me to know that so good a man is coming to take care of you and that it is no stranger but a friend of my own..."

'"What I can do to fill the void which [Mr Harding] left here, I will do," [Mr Quiverful said]. "But to you who have known him I can never be the same well-loved father that he has been."

'"No sir, no," said old Bunce, "no one can be that. Not if the new bishop sent a hangel to us out of heaven."'

(From *Barchester Towers* by Anthony Trollope)

Bestow on me, O Lord, a genial spirit and unwearied forbearance, a mild, loving, patient heart, kindly looks, pleasant, cordial manner ... that I may give offence to none, but, as much as in me lies, live in charity with all. – Johann Arnott 1558-1621

25 April

Oliver Cromwell was born on 25 April 1559.

'Take away this bauble!'

There was not a moment to lose. Oliver Cromwell did not even wait to change his grey worsted stockings for something more suitable for parliament. Even now the vital bill was being debated and only an urgent summons from a friend had brought him to the House in time.

Cromwell posted a guard within call, then entered and waited for the Speaker of the House to put the motion that 'this bill do now pass.' Then he intervened. He reminded the House of the abuses they had fought in battle to abolish. Now they wanted to maintain parliament in their own hands as a permanent body, with no freely elected members.

Cromwell paced up and down. 'The Lord has done with you,' he concluded and, calling the guard, ordered the Speaker to step down. Finally, the Speaker and all the members filed out of the chamber, leaving Cromwell and his soldiers in possession.

'Take away this bauble!' Cromwell shouted, snatching up the mace from the table. He was determined that a new rule of justice should begin.

Cromwell's last prayer

Lord, I come to thee for thy people. Thou hast made me, though very unworthy, a mean instrument to do them some good. Lord, however thou do dispose of me, continue and go on to do good to them. Give them consistency of judgement, one heart and mutual love: go on to deliver them and make the name of Christ glorious in the world. Amen.

Oliver Cromwell.

The tolerant Protector

When the new parliament assembled, Cromwell told them, 'You are called with a high call and why should we be afraid to think that this may be the door to usher in the things that God has promised?'

But in spite of the confidence that God was on his side, he was determined that others who thought differently should be left in peace. He refused to punish Roman Catholics in England who did not observe the state form of worship. He dealt kindly with the new Quaker movement and showed sympathy for the Jews, who had been cruelly persecuted by Christians for centuries. After a 300-year ban, they were again allowed into the country and given freedom to worship.

Cromwell's sympathies were with ordinary people who had no power or influence. He immediately pardoned some small-time criminals who had been sentenced to death. He hated the practice of hanging a person for committing a petty crime. 'To hang a man for six and eightpence and I know not what, to hang for a trifle and acquit for murder – to see men lose their lives for petty matters, this is a thing God will reckon for.'

'If we will have peace without a worm in it, lay we the foundations of justice and good will.' – Oliver Cromwell 1599-1658

27 April

On 27 April 1994 elections took place in **South Africa**, the first in which black as well as white people were allowed to vote.

Freedom!

'I folded my ballot paper and cast my vote. "Wow" I shouted, "Yippee!"' Archbishop Desmond Tutu vividly describes his emotions as he voted in his country's elections for the first time. When he went outside, people were cheering and dancing as if it were carnival time. He had waited until he was sixty-two to cast his vote and Nelson Mandela until he was seventy-six. Waiting seemed the keynote of voting day too. Many people queued for hours to vote due to hitches of one kind or another. But as they waited, people of all colours and social standing queued together. It seemed as if the barriers had come down at last and the people of South Africa were beginning to recognise that they were one people.

Desmond Tutu tried to describe his experience and that of his fellow black and coloured people that day: 'How do you convey that sense of freedom that tastes like sweet nectar the first time you experience it? How do you describe it to someone who was born into freedom? It is impossible, like trying to describe the colour red to someone born blind. It is a feeling that makes you want to laugh and cry, to dance with joy and yet at the same time you fear that it is too good to be true and that it might just all evaporate ... That's how we felt.'

Tutu believes that white South Africans were transformed by the experience too. They were set free from the burden of guilt caused by years of unjust oppression of others. They could only be set free when black people were free too.

(From *No Future Without Forgiveness* by Desmond Tutu)

Unless we learn to live together as brothers, we will die together as fools. – Martin Luther King Jr

Anthony Ashley Cooper, seventh Earl of Shaftesbury, was born on 28 April 1901.

'The cause of the poor and friendless'

Anthony Ashley Cooper was about fourteen at the time and a pupil at Harrow School.

'Walking one day down Harrow Hill, he heard from a side street the sound of a low song. He watched in fascinated horror as a party of drunken men came staggering round the corner carrying a rough coffin. Suddenly they let the coffin fall to the ground and broke into a flood of oaths and curses.'

The boy was shocked and appalled. There and then, according to his first biographer, 'Before the sound of the drunken song had died away, he had determined that with the help of God he would devote his life to pleading the cause of the poor and friendless.'

Despite his privileged birth into a wealthy family, Ashley Cooper knew what it was to be desperately unhappy. His parents were uncaring and his early school-life pure misery. Only one person loved and cared for him – a servant girl who had become housekeeper in the family's London home. She gave little Anthony all the love he needed and taught him to share her faith in a loving, caring God. He was only seven when she died, but he never forgot her teaching and her example. He did not picture God as a stern disciplinarian, like many in his time, but as a loving Father. His own unhappiness made him compassionate and his deep Christian commitment led him to do more to lessen the misery of others than any other person in England.

Prayer

Oh God, the father of the forsaken, the help of the weak, the supplier of the needy ... open and touch our hearts that we may see and do ... Strengthen us in the work which we have undertaken; give us wisdom, perseverance, faith and zeal ... for the love of your Son, Christ Jesus.

Lord Shaftesbury 1801-1885

---

29 April

Utchunu, a Hixkaryana Indian, living on the river Nhamunda, a tributary of the Amazon, died at the end of April 1971. Des and Grace Derbyshire lived with the Hixkaryana for nearly twenty years, learning the language, constructing a written language and telling the people the good news of the Christian Gospel. They were part of the international team of Wycliffe Bible Translators. Des eventually became an adviser to other translators and gained a Ph D at London University in his specialist field of linguistics study.

From fear to faith

Utchunu, quick-witted and intelligent, was the ideal person to help Des in his attempts to master the Hixkaryana language. He advised him too as he began to translate the New Testament into a language never before written down.

Utchunu was still busy hunting and fishing, collecting brazil nuts in the rainy season and clearing a new little bit of the forest every year for planting crops. He took time to make up his mind about this new religion and it was a while before he decided to commit himself wholly to love and follow Jesus Christ.

When he became a Christian his life was transformed. He no longer went to the shamans or witch-doctors for healing and ceased to live in fear of the evil spirits which were said to haunt everything around and bring illness and bad luck.

Before his death from cancer, he wrote a journal describing his experiences. He did not reject the culture of his own tribe, nor did he accept Western values, but his life changed because, in his own words, 'When we belong to Jesus, we have to be different.' The old hates and fears gave place to love and trust in God.

'Go good – I am with you'

Utchunu lay desperately ill in the hospital at Belem in Brazil. But he was not afraid.

He had lived all his life in the remote Hixkaryana village which was two hours' canoe-trip from the next village upstream, but when he fell ill he decided to hitchhike by boat to Belem, the big city 700 miles away, at the mouth of the Amazon. When he arrived for the first time in a city, with its huge buildings and the bewildering noise and bustle, Utchunu prayed. 'Father, I am going to this important man because I want to get into hospital. Send your Spirit ahead of us.' God answered him, 'Don't worry. Go good. You are with me and I am with you. I have brought you here because you are one of my people.'

Then, on top of the illness that had brought him to Belem, Utchunu caught smallpox. For forty-five days he was so ill that he was 'completely unable to eat meals, unable to see or talk, in a state of paralysis, not able to move at all,' as he described it later.

But he told the doctor, 'God will help me get better, if it is his will.'

The doctor said, 'Forget about God. He can't help you.'

Utchuna replied, 'God has let me be sick so that he can show you his power. He will make me well again so that you can see his power.'

And Utchunu was healed of his smallpox.

(Dialogue taken from *Utchunu's Journal*)

Postscript: Des Derbyshire translated the New Testament into Hixkaryana and has completed sixty per cent of the Old Testament, with the help of Hixkaryana volunteers. At present it is they who do the first draft which they send with their notebooks to Des, now in the UK. Sadly, Grace has died, but Des visits the tribe regularly for long visits so that all the translators can make revisions together. 'I learn a lot from them,' he insists.

1 May

On 1 May 1851, Queen Victoria opened the **Great Exhibition** in Hyde Park, London. It was a showcase for Britain's engineering and manufacturing achievements, housed in the Crystal Palace, designed by Sir Joseph Paxton and made of glass on a framework of iron. In 1854 the Palace was dismantled and re-erected in South London, where it was used as an exhibition and entertainment centre until it burned down in 1936.

For time – or for eternity?

'Dear Friend

'It is there! The Crystal Palace is before you in all its glory; its banners are waving in the breeze and the light of heaven is shining through its walls.'

These were words that a visitor to the Great Exhibition, strolling through Hyde Park, might have idly read from a leaflet politely pressed into his hand by a young man. George Williams and his friends in the newly-formed YMCA decided that the Great Exhibition would provide a splendid opportunity for them to spread the gospel. Thousands of visitors from far and wide would throng London for the occasion.

They set about the operation in a businesslike way. London was divided into thirty-six districts and each put in the charge of two young men, who were furnished with a printed plan. Every Sunday, sixteen thousand Christian tracts were to be distributed to the crowds converging on Hyde Park. The tracts were carefully written to capture attention and engage the interest of those who took them. In some, the writer contrasted the splendour of the Crystal Palace – which would pass – with the far greater splendours of God's kingdom, which would never end. Then came the challenging question:

'Are *you* safe for eternity?'

Leonardo da Vinci died on 2 May 1519. Born in 1452, he was the illegitimate son of a young Florentine noble and a country girl. He is probably the most versatile genius that ever lived. He studied music, painting and poetry, then at fifty-four began a career as an engineer. Centuries ahead of his time, he suggested the parachute, man-powered flight, the centrifugal pump and hydraulic press. He wrote pop songs and musicals. He painted the famous portrait of the Mona Lisa and the mural of The Last Supper.

Tested by experiment

The guests were enjoying themselves enormously. Leonardo was official Master of Revels at the court of Milan and always provided brilliant entertainment. They gazed in wonder at this latest party trick of his. Charming little figures were actually floating around the room above the table where they sat.

For Leonardo himself it was perhaps less of a party trick and more of an experiment. He had filled hollow wax figures with hot air to make them float, and had hit upon the principle that would launch the hot air balloon in the future.

Leonardo was not a fanciful or unrealistic inventor. His engineering drawings – like his anatomical drawings – are models of accuracy. His advice to all scientists and engineers was, 'Before you make a result a general rule, test it by experiment two or three times, to see if you get the same result each time.' Many times in his writings, the comment beneath reads, 'Tested by experiment'.

Iron rusts from disuse; stagnant water loses its purity and in cold weather becomes frozen; even so does inaction sap the vigour of the mind. – Leonardo da Vinci

3 May

In May 1999 **Leonardo**'s 'The Last Supper' was back on display in Milan. The latest restoration took 22 years – five times longer than Leonardo took to execute the original fresco(1498). He had been commissioned to do the work on bumpy, dry plaster; he experimented, using pigments mixed with egg and oil which quickly flaked. By 1566 the fresco was already decaying. The monks too, neglected their treasure and it was vandalised by invading soldiers. Critics are divided on their verdict on the latest restoration. 'It's 18 to 20 per cent Leonardo and 80 per cent by the restorer,' one says, but the person who oversaw the work insists that their techniques have restored Leonardo's original bright colours as well as some of the artist's work, long covered over by earlier restorers.

Unfinished portrait

The Dominican prior in Milan was growing impatient. He complained to the duke, who was Leonardo's patron, that the artist was taking far too long to complete the mural in his monastery. The duke tried to calm him down.

'Men of genius are sometimes producing most when they seem to be labouring least,' he reassured him. The fresco was to depict the Last Supper, at the moment when Jesus said, 'One of you shall betray me.' Two of the faces presented a challenge that even Leonardo found it hard to meet – the treacherous face of Judas Iscariot and the face of Christ, for which he could find no model.

He suggested to the duke that he could use the head of 'that troublesome and impertinent prior' as the model for Judas. He did complete that figure, but the head of Christ was never completed. Even Leonardo, a genius, felt unable to interpret Jesus through art.

The Council of Constance, meeting on 4 May 1415, decreed that the remains of **John Wyclif**, Bible translator, should be dug up and burned.

Burned with a Bible round their necks

No one could understand a word of the Bible or of the services in church. For a start, it was in Latin, which was fine for scholars and rich people, but totally incomprehensible to peasants and ordinary people. And the priests mumbled, so that even to those who could understand it, their Latin made no sense.

John Wyclif, who was a priest and a scholar, determined to make the Bible understood by everyone. First he sent his followers, two by two, to preach the gospel in the countryside round about. Their enemies dubbed them 'Lollards', or 'mutterers'. The Lollards took with them the New Testament in English, that Wyclif had translated, often with their help. Since it was before the days of printing, each copy had to be laboriously written out by hand. It took about ten months and cost about £40 to produce one. Amazingly, some 170 copies still survive.

It was dangerous to possess or even be found reading the English New Testament. Many Lollards were arrested and their Bibles burned. Some were themselves burned, with their Bibles round their necks. Wyclif was declared a heretic and though he died from natural causes, his body was dug up and burned. But his Bible survived.

Part of the Lord's Prayer (Luke 11:2-4) in the Wyclif Bible (about 1384)

Fadir, halewid be thi name. Thi kingdom come to. Give to us today oure eche dayes breed. And forgyve us oure synnes, as and we forgyven to each owynge to us. And leed not us in to temptacioun.

5 May

On 5 May 1659 **St Helena** was occupied by the East India company and became a British colony. St Helena has no air-strip and is more than a thousand miles from the African coast. But before the building of the Suez canal, more than 1000 ships a year would put in at St Helena for supplies. Napoleon was exiled and died there in 1821.

Far from home

The photo in the newspaper showed a genial bearded sea-captain, standing beside a teenage African boy, who frowns a little, as if uncertain what the future holds.

The March 2000 supply ship had arrived at St Helena with an unexpected passenger on board. Sixteen-year-old Alain had emerged from his hiding place in the ship's funnel when they were three days out to sea. He was covered in soot, thin and dehydrated. His story was horrific. His Hutu family – grandparents, parents and twelve brothers and sisters – had been massacred by Tutsi troops in Burundi, while he lay beneath their bodies, pretending to be dead. Then he made his escape, travelling five thousand miles, over four countries, avoiding patrols, and finally stowing away aboard *RMS St Helena* at Cape Town.

His arrival made front-page news and the islanders responded immediately. 'Everyone took him to their hearts,' the captain said. Passengers and crew on the supply ship raised enough money to buy Alain clothes, islanders sent parcels to the boat and offered free accommodation, even adoption. St Helena was ready to give a big welcome to their first asylum seeker. But Alain began to wonder; could he make this unfamiliar island his home?

Prayer

We bring before you, O Lord, the troubles and perils of people and nations, the sighing of prisoners and captives, the sorrows of the bereaved, the necessities of strangers, the helplessness of the weak, the despondency of the weary, the failing powers of the aged. O Lord, draw near to each; for the sake of Jesus Christ our Lord. – St Anselm 1033-1109

James Hudson Taylor, missionary to China, was born in May 1832. He was converted at 17, but later made a further, total commitment to God. He was sure that God wanted him to go to China. In preparation he began to study medicine and learn Chinese.

Faith that works!

'After various experiments,' Hudson Taylor wrote, 'I found that the most economical way was to live on brown bread and water.' A few apples for lunch supplemented James's meagre diet as he walked the four miles each way from his Soho lodgings to the London Hospital. One morning the students were dissecting the body of a man who had died of fever. They were warned not to cut themselves but James forgot that he had pricked his finger the night before. By the end of that day he was very ill and was bluntly told, 'you are a dead man.'

'My first thought,' he wrote, 'was one of sorrow that I could not go to China; but very soon came the feeling, "Unless I am greatly mistaken, I have work to do in China and shall not die."' Once back at his lodgings, he lanced the swelling himself, then fainted clean away. His uncle was summoned and called a doctor. James was so certain that he would recover that he asked that his parents should not be told. After weeks of illness, he was able to leave his room. He could not pay his fare home to Yorkshire, to convalesce, but felt constrained to go to a shipping office where he was owed some money. But that was two miles away and James hardly had the strength to walk downstairs, so 'I reminded the Lord that I could not afford to take a conveyance ... I asked in the name of Christ that the strength might immediately be given: and sending the servant up to my room for my hat and stick, I set out not to *attempt* but to *walk* to Cheapside.'

Next day, the doctor, (who refused payment), also refused to believe that Hudson Taylor had walked that distance. When he heard of the young man's prayers and that the money he had unexpectedly been paid was enough for his expenses and fare home, he said, with tears in his eyes, 'I would give all the world for a faith like yours.'

(Source: *Biography of James Hudson Taylor* by Dr and Mrs Howard Taylor)

7 May

On 7 May 1747 *Johann Sebastian Bach* arrived at
the court of Frederick II of Prussia.

Musical Offering

The King called for the music to stop. He wanted to hear
Johann Sebastian play on the king's latest and newest
pianofortes. Johann had come to visit his first grandson, who
was a musician at the King's court. Afterwards the King gave
Bach a theme on which he asked him to improvise. Bach
composed a trio for flute, violin and clavier and sent it to
Frederick, with the title of *The Musical Offering*.

But years of copying music scores had damaged Bach's
sight and two years later, when he died, he was almost totally
blind. But he was still working, dictating where he could not
see, engaged on his series of fugues for keyboard, *The Art of
Fugue*.

Bach was buried with no memorial and for almost fifty
years after his death his music was forgotten. His
contemporaries regarded him as just another organist and
nearly a century passed before he was recognized as a great
composer. Mendelssohn gave the second performance of the
St Matthew Passion in Berlin in 1829, one hundred years after
its first and only performance. He and Schumann campaigned
to make Bach's work known and formed the Bach Society. As
a result, by 1900 all of Bach's works had been published.

Bach's life was spent in what he described as: *'the object which
concerns me most, the betterment of church music.'* He wrote,
with simple modesty: *'Anyone could have done as much as I
have done if he had worked as hard.'*

(Source: *Bach and his World* by Cynthia Millar)

Henry Dunant was born in Geneva on 8 May 1828.

The man in white

Henry Dunant was a man with a conscience about the poor and underprivileged of his day. He travelled to Italy to meet the Emperor, Napoleon III, suitably dressed in a white suit. He hoped to gain his sympathies for his cause. Napoleon was leading his army against the Austrian rulers of Italy and he invited Dunant to come and watch the battle. He agreed, but was horrified by what he saw at Solferino.

Worse was to follow. After twelve hours of fighting, over 40,000 men lay dead or wounded. The wounded were carried on carts or strapped to the pack-saddles of mules and taken – if they survived – to the town of Castiglione. Even when they got there, not much was done for them. There were too few trained helpers and not enough organisation to make sure that everyone received even the food and water available.

Still in his white suit, Dunant set about improving conditions. He set up headquarters in a church and began to wash and bandage the wounded himself. He sent the boys in the town to fetch fresh water and clean straw for bedding and even cajoled tourists to give him a hand. In the end he had 300 helpers.

At first, the women in the town would care only for the French wounded – their allies. But they saw that Dunant made no difference, but cared for French and Austrian wounded alike. His helpers soon began to do the same and helped both 'friend' and 'enemy' alike.

9 May

On 9 May 1979 the *Bible Society* celebrated its 175th anniversary.

Red for danger!

A red cover seemed right, the Bible Society decided, for this translation of the New Testament. For the Maasai people of Kenya, red - the colour of blood – is specially important. So in 1983 in Kenya a little red book began to appear that was certainly not *The Thoughts of Chairman Mao*. It was the New Testament in the Maasai language. But the elders seemed to think that it was every bit as dangerous as the one-time communists' Bible. They noticed the effect the Bible had on the people who began to read it. For example, young warriors stopped stealing cattle from their neighbours and even old men were seen to be crying when they heard the words from this little book. So the elders warned the people, 'When the Christians talk to you, listen. But when they open the little red book, run away!'

One day Joel ole Kima – a Maasai pastor – met two men on the road. As usual, they began to 'chew the news' – which means to talk about their cows and their families. But Joel noticed that one of the men would not speak to him – something normally unheard of. When Joel asked him why he was silent he admitted that he had been forewarned. 'When Joel starts chewing the news,' the people in a nearby village told him, 'he always gets into the little red book'. This man had also heard that the words from the red book could change people. 'I don't want to take that risk,' he admitted.

(Source: *How the Bible Came to Us*, Bible Society)

O thou great Chief, light a candle within my heart

that I may see what is therein

and sweep the rubbish from thy dwelling place

Prayer of an African girl

Jonathan Edwards, British athlete, was born on 10 May 1966.

Handling success

1995 was an amazing year for Jonathan, who was already a world-class athlete. He says himself: 'I can't really explain it. I was running faster, I was stronger, I improved my technique, but it still did not add up to what happened. It was still a big surprise to me. I look back and shake my head.'

That memorable year Jonathan won all fourteen of the fourteen competitions he entered; achieved a new British record five times and a world record three times as well as winning the World Championship Gold Medal. On top of success in actual events, Jonathan picked up numerous awards including International Athlete of the year and BBC Sports Personality of the year. But Jonathan keeps his cool and doesn't let success go to his head. How does he manage that? He gives some of the answers himself:

'I think you can be terribly serious about sport. It can become the be-all and end-all, but when you reduce it to its fundamentals – rationalise it – it's sometimes given too much pre-eminence. In athletics, jump three times into a pit and measure the distance and suddenly you're famous. Sport does give people enjoyment and is an important part of life, but there are many more important and serious issues.'

Jonathan is quite outspoken about what for him is a more important issue. It is his commitment to Jesus Christ. 'I was brought up in a Christian home,' he explains; becoming a Christian himself was a natural progression from the reality he saw in his parents' lives. He reads the Bible and hears God speaking to him through it. 'If I'm looking for an attitude or I have a big decision to make, I'll pray, but I also need to know God's word and find out how other people in similar circumstances act.'

Jonathan's Christian faith helps him to keep his outstanding success in perspective. He says, with genuine modesty: 'I'm just Jonathan. I jump into the sand-pit for a living.'

11 May

Handling failure

If 1995 was a year of incredible success for Jonathan, 1992 was one of devastating failure. That was the year that he went to Barcelona, with high hopes of an Olympic medal in the triple jump. To his chagrin, he failed even to qualify, jumping well below his normal length. So how did he feel about that?

'It was probably the worst year of my life athletically. I was absolutely devastated. All my hopes and dreams had been blown out of the water. I remember going to bed in the evening thinking I'd wake up in the morning finding it had all been a dream. This wasn't the way it was supposed to happen. I was taken to depths that I hadn't known previously.'

But, surprisingly perhaps, Jonathan looks back on that painful time and sees it as an important part of his maturing as a Christian. 'I think at that stage it was the first real crisis I had faced as a Christian,' he admits. He had to stop and decide whether God did come first in his life and whether he was prepared to go one hundred per cent for God, come what may, win or lose. 'Is God first?' he asked himself, 'Am I going to glorify him and give my best to him, regardless of results?' Facing up to that decision laid the foundation, he believes, for the years that followed both spiritually and in the field of athletics.

Jonathan is only too aware of the problems that fame and fortune can bring. Both money – or the love of it – and the glamour of being a star, could shift his focus from glorifying God and take him away from his family. In spite of the pain of failure, Jonathan is honest enough to recognise: 'Having had disaster as well as incredible success, I certainly feel that success represents the biggest threat to my walk with God.'

In Jonathan's case, forewarned is forearmed.

(Grateful thanks to Stuart Weir of *Christians in Sport*)

Florence Nightingale was born on 12 May 1820.

Waiting time

Florence Nightingale knew exactly what she wanted to do. She had made up her mind to be a nurse. That seems an ordinary enough career choice for a girl today, but in 1842 it was quite extraordinary, especially for someone from Miss Nightingale's social class.

Seven years earlier she had received a call from God. She never forgot that occasion and kept the anniversary of the experience to her dying day. She had waited, then, to find out what God wanted her to do. But when she *did* know, she kept quiet about it, and for very good reasons.

The first was her family. Florence came from a wealthy, well-connected family; daughters were expected to help their mothers in the social round, then get married. Florence actually fell ill with the frustration of such a trivial life-style. Yet she dreaded the rows and scenes that would follow if she tried to break free. So she waited.

But she did not waste the years of waiting. She got up early to study mathematics and also to organise the store cupboards of their large household. At Lord Shaftesbury's suggestion, she also studied public health records and hospital reports. Long before she ever went into one, she knew all about the running of hospitals.

The second obstacle in the way of Florence becoming a nurse was the image that nursing had. Hospitals were places of unimagined filth; nurses were almost always drunk and often immoral. They had to eat and sleep in the hospital corridors. Training for nurses was unheard of. In fact, what is incredible is not that Florence waited so long before embarking on her God-given vocation, but that she ever became a nurse at all.

13 May

On 13 May 1992 'Aunt Flo' mysteriously met her death and **Sheila Bowler**'s nightmare began. Sheila Bowler, a piano teacher who had recently been widowed, fetched her late husband's elderly aunt from a residential care home, to take her to her own home in Rye.

No tears – no feelings?

What a time for the tyre to go flat, with Aunt Flo on board! Sheila hurried back to her car in the darkness, accompanied by the people she had called on for help. But the passenger seat was empty – Aunt Flo had gone! Sheila was certain that the old lady could not have walked unaided, but they searched the lanes – in vain. When the police took charge, Sheila could only go home and wait.

What followed seemed unbelievable – to Sheila and to everyone who knew her well. When Aunt Flo's dead body was discovered in the river next morning, Sheila became chief suspect. If Aunt Flo could not have walked the distance, then Sheila must have taken her there to murder her.

Sheila Bowler had everything in her favour – an unimpeachable character and a well-deserved reputation for showing the utmost kindness to her husband's aunts over many years. She was not in need of money, nor was Aunt Flo wealthy. Why did she end up in the dock? Why was she declared guilty?

Sheila was probably her own worst enemy. She was scrupulously honest and straightforward, in a society unused to plain speaking; she was also sharp and did not suffer fools gladly. Above all, she did *not* wear her heart on her sleeve. Because she did not cry or outwardly show any grief, it was wrongly assumed that she was unfeeling and callous. Therefore she could be a murderer. But justice was neither done nor seen to be done by those who knew her best.

(Source: *Anybody's Nightmare* by Angela and Tim Devlin)

Mary Seacole died in England on 14 May 1881. She was a Jamaican woman of great ability and energy as well as kindness and compassion. Her mother had been famed as a 'doctress' attending British officers and soldiers in Jamaica and Mary learned her skills. She seems to have had the travel bug and went to Panama more than once as well as visiting England.

Daughter of the 'doctress'

There could be no doubt about it – the patient was suffering from cholera. Mary Seacole had seen too much of the disease at home in Jamaica not to recognise the symptoms now. When cholera had broken out in Jamaica in 1850, Mary had developed a medicine that produced remarkable results. Now she was in Panama, where she had come to visit her brother. But instead of paying a social visit, Mary soon found that she was back at her familiar task of nursing the sick. She used the medicine that had been so successful in Jamaica, and brought relief to many cholera sufferers who had been reluctant at first to have medical help from a foreigner – and a woman at that.

Mary had years of experience behind her. Her mother, who had kept a house for army officers and their wives, was known locally as the 'doctress'. She had great skill in dealing with the sick, and not surprisingly Mary learned from her. She also learned by watching the army doctors and surgeons at work. She even conducted a post-mortem examination on a baby in Panama who died of cholera, so that she could learn more about the disease.

Afterwards, the Americans honoured her work at a 4 July banquet. They drank a toast to her, adding their regrets that she wasn't white. Mary was a match for them. In her reply, she drank to them and to 'the general reformation of American manners'!

15 May

On 15 May 1919, *Eglantyne Jebb* appeared in court. Publicity from Eglantyne Jebb's trial – at which she was convicted and fined £5 – brought money flooding in, and the Save the Children Fund was set up. Before she died at fifty-two, worn out with hard work, she told her sister: 'I can trust God with the future of the Save the Children Fund. How very odd, how ridiculous it would be if I could not.'

Save the children

They stare at us from newspapers and hoardings; wistful faces and thin, emaciated bodies – the starving children of our world. The very first such photographs were distributed on a handbill in 1919 by a beautiful and determined woman called Eglantyne Jebb. She had heard, through the reports of the Red Cross and overseas newspapers, that thousands of children were dying of hunger. It was the direct result of the blockade imposed by the victorious Allies on the defeated nations after World War I. Eglantyne Jebb had only £10, so she spent it on printed handbills which would tell the tragic story of these children to the people in Britain.

As a result of this action, she was charged in court with distributing her handbills without the permission of the censors. Many branded her as a traitor to the Allies, because she wanted to help the children of the 'enemy'.

The prosecutor read out the charge against her, and in the interval Eglantyne walked across to him. There was a whispered conversation, then, back in the dock, the prisoner announced to the court triumphantly, 'He has promised to contribute to my fund for the children once the trial is over!'

On 16 May 1763 **James Boswell** met Dr Johnson for the first time.
James Boswell was born in 1740 the son of a Scottish lawyer and
landowner. He resisted his father's overbearing plans and
escaped to London. His *Life of Samuel Johnson*, for which he is
best-known, is vivid and immediate. He brings his hero
wonderfully alive for us. Johnson's wit, kindness, irascibility and
clear thinking are all displayed in its pages.

A very fine cat indeed

'I shall never forget the indulgence with which he
treated Hodge, his cat: for whom he himself used to
go out and buy oysters, lest the servants having that
trouble should take a dislike to the poor creature. I
am, unluckily, one of those who have an antipathy to
a cat, so that I am uneasy when in the room with
one; and I own, I frequently suffered a good deal
from the presence of this same Hodge. I recollect
him one day scrambling up Dr Johnson's breast,
apparently with much satisfaction, while my friend
smiling and half-whistling, rubbed down his back
and pulled him by the tail; and when I observed
that he was a fine cat, saying, "why yes, sir, but I have
had cats whom I liked better than this;" and then as
if perceiving Hodge to be out of countenance,
adding, "but he is a very fine cat, a very fine cat
indeed."

'This reminds me of the ludicrous account
which he gave Mr Langton, of the despicable state
of a young Gentleman of good family. "Sir, when I
heard of him last, he was running about town
shooting cats." And then, in a sort of kindly reverie,
he bethought himself of his own favourite cat, and
said, "But Hodge shan't be shot; no, no, Hodge shall
not be shot."'

(From *The Life of Samuel Johnson* by James Boswell)

17 May

Edward Jenner was born on 17 May 1749. Sixty million people died from smallpox in Europe in the eighteenth century. In ten years nearly 250,000 died from it in London alone. Inoculation with smallpox virus was practised, but could result in serious illness or death.

A dairymaid with cowpox

It all began when Edward Jenner was a young apprentice doctor. He heard a dairymaid who was being treated for a skin eruption, say, 'It can't be the smallpox because I've had cowpox.'

'Just an old wives' tale,' doctors commented, 'like carrying a potato to get rid of rheumatism.' But Jenner determined to try out the theory. This just might be the key to preventing the world's greatest scourge.

Sometimes cows developed blister-like spots on their udders, and the girls who milked them developed similar blisters on their hands and felt off-colour for a few days. If Jenner could prove that a dose of cowpox made the sufferer immune to smallpox, he could inoculate people with the mild cowpox virus and so save patients from the danger of contracting deadly smallpox.

All he needed to carry out his research were some outbreaks of cowpox, and he eagerly followed up every case at farms nearby. He collected the cowpox vaccine, inoculated volunteers with it, then later inoculated them with smallpox virus. None of those inoculated with cowpox vaccine reacted to the smallpox. They *were* immune!

Jenner was a Christian and he believed that God might use him to wipe out this terrible disease. His theory took years to confirm and the medical men of his time took a great deal of persuading. But thanks to Jenner and cowpox, what was once the world's worst killer has now been officially eradicated.

Rick Wakeman, rock keyboard player and composer, was born on 18 May 1949. He is best known for his compositions and brilliant keyboard wizardry, performing solo and with the *Strawbs* and *Yes* – among other bands.

Inimitable 'YES' man

Rick Wakeman rocketed to fame and wealth and plummeted to near bankruptcy – not once but several times. Yet the story of his life is shot through with wit and humour that makes for laughter as well as for tears.

Rick was an outstandingly musical child and went from childhood successes to study at the Royal College of Music. But he relinquished the classical concert hall for the exciting but uncertain career of a rock musician.

In the hectic programme of a composer and performer, on tour overseas and at home, no room was left for his earlier Christian commitment. Heavy drinking, two failed marriages and a coronary at twenty-five all failed to bring about the radical changes that his lifestyle so badly needed.

When his third partner, the ex-model Nina Carter, wanted a church wedding, he felt sure that no minister of religion would agree to marry them. But Graham Long, a United Reformed Church minister, quietly listened to their story and invited them to church. Later he agreed to conduct their wedding. His openness, honesty and compassion sowed the seeds for Rick's return to faith. 'Graham's faith in Nina and me,' he says, 'started me rethinking my Christian values.' A year or so later Rick decided to put his life back into God's hands. He asked for God's forgiveness and strength and soon afterwards made the decision to give up drinking entirely. Life did not immediately become easy but now, as Rick says, he has exchanged the aimless roller-coaster of life for 'the roller-coaster ride of Christianity, which is never-ending.'

(Source: *Say Yes!* By Rick Wakeman)

19 May

James Hudson Taylor was born in May (21ˢᵗ) 1832 and was called by God to take the gospel to China. His austere way of life in England prepared him for hardships ahead.

Contextualising the Gospel

A group of new missionary arrivals to China were waiting to meet the great man when one of the group who knew him, exclaimed, 'There is Mr Taylor!'

'We looked', one wrote afterwards, 'but could only see a Chinaman on a wheelbarrow. The barrow stopped and the figure advanced towards us. It was a good thing that there was someone to do the introducing, for we should never have recognized Mr Taylor. The weather was cold, and he had on a wadded gown and jacket. Over his head he wore a wind-hood with side-pieces which fitted close to the face, leaving nothing but a medallion-shaped opening for nose, eyes and mouth. In his hand he grasped a huge Chinese umbrella … In his wadded clothes he looked almost as broad as he was long, and to our foreign eyes was the oddest figure we had seen.'

Hudson Taylor was strongly criticised by nineteenth century Europeans for adopting Chinese clothes and customs. The idea of conforming to Chinese ways was repellent and there was indignation at the idea that English women should wear Chinese dress and live in the interior. But Taylor was acting from conviction. He wrote to his mother: 'I am not alone in the opinion that the foreign dress and carriage of missionaries (to a certain extent affected by some of their pupils and converts), the foreign appearance of chapels, and indeed the foreign air imparted to everything connected with their work has seriously hindered the rapid dissemination of the Truth among the Chinese. And why should such a foreign aspect be given to Christianity?'

'On Thursday last at 11pm,' he had written to his sister some time before, 'I resigned my locks to the barber, dyed my hair a good black, and in the morning had a proper queue (pigtail) plaited in with my own, and a quantity of heavy silk to lengthen it out according to custom. Then, in Chinese dress, I set out.'

(Source: *Biography of James Hudson Taylor* by Dr and Mrs Howard Taylor)

Rose Macaulay, novelist and essayist, writes to Father Hamilton
Johnson on 20 May 1951.

Return of the wanderer

'If someone has got to housekeep, there is no reason why it
should be a woman rather than a man,' Rose Macaulay wrote.
She insisted too that 'a house unkempt cannot be so
distressing as a life unlived.' She was unperturbed by the
clutter of books and papers in her own flat. She held views
ahead of her time in other ways. In 1951 it was unusual for
churches of different persuasions to meet together. She
expresses approval for such early ecumenism.

Rose did not marry and her lifelong love affair with a
former Catholic priest, already married, led her to
excommunicate herself from the Church of England. These
letters, written to Father Hamilton Johnson, an Anglican monk
living in the United States, tell of her return, after thirty years,
to the Anglo-Catholic fold.

'Dear Father,

I took away with me for the week-end your letter of
11th May, but not my typewriter, so will write to you in my
very best hand instead. I am sitting in a beautiful library,
looking out on a beautiful garden…

'Your phrase "nowhere to come back to": it called up a
vision of desolation, of perpetual wandering homeless o'er
moor and fen and crag, with no kindly light to lead: a kind of
waste land. Yes: I am glad I didn't reject confirmation …

'Just now there is [a dissension] about a United
Church's Rally in Hyde Park (yesterday afternoon), led by the
Arches of Canterbury and York and the Bp. Of London and
other bps. … Many Anglo-Catholics … I believe, held a
protest meeting … I don't myself see anything
compromising in "rallying" with the free churches – it doesn't
imply any abandonment of church principles, only Christian
fellowship. People wrangle too much … Walking in bluebell
woods, with cuckoos and wood-pigeons uttering their May
songs, makes me feel very peaceful.'

(From *Letters to a Friend 1950-52*)

21 May

Elizabeth Fry, Quaker reformer, was born on 21 May 1780 in Norwich into a wealthy Quaker family. She was 17 when she decided to dedicate her life to God. She began a school for 60 poor children. At 20 she married Joseph Fry, also a Quaker and banker. She had eleven children but still continued her teaching. In 1813 she visited Newgate prison, having heard about the terrible conditions there.

The gate to Hell

'Of all the seats of woe on this side Hell, few, I suppose, exceed or equal Newgate.'

(From a letter to *The London Chronicle*)

Elizabeth argued patiently with the turnkeys of Newgate prison. They refused to let her into the women's yard. The screams of the prisoners almost drowned their whispered dialogue. One woman rushed from a doorway and snatched the caps off the other prisoners with shrill laughter.

'They'll do the same to you, Ma'am,' the turnkey warned.

'I am going in to them,' Mrs Fry insisted. 'Here is my letter of authorisation from the governor.'

'At least take off your watch,' they begged. But Elizabeth refused, saying that it went everywhere with her.

Reluctantly the men opened the gate against the press of women, and Elizabeth Fry, in her sober Quaker dress, went through. The gate clanged behind her. There was a moment's hush, then the whole crowd of prisoners surged towards her and nothing could be seen but the tip of her white cap. But no one bit or scratched or tore at her clothes. Her gentle, quiet firmness had its effect.

She stooped and picked up a tiny child. Then she talked to the women as mothers, like herself, and began to make plans for their children. She told them a story about Jesus, then promised to come again. When she went out through the gates, the wretched women she had left inside began to have hope.

Elizabeth Fry visited Newgate regularly. In the face of opposition from the authorities she was able to show that better treatment of prisoners led to better behaviour. Through her recommendations women guards were employed for women prisoners, accommodation was improved and prisons were regularly inspected. She visited other prisons in Britain and on the continent. Her ideas for reform were welcomed in these countries too.

Patchwork in prison

Elizabeth Fry hated delay. She began at once to plan a school for prisoners' children and for young prisoners in Newgate. It did not cost much nor did it require an Act of Parliament to put such practical matters into action. But the London authorities and the Governor of Newgate thought otherwise. They believed that it was useless and wrong to try to help such wicked women. Besides, there was no space for a school.

The prisoners themselves suggested a small room that could be used and proposed that one of the prisoners who was well qualified to teach should take on the job. The mothers tidied up their children and got them ready for school.

When the thirty children, most of them under seven, had squeezed into the narrow room, a crowd of prisoners stood outside and begged to be allowed to learn to read and write too. Elizabeth determined to help them and also to find work for the prisoners who had nothing to do all day but to drink and cause trouble. Permission was at last given for her to use a large laundry-room, but no money was allowed for materials. But in response to Elizabeth's pleas, Quaker merchants provided thousands of scraps of material – just right for patchwork.

Supervised by helpers, the prisoners of Newgate began to make patchwork quilts and Elizabeth found a ready market for them. English settlers in New South Wales, Australia, bought them gladly; perhaps they were a welcome reminder of home. In exchange, the prisoners received small payments and were able to buy soap, tea and sugar. With work and some small earning power, they began to gain some self-respect.

---

23 May

Mother's Day in the United States is held in May. **Anna Jarvis** was born on 1 May 1864 in West Virginia. The house became a focal point in the Civil War when General McClellan used it as his headquarters. It has now been restored as the Anna Jarvis Birthplace Museum.

Celebrating Mother's Day

When the Civil War was over, there was work to be done to bring together families that had been torn apart by the war. Anna's mother organised a Mother's Friendship Day in 1868 to try to unite Confederate and Union families. Anna was a small child then, but when her mother died in May 1905, Anna began promoting the second Sunday in May as a special day to honour mothers. In 1915, following an act of Congress, president Woodrow Wilson officially proclaimed that Sunday Mother's Day.

In a Women's History course on the Internet in 2000, students were invited to write in about the best commercial gift they ever gave or got for Mother's Day. One said that in her family they preferred to give each other little things all the year round and commented that 'Being consistently generous and sweet is the best way to celebrate your mother, isn't it?'

Nancy Coulter wrote about this mutual giving of gifts:

'It was probably something I made back in elementary school … my mom saved all of that stuff. When I was older and was snooping around (like any good child does) I found a box of all the things I made in school. My mom kept everything I ever made. That made me realize how much my mother does love me and cherishes everything I do.

'Not only did I give her great handmade gifts, but she gave me a gift myself by keeping all of those things.'

'All that I am and ever hope to be, I owe to my angel Mother.' – Abraham Lincoln

24 May

Victoria Day, in honour of Queen Victoria, is still celebrated as a holiday in Canada on 24 May. *Joseph Scriven* emigrated to Canada in 1845. He was born in Dublin in 1820. He hoped to go into the army but was not physically fit enough and endured ill-health until his death in 1886.

'We did it between us!'

Not long before he died, a friend picked up a sheet of manuscript lying among Joseph Scriven's papers. The words were new to him and he asked his friend where they came from. Joseph explained that he had written them to comfort his mother back in Ireland when she was going through a time of great sadness and sorrow. 'Did you write the words without anyone else's help?' his friend asked. 'The Lord and I did it between us,' Scriven replied.

Joseph Scriven had been through much sorrow himself. His bride had drowned the night before their wedding and it was after that bereavement that he emigrated to Canada. He settled in Ontario where he earned his living as a tutor as well as doing much voluntary work among people in need. He became engaged again but his fiancée died after a short illness. Perhaps Scriven's hymn *What a friend we have in Jesus,* has been a perennial favourite because it rings true. The writer wrote from his own experience. Today it is no longer a *fashionable* hymn, but it is still a firm favourite with many people and a source of comfort and strength.

What a Friend we have in Jesus
All our sins and griefs to bear;
What a privilege to carry
Everything to God in prayer!
Oh what peace we often forfeit,
Oh what needless pain we bear;
All because we do not carry
Everything to God in prayer.

Joseph Scriven 1820-1886

25 May

The **Venerable Bede** died on 25 May 735. Bede was born in Northumberland in 673 and became a monk at Jarrow, where he passed his whole life. He said of himself: 'I have devoted my energies to the study of the Scriptures ... study, teaching and writing have always been my delight'. Bede's tomb is in Durham Cathedral. His *Ecclesiastical History of the English People* tells many wonderful stories of the saints and preachers in Britain.

'It is done'

It was Ascension Day in the year 735 in the monastery at Jarrow. An old man's voice murmured on, so faintly and feebly now that the young scribe, busily scratching with his quill across the vellum, had to turn his head to catch each word. He wrote hurriedly, anxiously, aware of the urgency to finish.

They had reached the last chapter of St John's Gospel, which the learned monk was translating into English. But the Venerable Bede was dying.

'Write quickly!' he urged and the dictation continued until the chapter was almost finished. Then Bede stopped and sent for the other monks. He received each in turn and gave each some small gift – a few peppers and some napkins – and said goodbye. They left the room and the scribe wondered if his master would be able to finish the task.

'There is still one sentence to be written,' he said. With a final, supreme effort, Bede dictated the closing words of the Gospel.

'It is done,' he said. His work and his life were finished.

Prayer

I beseech thee, good Jesus, that as thou hast graciously granted to me here on earth, sweetly to partake of the words of thy wisdom and knowledge, so thou wilt also vouchsafe that I may some time come to thee, the fountain of all wisdom, and always appear before thy face; who livest and reignest, world without end. – The Venerable Bede 673-735

26 May

On 26 May 1780 an eyewitness described a Shaker meeting in America. **The Shakers** left England for America in 1774. Their leader, Mother Ann Lee, prophesied that they would see 'great numbers' joining them and by 1803 there were sixteen hundred converts – a figure which doubled in the next twenty years.

Revival!

Valentine Rathbun, a Baptist minister and leading citizen, was attracted to the Shakers at first, but later became a bitter opponent. He describes the welcome he was given when he visited their settlement. His hosts assured him that they knew he was coming, then gave him a good meal. One of them began to 'speak many good words, saying, I must hate sin, love God and take up my cross.' Then he describes their worship:

'When they meet together for their worship, they fall a groaning and trembling, and everyone acts alone for himself; one will fall prostrate on the floor, another on his knees and his head in his hands; another will be muttering over articulate sounds ... Some will be singing, each one his own tune ... some will be dancing, and others standing laughing, heartily and loudly; others will be drumming on the floor with their feet ... Others will be agonizing, as though they were in great pain; others jumping up and down; others fluttering over somebody, and talking to them; others will be shooing and hissing evil spirits out of the house.'

Preaching and signs – usually the healing of some present – would follow. Not everyone, like Rathbun, dismissed the meetings as 'bedlam'. Some saw God at work in the Shakers' strange amalgam of restraint, abstinence, and free expression. Issachar Bates joined the Shakers because they were 'the only people who did not live after the flesh.' He sums up his conversion briefly and neatly:

'My whole stay was not much over an hour, for we did business quick. I ate quick and talked quick, heard quick and started home quick, for I was quickened.'

(Source: *The People called Shakers* Edward Andrews)

27 May

27 May is the Feast Day of the **Venerable Bede.** He is thought to have been
the first person to draw up a calendar of the Christian year in England.

Special days

The year is full of days that are special to us personally or as a
community. Birthdays and anniversaries remind us of friends
and relatives. The early Christians wanted to keep certain days
special to remind them of outstanding leaders, martyrs and
saintly people whose example they should follow. They used
the Roman calendar – based on the sun – for these days, so
they come at fixed dates each year. The date chosen is often
the day of their death.

But the church also wanted to commemorate the great
historic events of the Christian faith: when Jesus died, rose
again, ascended to heaven, and when the Holy Spirit was given.
These happenings are linked to the Jewish calendar, which is
calculated by the moon. For example, the Jewish Feast of
Passover, which was the time at which Jesus was crucified,
varies from year to year, according to when the full moon
occurs in the month.

So the Christian calendar is a mixture of fixed feasts and
so-called movable feasts. Those are the ones that can fall on
different dates in different years.

Prayer

*Grant me thy grace, O Christ I beseech thee, that thy good spirit
may lead me in the right way and move far from me him who
cometh to destroy, that casting away all malice of evil, I may
search into the commandments of my God, and with the eyes of
my mind awakened, go forward faithfully to read and to weigh
the marvels of the holy law.* – The Venerable Bede 673-735

Canon Rawnsley died on 28 May 1919. Rawnsley, like many Victorians, seemed to have unlimited vigour and enterprise. He had a finger in a great many pies. He fervently embraced the 'green' cause. He campaigned for streams to be unpolluted, and championed the cause of organic farming.

In trust for the nation

It all began when the landowners threatened to close a footpath. It was 1885 and two high-handed autocrats had actually put up barriers to stop the public from exercising their rights and walking along the paths beside Lake Derwentwater. Canon Rawnsley was up in arms. He began by writing some strong letters of protest to the two offenders, but these were completely ignored. So he headed a crowd of peaceful protesters numbering four hundred people, in a march that fetched up at the home of one of the guilty landowners. The next public march he led was two thousand strong, and they followed a route along the newly prohibited path.

But Canon Rawnsley was not prepared to keep the issue local. He held protest meetings in London and other big cities to make the cause known, then finally he took the landowners to court, triumphantly winning the case.

Rawnsley had spent most of his life in the Lake District and he was determined to protect and preserve this beautiful area of England. Wordsworth – another 'local' – and John Ruskin had both *talked* about the need to form some kind of body to protect the Lake District but it was Rawnsley who took the action. He joined with two other campaigners who were friends of his – Octavia Hill and Sir Robert Hunter. They met together at the Duke of Westminster's home, and between them hatched up the idea for the National Trust – a body that would buy up and rescue for the nation places of special beauty and importance.

In 1895 the National Trust was granted legal status, with the Duke of Westminster as its first president and Canon Rawnsley as secretary, a position he was to hold for the next twenty-five years.

29 May

Gilbert Keith Chesterton was born on the 29 May 1874. G K Chesterton, critic, novelist and poet, was born in London and studied art at the Slade School. He became a Roman Catholic in 1922. His writings are witty, amusing and thought-provoking; he was a brilliant defender of goodness and of the Christian faith. He became widely known for his detective novels featuring Father Brown – a Roman Catholic priest – as sleuth.

Looking through windows

Chesterton strolled out to the downs one morning with some bits of chalk in his pocket, in order to draw the soul of a cow, which, he said, 'was all purple and silver, and had seven horns and the mystery that belongs to all the beasts.'

G K C was a larger than life in every sense. His big shambling figure in shovel hat, with caped coat billowing out behind, was instantly recognizable on the London streets. Unlike some writers and poets, he did not create a fantasy world but recognized and described the unseen world which be believed lay about us all. 'A mirror is a mystical thing,' he wrote, 'but it is not so wonderful as a window.' He looked through windows and saw the transcendent and the spiritual dimension in every place and person.

Father Brown in the *Father Brown Stories* seems absent-minded – like his author – but he is that rare fictional creation – a character who is both good and attractive. Creating good people convincingly is far harder than creating evil characters. Father Brown may appear to be naïve and gullible, but he is no stranger to the darker side of human nature. He is able to recognize both good and evil in men and women and to put his finger on the mainsprings of their action. He is also skilled at catching the villain of the piece.

Chesterton is largely forgotten today, but he will be revived and read again for his wit, his impressive logic and his transparent goodness.

On 30 May 1431 **Joan of Arc** was burned at the stake in the old market-place of Rouen.

Death of the Maid of Orleans

'The judges there present and even several Englishmen were provoked to tears and weeping and indeed most bitterly wept at it.' Joan had just spoken her final words in the Old Market, where she had been taken by more than eight hundred men of war with swords and axes. Joan deeply regretted being handed over to the secular instead of the ecclesiastical court because it meant that she would be burned at the stake instead of being executed. She dreaded the burning of her body to ashes.

Joan had been obedient to the voices that first instructed her to leave her country home and go to relieve the British siege of Orleans. She had escorted the timorous Dauphin through English-held territory to be formally crowned in Reims Cathedral and taken command of his faltering army in a bid to expel the British from French soil. With amazing skill and single-minded courage she carried out her orders but after a run of success she was captured by Burgundian troops who sold her to their English allies.

For a year Joan languished in prison. Then followed interminable interrogations; she was handed over to the secular power, then sentenced to burning. In the end, her chief offence in the eyes of authority was her wearing of men's clothes.

The usher who was with her to the last recorded that Joan asked for a cross to hold and an Englishman made a little cross from two wooden sticks and gave it to her. At her request the cross from the nearby church was fetched and held before her eyes. 'Being in the flames she ceased not until the end to proclaim and confess aloud the holy name of Jesus'.

'I would that my soul were where I believe this woman's soul to be.' – Canon of Rouen, present at Joan's death

(Source: *Joan of Arc* by Régine Pernoud)

---

31 May

Terry Waite was born on 31 May 1939. He grew up in the country, a policeman's son. After serving in the Grenadier Guards he joined the Church Army. He became the Archbishop of Canterbury's special envoy. It was when he went to Beirut to visit American hostages that he himself was taken hostage and kept captive for 1,763 days, almost four years of which were in solitary confinement.

Without pen and paper

Prison seems to offer the ideal opportunity to write a book. There is time in plenty and fairly few interruptions. John Bunyan wrote *Pilgrim's Progress* during his imprisonment on religious grounds in Bedford jail. But Terry Waite was in the dark, in a room that was shuttered and barred, chained to a wall and with no pen and paper. But still he wrote his book.

From the time that he was captured Terry was determined to keep sane in a situation where many would go mad. He made three resolutions: to indulge in no regrets, no sentimentality and no self-pity. Then he set about surviving the boredom as well as the uncertainty. He would recreate his life up to that time, ready to set it all down once he was free. He began with his earliest memories and re-enacted the scenes of childhood, the years of adolescence, youth and manhood. He tried to face every memory with honesty and courage, not hiding from himself the truth about all that he had experienced. Later he wrote, 'It's painful to be intro-spective, to see myself in the light of truth. In this solitary dark space the light of truth shines brightly, so brightly that it hurts.'

After his release, Terry did indeed write down the book he had so carefully prepared and constructed in the dark days of captivity. In the retelling he is honest about everything – and that includes his moments of doubt and uncertainty. He does not pretend in retrospect, as he so easily could, that he sailed through on a cushion of faith. But he does affirm that however bad things were, he recognised that he was in the hands of God and he had hope.

(Source: *Taken on Trust* by Terry Waite)

The Revd Henry Francis Lyte was born on 1 June 1793. Henry Lyte, author of the hymn 'Praise my soul the King of heaven', had hoped to train as a doctor, but was not fit enough physically. He was ordained and appointed to the quiet Devon living of Brixham. He died at the age of fifty-four, after years of ill-health.

Abide with me

Those who haven't sung that hymn in church have probably heard it sung at FA Cup Finals. But Henry Lyte had other things in mind when he first wrote *Abide with me*. He was thinking about death. He had visited a fellow clergyman who was dying and was struck by his friend's repeating the words, 'Abide with me.' He may have written his hymn then.

Another story tells how he went for a walk by the sea, late one Sunday afternoon, and saw a beautiful sunset. He had only a few more days left in England; he had been ordered abroad for the winter because of his health. Lyte went home and wrote his famous hymn, or retrieved it from his notes of many years before. Then he insisted, against his family's advice, that he would preach that evening. His daughter reported, 'he did preach, amid the breathless attention of his hearers.'

Before he went to bed, Lyte gave the copy of his hymn to a close relative. He died a month or two later in Nice.

> Abide with me; fast falls the eventide;
> The darkness deepens; Lord, with me abide!
> When other helpers fail, and comforts flee,
> Help of the helpless, O abide with me.
>
> Swift to its close ebbs out life's little day;
> Earth's joys grow dim, its glories pass away;
> Change and decay in all around I see;
> O thou who changest not, abide with me.

Henry Lyte 1793-1847

2 June

Lord George Gordon led the 'No Popery Riots' on 2 June 1780. The Trouble began when Lord Gordon led a Protestant march against the House of Commons in an attempt to have the Catholic Relief Act repealed. It was a hot summer and feelings ran high. Mob violence spread and Roman Catholic churches and houses were burned down. When some of the rioters were put into Newgate prison, the mob set fire to the gaol. There was no such thing as a police force then, so troops were called in to restore order. At least 450 people died in the riots.

Religion of hatred?

The eighteenth century poet, George Crabbe, was one of those who witnessed the terrible scenes in that week of riots. This is part of his description of it:

'Never saw anything so dreadful. The prison was a remarkably strong building; but determined to force it, they broke the gates with crows and other instruments and climbed up the outside. They broke the roof, tore away the rafters and having got ladders they descended, flames all around them. The prisoners escaped – they were conducted through the streets in their chains. Three of them were to be hanged on Friday. You have no conception of the frenzy of the multitude.'

William Blake, the poet and artist, was another spectator. The fire started near his home. Someone has suggested that 'perhaps the terrible flames and prisons, smoke and chains that appear in Blake's pictures and his poetry owe some of their grim reality to this time of violence.'

Television has made us all spectators – more than two hundred years later – of even more widespread scenes of violence, death, fire and destruction caused by religious hatred and intolerance.

Pope John XXIII died on 3 June 1963. Pope John XXIII, born Angelo Guiseppe Roncalli, was the eldest son of poor tenant farmers in Northern Italy. He was elected Pope in 1958 on the twelfth ballot. His five years in office brought about lasting changes. He convened the second Vatican Council, worked for unity among Christians and sought reconciliation between East and West.

Unity and contentment

The newly-elected Pope strolled through the Vatican gardens, stopping to chat with a group of gardeners. He looked at what they were doing with interest, then asked about their families and how much they earned. The Pope thought that their wages were too low and saw to it himself that they were given a rise.

Inside the palace, Pope John was a splendid host to his many visitors. He always insisted that the guest should have the best bedroom – which was his own. So he would turn out and sleep in a little room adjoining his study.

Pope John woke one night with a problem on his mind. 'I must take this up with the Pope,' was his first waking thought. 'But I *am* the Pope! Then I must take it up with God!'

'In the five years I spent working with him I never saw him angry, impatient or upset. On the contrary, he accepted everything with contentment.' – Archbishop Bruno Heim, speaking about Pope John XXIII

'The accumulation of vast wealth while so many are languishing in misery is a grave transgression of God's law, with the consequence that the greedy, avaricious man is never at ease in his mind: he is in fact a most unhappy creature.' – Pope John XXIII

'Perfume all your actions with the life-giving breath of prayer.' – Pope John XXIII

---

4 June

Full sovereignty was re-established for **Tonga** on 4 June 1970. Tonga – named the 'Friendly Isles' by Captain Cook – is made up of some 71 far-flung islands, though fewer than forty are inhabited. Tonga is the only South Pacific country never to be colonised by Europeans. Wesleyan Methodist missionaries brought the Christian Gospel to the islands and a clergyman helped to devise their just and liberal constitution. They have remained a strongly Christian community.

Smiling in the rain

The rain poured down but Queen Salote beamed and waved at the cheering crowds who lined the London streets. Everyone who saw her or watched on television was captivated by the delightful and exuberant Queen of Tonga. She was in London for the coronation of Queen Elizabeth II, which took place on 2 June 1953. According to Tongan etiquette it is not courteous to imitate someone you hold in respect, so out of deference to Queen Elizabeth, whose carriage was covered, Queen Salote faced the elements unprotected.

It was not just British hearts that the Tongan monarch won. In her own country Queen Salote was loved and admired. She cared for her people and made it her concern to improve medicine and education in Tonga. Her Christian faith shone through her life and rule.

Tonga was the first time-zone to greet the new millennium. As the television cameras focused on their country, the choir could be seen and heard singing Handel's *Hallelujah Chorus* with heart and soul. A Christian welcome for a Christian celebration.

5 June is the Feast Day of **St Boniface of Crediton**, who died in Friesland in 754 or 755. St Boniface was christened Wynfrith but later used the name Boniface. Born in Devon, he left England when he was forty and never returned.

'A great and loveable man'

Boniface had one overriding ambition – to tell others the good news about the Christian faith. Until he was forty, he was a monk, keen to study the Bible and pass on what he learned to others. But the urge to evangelise was strong and, as an Anglo-Saxon, he felt especially keen to pass on the gospel to his fellow Saxons on the continent. He left England in 718 and travelled all over Saxon Germany. Later he sent for others from Wessex – women as well as men – to help him in his missionary work.

When he was an old man of over seventy he still went on with his travels, eager to reach other tribes that had not yet heard the gospel. He and his companions went to Holland where they were set upon and murdered by a band of heathen Frieslanders. Boniface was sitting in his tent quietly reading when the men broke in and killed him.

Cuthbert of Canterbury wrote: 'We in England lovingly reckon Boniface among the best and greatest teachers of the faith.' He is still remembered and honoured in the land where he preached and taught.

The last words of St Boniface of Crediton: *'This now is that very day we have long dreamed of. That moment of freedom we have yearned for is now here. So be heroic in the Lord and suffer this royal grace of his will gladly. Keep your trust in him and he will set your souls free.'*

6 June

6 June is the Feast Day of **St Philip the Deacon**. Philip, who features in *The Acts of the Apostles*, was one of seven men, known as deacons, chosen to superintend the care of widows in the early church in Jerusalem. He also led a preaching campaign in the nearby country of Samaria.

Journey into faith

The man was sitting in his carriage and reading from the scroll on his lap, unaware of the jolts and bumps. He was an African, splendidly dressed, and judging by his retinue a person of importance in his own country.

Philip ran up alongside the carriage. He was not on this desert highway by accident but because God had directed him there. The important-looking stranger was reading aloud, as the custom was, and seemed puzzled by the words, so Philip broke in and asked, 'Do you understand what you are reading?'

The man looked up, startled, then exclaimed with some impatience, 'How *can* I understand unless someone explains to me? I don't know who the writer is talking about. Is he describing himself or referring to someone else?'

He was reading about God's servant in the book of Isaiah: 'He was led like a lamb to the slaughter; like a lamb that is dumb before the shearer, he does not open his mouth. He has been humiliated and has no redress. Who will be able to speak of his posterity? For he is cut off from the world of the living.'

Starting at that very passage, Philip began to tell the African courtier about Jesus. *He* was the perfect servant of God. He had led a good life, teaching and healing people, yet the authorities had put him to death. But his death had been part of God's plan and God had raised him from death; he was alive. He was the Son of God, the long-awaited Messiah and the Saviour of the world.

The man listened open-mouthed. In his own land he was a person of high rank, but he was also a humble searcher for truth. He had been to Jerusalem to learn more about the true God. Now God had met him on the desert road by sending Philip to tell him about Jesus.

(From *Acts 8: 26-40*)

Sir James Simpson was born on 7 June 1811, the seventh son of a baker in Bathgate near Edinburgh. He trained as a doctor and specialised in midwifery. Although he became a fashionable physician, attending royal and titled people, he made no distinction between rich and poor patients, seeking only to relieve pain and save life.

'Miss Anaesthesia'

It was supper-time in the Simpson household and Dr Simpson and two colleagues were waiting for their meal after a late night at work. As Simpson searched among his papers for something he wanted, he came across a sample of chloroform that the local pharmacist had given him to test. Impressed by early trials of ether to anaesthetise patients during operations, Simpson was always on the lookout for some improved substance, suitable for mothers, to relieve the pain of childbirth. The only way to test a new substance was to try it himself.

Simpson poured the liquid into a tumbler and the three doctors took a good sniff at it. When Mrs Simpson came to call them to supper, she found all three of them under the mahogany table! Simpson recovered consciousness first, delighted to have found something so effective. Five days later he used chloroform in a midwifery case. He later kept a photograph on his desk of the little girl born so painlessly. He nicknamed her 'Miss Anaesthesia'.

8 June

Dr James Simpson's desire to relieve pain and suffering sprang from his Christian faith. When he was dying, he said to his nephew: 'From extreme pain, I have not been able to read or even to think much today, but when I think, it is of the words "Jesus only", and really that is all that is needed, is it not?'

Pain – a necessary evil?

We take it for granted today that pain is to be relieved whenever possible. In Simpson's day, many thought differently – especially about pain in childbirth. They quoted from *Genesis 3* where God told Eve: 'In sorrow shalt thou bring forth children.' They interpreted 'sorrow' as 'pain' and insisted that pain was divinely intended in childbirth. No doubt those that held that view were men.

Simpson refused to be quelled by such 'theologians', and wrote pamphlets, explaining that the word 'sorrow' meant 'toil' not pain. If, he argued, drugs were used to ease pain in ordinary illness, how could it be wrong to relieve the pain of mothers too?

Most, but not all, doubters were convinced by Simpson's humane attitude. And when Queen Victoria herself accepted chloroform at the birth of her ninth child, Simpson's cause finally triumphed.

Another doctor, a century later, demonstrates that pain is not always an enemy. Paul Brand has worked among leprosy sufferers in India, whose limbs are burned and lacerated because the disease has blocked off the pain that warns of impending damage. 'My work with pain-deprived people has proved to me that pain protects us from destroying ourselves,' he says. 'Rather than trying to "solve" pain by eliminating it, we must learn to listen to it and then manage it.'

St Columba died on 9 June 597.

White martyr

There is more than one way for a Christian to lay down his life. The Celtic church talked of white martyrdom – the sacrifice made by a Christian who undertakes a costly journey in order to gain eternal life. The journey in miles may not be long, but it is a symbol of the spiritual journey of all Christian seekers on the way to God.

Columba was born, of royal blood, in Donegal in Ireland in about 521 and educated for the priesthood. He preached and founded monasteries for some fifteen years after his ordination. He was described as tall and commanding with a voice 'so loud and melodious that it could be heard a mile off.' Then in 563 he left his country as penance for causing a bloody clan battle in which three thousand people were killed. Columba vowed publicly, 'I will not rest until I have won for God the souls of as many men as have fallen in this battle.' But it was hard to leave his own country. He said, 'It is like the parting of soul and body for me to leave my kinsmen and my fatherland, and go from them into strange and distant places in everlasting exile.'

Columba's boat landed on Iona, the remote and barren island off the Scottish coast and Iona became his home for over thirty years. From there he made his missionary journeys among the Picts, often with great success. The fiery and impetuous young priest became a man of peace and a man of prayer. His biographer wrote: 'In the midst of all his toils, he appeared loving unto all, serene and holy, rejoicing in the joy of the Holy Spirit in his inmost heart.' He died on the altar steps of the oratory in Iona, his white martyrdom accomplished.

> Alone with none but thee, my God,
> I journey on my way.
> What need I fear, when thou art near
> Oh king of night and day?
> More safe am I within thy hand
> Than if a host did round me stand.
>
> St Columba 521-597

---

10 June

Charles Dickens was born on 9 June 1812. In *Great Expectations* – perhaps his greatest novel – Pip, brought up by his sister and his kind-hearted brother-in-law, Joe Gargery, is spoiled by unexpected money and privilege. He is ashamed to own his poor relations. But Joe, too loving and self-effacing to take offence, comes to Pip when he is alone and sick.

'A gentle Christian man'

Pip tells the story:

'After I had turned the worst point of my illness, I began to notice that while all its other features changed, this one consistent feature did not change. Whoever came about me, still settled down into Joe. I opened my eyes in the night, and I saw in the great chair at the bedside, Joe. I opened my eyes in the day, and sitting on the window-seat, and smoking his pipe in the shaded open window, still I saw Joe. I asked for cooling drink, and the dear hand that gave it me was Joe's. I sank back on my pillow after drinking, and the face that looked so hopefully and tenderly upon me was the face of Joe.

At last, one day, I took courage, and said, "*Is* it Joe?"

And the dear old home-voice answered: "Which it air, old chap."

"'Oh Joe, you break my heart! Look angry at me, Joe. Strike me, Joe. Tell me of my ingratitude. Don't be so good to me!"

'For Joe had actually laid his head down on the pillow at my side, and put his arm round my neck, in his joy that I knew him.

"'Which, dear old Pip, old chap," said Joe, "you and me was ever friends. And when you're well enough to go out for a ride – what larks!"

'After which, Joe withdrew to the window, and stood with his back towards me, wiping his eyes. And as my extreme weakness prevented me from getting up and going to him, I lay there, penitently whispering: "O God, bless him! O God bless this gentle Christian man!"'

(From *Great Expectations* by Charles Dickens)

11 June is the Feast Day of **St Barnabas**. 'Barnabas' was the nickname given to Joseph, a Christian Jew from Cyprus. It means 'one who encourages'. We read about him in *The Acts of the Apostles*. It was Barnabas who persuaded the doubtful Christians in Jerusalem to welcome and accept Paul after his dramatic conversion. He also went with Paul on the first overseas missionary expedition.

Think positive

Barnabas was not the sort of person who quarrelled with others – and certainly not with his great friend and colleague Paul. He was the one to make the peace when tempers were frayed and it looked as if it might come to blows. But this time he stood his ground and the whole episode ended in a big disagreement.

It all began when Paul suggested that they should set sail from Antioch and their home church, and go back to visit again the little groups of Christians who had been converted to faith on their first overseas trip. Barnabas readily agreed.

'We'll take John Mark again,' he said.

'No, we most certainly won't,' Paul said sharply. 'Not after the way he let us down last time, turning back home when we needed him.'

'He'll be different this time,' Barnabas pleaded. 'He's learned his lesson and it's important that he feels we trust him again.'

But Paul would not budge. Every member of such a dangerous and demanding expedition had to be hand-picked. There was simply no room for passengers and they could not afford to risk someone who might be a liability. John Mark had left them in the lurch once, he wouldn't risk it happening again. But Barnabas was thinking of John Mark's need to be encouraged and trusted, not of streamlined efficiency.

The disagreement led to the two friends splitting up. Paul went without Mark or Barnabas, choosing a new companion, Silas. Barnabas took the dejected Mark with him on his own missionary trip to his beautiful home island of Cyprus.

(Adapted from *Acts 15*)

Postscript: We know from a letter written by Paul, that he was later reconciled to Mark and valued him highly.

12 June

Charles Kingsley was born on 12 June 1819. A country vicar, he felt strongly about the harsh and insanitary conditions in Victorian England. He joined the Christian Socialists, a group who encouraged fair dealing and justice between employers and workers. He also wrote books, exposing the terrible conditions that existed. *The Water Babies* is a moral tale for children, but it also highlights the way even small children were employed to sweep the narrow chimneys that no larger person could reach.

The little chimney sweep

'Once upon a time there was a little chimney sweep and his name was Tom ... He lived in a great town in the North country, where there were plenty of chimneys to sweep and plenty of money for Tom to earn and his master to spend. He could not read nor write, and did not care to do either; and he never washed himself, for there was no water up the court where he lived. He had never been taught to say his prayers. He never had heard of God or of Christ ... He cried half his time and laughed the other. He cried when he had to climb the dark flues, rubbing his poor knees and elbows raw; and when the soot got into his eyes, which it did every day of the week; and when his master beat him, which he did every day in the week; and when he had not enough to eat, which happened every day in the week likewise. And he laughed the other half of the day, when he was tossing halfpennies with the boys, or playing leapfrog over the posts, or bowling stones at the horses' legs as they trotted by, which last was excellent fun, when there was a wall at hand behind which to hide. As for chimney-sweeping, and being hungry, and being beaten, he took all that for the way of the world, like the rain and snow and thunder, and stood manfully with his back to it till it was over, as his old donkey did to a hail-storm; and then shook his ears and was as jolly as ever, and thought of the fine times coming, when he would be a man, and a master sweep.'

(From *The Water Babies* by Charles Kingsley)

Other Christians shared Kingsley's concern. **Lord Shaftesbury** had successfully put a bill through Parliament forbidding women and children under 13 from going down the mines. Later he took up the cause of the 'climbing boys'.

Death of a climbing boy

Washington Old Hall, in County Durham, now belongs to the National Trust, but it was once the home of the Washington family, forbears of George Washington, first President of the United States.

Visitors can look out of an upstairs room in Washington Old Hall at a nearby mansion, where in 1872, the local chimney sweep paid his customary visit. He brought with him little Christopher Drummond, seven years old and small enough to wriggle up the narrow twisting chimneys and clean them for his master. But this time something went wrong. Christopher got stuck half way up the chimney and could not move either way. The impatient sweep lit a fire in the hearth below to flush him out. But still Christopher could not struggle free and when they finally reached him he was dead. They laid out the tiny corpse in the front room of the nearby *Cross Keys*. But his death did not go unnoticed. When Lord Shaftesbury spoke in Parliament in favour of a bill to prohibit the use of climbing boys, he told the tragic story of Christopher Drummond. It was far more persuasive than any string of acts and figures could be. The bill was passed.

14 June

Harriet Beecher Stowe was born on 14 June 1811. Harriet Beecher, daughter of a well-known Christian minister, married Calvin Stowe, a college lecturer, and for eighteen years lived just across the river from a state where slavery was legal. She hid runaway slaves on their way to Canada. She wrote *Uncle Tom's Cabin* to lay bare the evils of slavery. First as a magazine serial and then as a book, her novel was an overnight success and was translated into many European languages. It contributed to the abolition of slavery in the Southern States and stopped enforcement of the Fugitive Slave Act.

Theory and practice

Mr Bird, returning from his duties as senator, was discussing with his wife the new Fugitive Slave Act; he had voted in favour of it, but his wife was horrified. She tried to convince her husband without success, that it would be un-Christian and inhumane to hand over a poor, suffering, exhausted human being to a ruthless and vengeful master.

At that moment, there was a commotion in the kitchen. A distraught girl, clutching her little son, had staggered into the house injured, after crossing from the slave state on the other side of the river. Mr Bird was as concerned as his wife. The runaway was fed, clothed and cared for, then taken to a house of safety by the master of the house himself.

High drama and personal involvement enlist the compassion of readers more than reasoned arguments. Because it is a good story, well-told, *Uncle Tom's Cabin* became a huge success and changed people's attitudes.

But not everyone approved. Some Black Americans objected to the patronising air of the white people in the book. They thought Uncle Tom a traitor to their cause because, out of his Christian convictions, he refused to stand up to his bosses or to run away. But the book helped to transform attitudes to slavery in the US and in Europe too.

Revd Wilbert Awdry was born on 15 June, 1911. Awdry grew up in a parsonage and followed his father into the church. A lifelong love of all things to do with railways – real and model – led naturally to his telling stories of trains to his small son Christopher. In time these were published and a total of twenty-six stories have delighted several generations of children, including the Prince of Wales.

The Thomas the Tank Engine Man

'It all began,' the author explained, 'when Christopher caught measles.' A story told to keep his small son happy became a favourite often repeated. After a time the child would correct his father when he used a different word. So Wilbert Awdry wrote the story down on odd scraps of paper, to make sure he got it right. No one could have foreseen that a generation or two later, there would be millions of copies of the books still in print.

Critics have both praised and condemned the books but children love them. And so do the parents who read them aloud over and over again. They bear repetition and have stood the test of time.

Revd Awdry cared about accuracy in all railway matters and he also cared about creating a moral universe for his engines. He never preaches, but the laws of cause and effect are clearly seen. When the engines – like humans – go their own way, they bring trouble on themselves and others. They need to be truly sorry and to accept punishment. 'But,' said their author, 'they are *never* scrapped.'

When Wilbert Awdry was asked in an interview how he would like to be remembered he said *'He helped people to see God in the ordinary things of life, and he made children laugh.'*

(Source: *The Thomas the Tank Engine Man* by Brian Sibley)

16 June

Alfred Fisher studied art in Liverpool and helped to create the stained glass windows in Liverpool Cathedral, where he had been a choir boy. He has made windows for churches and cathedrals in the UK and overseas as well as for civic buildings. He lately completed twenty windows for the Henry VII chapel in Westminster Abbey.

A tank engine in church

It is there to be seen by everyone – a blue tank-engine – known to all as Thomas – ensconced in the window of the church at Rodborough. It was the church that the Reverend Wilbert Awdry attended in his old age and when he was in his eighties he decided to commission a window to commemorate his engines and some of the other things he counted dear. Alfred Fisher seemed the ideal artist to carry out the project as he is not only a leading artist in stained glass but also a railway enthusiast.

'It wasn't an easy commission,' he admits. For a start, Revd Awdry had chosen a number of assorted themes for the window. As well as Thomas he wanted the window to celebrate nature and the joy of ordinary things. Children were to be included as well as his own family. There were further problems over copyright (of Thomas) and the inclusion of people still living, but somehow Alfred Fisher overcame the difficulties.

Sadly, Wilbert Awdry did not live to see the completed window. But the themes he asked for are all there. Thomas the tank-engine is being put into his shed for the last time. The shadowy form of a man in a cloth cap and a clerical collar prepares to close the door. Above, the moon shines – the end of the day has come. But at the top of the window the Dove of the Holy Spirit can be seen. He still breathes life and love into the works of creation, the handiwork of artists and the happiness of children at play. These things live on in the beauty of the window and in the stories which gave it being.

Diane Modahl was born on 17 June 1966. Diane was the youngest of a family of seven children, born to Jamaican parents who had come to Britain. Church, sport on TV and running races in the local park were an accepted part of a happy childhood. Exceptional talent, self-discipline and hard training eventually led to international success in the 800 metres race.

Winning the race

How does a top-class athlete prepare for an event? Diane tells us. In August 1994 she had arrived in Victoria, an island off Canada, where the Commonwealth Games were to be held. She had two weeks to prepare for the first race on 24 August. Training was an important part of each day, but Diane also relaxed in the beautiful surroundings and went to Bible Studies organised by *Christians in Sport*.

When the day itself arrived, her routine changed. She went for her usual early morning jog, savouring the quietness and solitude of the forest as she ran. But her mind was already planning the race ahead. She wrote, 'The race was playing through my head like a video tape that kept rewinding. I saw myself at the track, warming up, reporting and heading to the main arena. I could picture myself taking up the position I wanted and moving through the stages of the race.' It is a kind of action replay *before* the event.

Diane describes her state of mind – and that of every athlete before an important event – as 'tunnel vision.' Everything that is happening that could distract the athlete from the race ahead is blocked out – the race ahead, and only the race ahead absorbs every part of the consciousness. As well as this total concentration is the will and determination to win. Before the race, Diane wrote in her diary, 'I am confident to win, I'm strong to win, I'm determined to win.'

18 June

As well as gaining medals in British, European, Commonwealth and World athletics, **Diane Modahl** has run the 800 metres in under two minutes no fewer than eighteen times.

Disaster

Diane was never to run the race she had prepared for so well. Instead of triumph she faced tragedy. When she got back from her early morning run she was called to the team manager's room. What Sue Deaves had to say was unbelievable. Diane had failed a random drugs test; a large amount of testosterone had shown up. Her whole future in athletics was threatened.

The sheer impossibility of the charge and the monstrous implications sent Diane into deep shock. She passed out several times, lying immobile as if dead. The shame, the unfairness, the knowledge that she was incapable of such a flagrant and dishonest act, shook her to the core. She was sent straight home and spent the interminable journey back to the UK in a state of zombie-like shock. In spite of all precautions, news of her disgrace had leaked out and she was faced at Heathrow by a barrage of cameramen. Only when she was in her husband's comforting arms could she begin to unwind.

But a fierce battle lay ahead. She and her husband were determined to clear her name. Many other sportspeople spoke in her defence, knowing that Diane was morally incapable of such unsporting and dishonest behaviour. But it was a long fight to establish her innocence. In spite of many inconsistencies and unexplained details regarding the test samples, the nightmare lasted twenty months. Only then did the IAAF clear Diane's name.

Diane had friends and family who stood by her but with complete honesty she admits that she did wonder if God had abandoned her. At the time she asked, 'Why have I been the victim of an injustice so cruel and relentless that it robbed me of so much that I hold dear in life?' No answers came, only the hope remained that one day she may see things in a different light.

(Source: *The Diane Modahl Story* by Diane Modahl)

Blaise Pascal, French philosopher, mathematician and scientist, was born on 19 June 1623. Pascal loved mathematics and was encouraged by his father who taught his motherless children himself. At eighteen, Blaise invented a calculator, which worked on cogged wheels and could add and subtract. He was often ill and died when he was only thirty-nine, yet he wrote on geometry and physics and discovered the physical law that 'the pressure acting on a point in a fluid is the same in all directions' (Pascal's Law).

Surrender – to Jesus Christ

During the night of 23 November 1654, Pascal had a strange and wonderful vision of God. He was told to renounce the world and surrender to Jesus Christ. That night changed him, and for the rest of his life he wore round his neck a scrap of parchment bearing the date of his conversion. Over three hundred years later, he is known best not for his scientific or mathematical work but for his *Pensées* ('Thoughts'), the scattered sentences about his faith which he jotted down but did not live to revise or set in order.

Some of Pascal's 'thoughts'

'The God of Christians is not a God who is simply the author of geometrical truths, or of the order of the elements … the God of Christians is a God of love and comfort, a God who fills the soul and heart of those whom he possesses.'

'We can have an excellent knowledge of God without that of our own wretchedness, and of our own wretchedness without that of God. But we cannot know Jesus Christ without knowing at the same time both God and our own misery.'

'All men seek happiness. This is without exception. Whatever means they employ, everyone tends to this end. Some go to war, others do not; but all have the same end in view … Yet without faith no one ever reaches the goal of happiness to which we all aspire, even after years of trying.'

20 June

Extracts from **John Wesley**'s *Journal* for 20 June 1774 reveal the hazards of eighteenth century travel – and Wesley's courage. He was seventy-one.

Guardian angels

'About nine I set out from Sunderland. I took Mrs Smith and her two little girls in the chaise with me. About two miles from the town, on a sudden both horses set out, without any visible cause, and flew down the hill, like an arrow out of a bow. In a minute John fell off the coach-box. The horses went on full speed. A narrow bridge was at the foot of the hill. They went directly over the middle of it. They ran up the next hill with the same speed, many persons getting out of the way. Near the top of the hill was a gate which led into a farmer's yard. It stood open. They turned and ran through it, without touching the gate on one side or the post on the other. I thought, "the gate on the other side of the yard will stop them", but they rushed through it as if it had been a cobweb and galloped on through the cornfield. The little girls cried out; I told them, "Nothing will hurt you; do not be afraid"; feeling no more fear than if I had been sitting in my study. The horses ran on till they came to the edge of a steep precipice. Just then, Mr Smith, who could not overtake us before, galloped in between. They stopped in a moment. Had they gone on ever so little, he and we must have gone down together!

'I am persuaded both evil and good angels had a share in this transaction; how large we do not know, but we shall know hereafter.'

(From John Wesley's *Journal*)

Increase Mather was born in Massachusetts on 21 June 1639. Mather went to Harvard College at the age of 12, graduating at 17. He was ordained and became a minister at the North Church at Boston. He also became the first President of Harvard College. His book *Cases of Conscience Concerning Evil* helped end the Salem witch trials. He was a fierce advocate of American independence and pleaded the cause of his colony in England before the king.

Blazing stars

In November 1680 the people of Boston were amazed to witness a large blazing comet in the morning sky. What did it mean? Their minister, the Reverend Increase Mather, soon told them. If they had been alarmed before they went to church they were terrified by the time they left. In his sermon, *Heaven's Alarm to the World,* he told them that 'flaming vengeance is kindled and burning in Heaven against a sinful world.' The people had departed from the puritan way of life and Mather urged 'Reformation, reformation!' to escape God's punishment.

But the comet – which could be seen until mid-February – awakened Mather's interest in astronomy and cosmology and he consulted the work of Kepler and the new scientists. Then, two years later, a second comet appeared (now known as Halley's comet). Mather preached again, a sermon entitled *Signal Providences.* He still believed that the comet was a sign and a warning from God, but he also recognised that the comet came about through natural causes. It was a second warning. 'The Lord's usual method,' he told them, 'is first to speak to men by his Word, and if that taketh place, well and good: but if his Word be not regarded, then he speaks by signal Providences, one after another.' God works through science.

Reverend Increase Mather died on 23 August 1723. A codicil to his will states: I *do hereby signify to my Executor, That it is my Mind & Will that my Negro Servant called Spaniard shall not be sold after my Decease; but I do then give Him his Liberty: let him then be esteemed a Free Negro. Jun 4, 1719.*

22 June

Dame Cicely Saunders was born on 22 June 1918. Cicely Saunders was a student at Oxford when World War II broke out. She left to be a nurse and later trained as a medical social worker and as a doctor. She has received the OBE and the Templeton Prize for Progress in Religion for her pioneer work in hospices. She was made a Dame Commander of the British Empire in 1980.

Dying with dignity

David Tasma, a Polish patient, left Cicely Saunders £500 in his will, to be – as he put it – 'a window in your home.' David had become a friend as well as a client during his dying months, and shared her vision for a place where the dying could be cared for sensitively and in a positive spirit. Doctors and nurses often view a patient's death as failure, but Dame Cicely believes that dying is a natural part of living. What really matters is that the right kind of care should be offered to the terminally ill. They need to be listened to, nursed with sensitivity and their pain relieved.

Much more money was needed for the project and Dame Cicely realized too that she should train as a doctor and add to her nursing and medical social skills. Once qualified she began research on the relief and control of pain. Her patience at last bore fruit. In 1967 – some nineteen years after that first legacy – St Christopher's Hospice was opened in South London, the first of its kind.

Dame Cicely is motivated by a deep Christian faith but 'religion' is never forced onto patients. There is just someone always at hand to listen, and to talk over a patient's hopes and fears. Relatives and close friends are given support too. Death and dying have been given new meaning and dignity.

Dame Cicely on Listening

'You should listen to someone as if you are looking on water rather than looking on a mirror because you have to be very still if you are going to see in water, you can so easily disturb it.'

Midsummer Eve probably fell on 23 June in 1413. **Margery Kempe**, one of the most colourful women in medieval Christian history, dictated her life story, the first autobiography in English prose. She refers to herself in the third person.

On the road to Bridlington

'It happened one Friday, Midsummer Eve, in very hot weather – as this creature was coming from York carrying a bottle of beer in her hand and her husband a cake tucked inside his clothes against his chest – that her husband asked his wife this question…'

As Margery tells her story – warts and all – we relish the fascinating glimpse of a colourful and very human woman. That Midsummer Eve was one of the turning points in her eventful life. She was born in Norfolk and married a good burgess of the town, John Kempe, clothmaker. Margery's first pregnancy was difficult and following the birth she had a spell of madness. One night Jesus Christ appeared to her and she was restored to sanity and resumed her duties. But she did not give up her love of finery and her desire to be better-dressed than the other ladies. It was only when two ambitious business ventures failed, that she humbly and genuinely gave her whole life to seeking God. Her finery seemed paltry beside a vision that she had of heaven. One night she heard a sound so sweet that 'she thought she had been in paradise'. She jumped out of bed saying, 'Alas that I ever sinned! It is full merry in heaven!'

Friends were sceptical, commenting that she couldn't know about heaven as she had never been there and her husband was loath to accept the celibate lifestyle that she wanted them to lead. But three years later, on that hot summer journey from York, they stopped beside a cross in the field and struck a bargain. John would allow her to travel on pilgrimages and to live a celibate life if she would still lie in the same bed with him, eat with him on Fridays instead of fasting, and pay off his debts. Margery was soon to be off on her pilgrimages.

(Source: *The Book of Margery Kempe*)

24 June

On 24 June 1965 a special meeting of the **Salvation Army** was held in the Albert Hall to mark its one hundredth birthday.

A brass band!

'Mr Booth! A brass band!' exclaimed a young Salvation Army officer in the early days of the movement. She was used to singing her solos to the accompaniment of a chapel organ. 'I don't think I should like a brass band in connection with religious services,' she demurred.

But William Booth and other enthusiastic officers thought otherwise. A father and his three sons, who all played brass instruments, first decided that a bit of cornet and trombone playing might quell the noise of hecklers at open-air meetings. But the band not only drowned interruptions, it also drew the crowds. By Christmas 1879 a band had been formed in Consett, County Durham, in time to play carols for the local residents. Since then Salvation Army bands play carols in almost every town and feature in television plays and episodes of Christmas too.

Soon General Booth was issuing an order in the magazine *War Cry*. 'Bring out your cornets and harps and flutes and pianos and drums and everything else that can make a melody,' he wrote. 'Offer them to God and use them to make all the hearts about you merry before the Lord.'

Certainly the band characterizes the mood of the Salvation Army as a whole. 'I don't think I've ever seen a gloomy member of the Salvation Army,' the Archbishop of Canterbury declared at the centenary celebrations. And no one will disagree with that.

> Praise him with trumpets.
> Praise him with harps and lyres.
> Praise him with drums and dancing.
> Praise him with harps and flutes.
> Praise him with cymbals
> Praise him with loud cymbals.
> Praise the Lord, all living creatures!
> Praise the Lord!

(From *Psalm 150*)

The Reverend Sydney Smith was born in June 1771. Sydney Smith could not afford to read for the bar, so he entered the church, which was one of the professions open to the sons of gentlemen. He was a brilliant and witty writer, whose forthright views sometimes made him unpopular. But he also did much to help his parishioners.

Enough is enough

Food is an important feature of the good life enjoyed in the wealthy nations. It is the subject of many best-selling books and chefs are top stars in popular television programmes. But some people have a conscience about the fact that a few eat so well while the rest of the world cannot get enough to eat. Sydney Smith made the point in a letter to his friend Lord Murray, who seems to have eaten too well.

'If you wish for anything like health and happiness in the fifth act of life, eat about one half what you *could* eat and drink. Did I ever tell you my calculation about eating and drinking? Having ascertained the weight of what I could live upon, so as to preserve health and strength, and what I did live upon, I found that, between ten and seventy years of age, I had eaten and drunk forty-four horse wagon-loads of meat and drink more than would have preserved me in life and health! The value of this mass of nourishment I considered to be worth seven thousand pounds sterling. It occurred to me that I must, by my voracity, have starved to death fully a hundred persons. This is a frightful calculation, but irresistibly true; and I think, dear Murray, your wagons would require an additional horse each!'

26 June

Gilbert White died on 26 June 1793. The Reverend Gilbert White whose *Natural History of Selborne* recorded his observations of the flora and fauna of the countryside around Selborne, was also interested in pets. He himself kept a tortoise.

Maternal instinct

'My friend had a little helpless leveret brought to him, which his servants fed with milk from a spoon, and about the same time his cat kittened and the young were despatched and buried. The hare was soon lost and supposed to be gone the way of most foundlings, to be killed by some dog or cat. However, in about a fortnight, as the master was sitting in his garden in the dusk of the evening, he observed his cat, with tail erect, trotting towards him, and calling with little short inward notes of complacency, such as they use towards their kittens, and something gambolling after, which proved to be the leveret that the cat had supported with her milk and continued to support with great affection.

'Why … a cat should be affected with tenderness towards an animal which is its natural prey, is not so easy to determine … This strange affection was probably occasioned by … maternal feelings which the loss of her kittens had awakened … till she became as much delighted with this foundling as if it had been her real offspring.'

In the *Advertisement* to his *Natural History of Selborne,* Gilbert White wrote in 1788:

'These pursuits, by keeping the mind and body employed, have, under Providence, contributed to much health and cheerfulness, even to old age'.

Helen Keller was born on 27 June 1880.

Teacher and taught

Anne Sullivan put Helen's hand gently under the pump and let the water trickle over her fingers. Then, as the water was running, she traced the letters w-a-t-e-r on Helen's other hand. At last Helen understood. The symbols on one hand represented the cool water on the other.

Helen Keller had a serious illness when she was nineteen months old. When she recovered she had lost her sight and her hearing. Although she used her sense of touch and smell and tried to communicate with signs she invented she was often desperately frustrated and flew into terrible rages. Her mother determined to try to find some way to free the child from her painful isolation. She took her to see Alexander Graham Bell (inventor of the telephone) who was professor of vocal physiology at Boston and devoted time to teaching those who were deaf and mute to speak. He helped to find a teacher for Helen.

Helen was six when Annie Sullivan arrived. She began by teaching Helen obedience and proper manners, and gradually turned the wild creature into a biddable child. But although she traced letters on Helen's hand, she could not make the child equate the letters with the object the symbols represented, until the day that Helen made the connection between the water from the pump and the word traced on her hand. Soon Helen knew hundreds of words and began to read and write in Braille. She learned to speak by tracing Annie's lips and tongue and imitating them. She went to university – accompanied by Anne – and in time became a distinguished scholar, lecturer and writer, making known the needs of those like herself, who were unable to see or hear.

When one door of happiness closes, another opens; but often we look so long at the closed door that we do not see the one that has been opened for us. – Helen Keller 1880-1968

28 June

John Wesley was born on 28 June 1703. Wesley declared that the world was his parish. He did not stay inside church preaching to wealthy congregations but went out and about among ordinary people often addressing huge crowds in the open air. He never forgot how his own heart had been 'strangely warmed' when he 'trusted in Christ and Christ alone for salvation.' It was the gospel message of forgiveness and new life in Christ and of holy living to follow, that he preached to rich and poor alike. As a result, lives were transformed and eighteenth century Britain was changed too. He travelled 250,000 miles and preached 40,000 sermons yet he still found time to write a journal.

Secrets of a healthy old age

More and more people are living to be one hundred years old or more. Wesley lived at a time when the average life expectancy for a man was only forty years yet in spite of a gruelling programme of travel and preaching, he lived to be eighty-eight. Like many people who live to a great age, he had his own theories as to the secret of his continued health and strength.

'This being my birthday, the first day of my seventy-second year, I was considering how is it that I find just the same strength as I did thirty years ago? That my sight is considerably better now and my nerves firmer than they were then? That I have none of the infirmities of old age and have lost several that I had in my youth? The grand cause is the good pleasure of God who doeth whatsoever pleaseth him. The chief means are:

'1) My constantly rising at four for about fifty years;

2) My generally preaching at five in the morning, one of the most healthy exercises in the world;

3) My never travelling less, by sea or land, than four thousand five hundred miles in a year.'

Prayer

'O Lord, let us not live to be useless, for Christ's sake. Amen.' – John Wesley

29 June is the Feast Day of **St *Peter*** the apostle.

Never mind about other people!

They strolled across the stony beach beside the lake. Peter felt warm and comfortably full after the good breakfast Jesus had cooked for him and the other disciples. The cold and frustration of the night's fruitless fishing expedition were all forgotten. But the deep sense of his failure and denial of his master still weighed heavily on Peter's mind. Then Jesus asked,

'Peter, do you love me?'

'You know I do, Lord!' Peter answered quickly. Twice more Jesus asked him the same question and three times Peter was able to affirm his love, nullifying the three times he had denied any knowledge of his Lord.

'Feed my sheep,' Jesus told him. Then he went on: 'Following me won't be easy Peter. When you are old you will find yourself at the mercy of others who will take you where you don't want to go.'

Peter did not flinch. He guessed that Jesus might be foretelling a future of suffering and death but he was glad to have the chance to show that now he *was* ready to face arrest or death for the Master. But he couldn't help wondering what the future had in store for the rest of the group. There was John, now, walking a bit behind them.

'What about him?' he asked Jesus, with a jerk of his head in John's direction.

'Never mind about other people,' Jesus replied, 'what happens to John is not your concern. What matters is that *you* follow me.'

Peter did indeed suffer martyrdom but he spent the rest of his life doing what Jesus had asked; following in Jesus' steps and caring for his sheep – all the men and women who made up the flock, or church, of Jesus, the Good Shepherd.

(From *John 21*)

---

30 June

Stanley Spencer was born on 30 June 1891 in Cookham in Berkshire, where he lived for most of his life. He died there in 1959. He was one of a large musical family but Stanley and one brother, Gilbert, became artists.

'A holy suburb of Heaven'

Spencer and Cookham belong together and when Stanley was a star pupil at the Slade School of Art, he was affectionately known as 'Cookham'. In his heyday local people were used to seeing him pushing a pram chassis down the village street, loaded with his easel and canvas.

At that time, so his brother Gilbert wrote, Cookham was 'strongly imbued with a spirit of independence, of a kind which is more usually associated with islands.'

Stanley and Gilbert received an informal education in an improvised schoolroom set up in a shed at the bottom of their garden, taught by their older sister and father. He read to them a great deal from the Bible and the young Stanley envisaged the Bible stories in his own setting, located in their house, village or the surrounding landscape. When Stanley heard the murmur of the maids' voices from the attic, it seemed to him to be communion with the angels.

After a brilliant career at the Slade, and a spell as a soldier in combat and as a war artist, Spencer went back to Cookham, the village that he called a 'holy suburb of Heaven'. When he painted *The Centurion's Servant* he returned to the attic where the maids had chattered and painted the very same brass bedstead peopling it with his childhood companions. When he painted his *Passion Cycle*, the way of the cross was along Cookham High Street and the famous Resurrection picture exhibited in 1927 takes place in Cookham churchyard. Instead of a theology that is remote, belonging to a different age and culture, Spencer brought the eternal into our own backyard.

(Source: *Stanley Spencer* by Gilbert Spencer)

On 1 July 1535 **Sir Thomas More** was tried for treason. He was born in London in 1478, the son of a judge. He was a scholar, writer and statesman. He became Henry VIII's Lord Chancellor but fell from favour and was tried, imprisoned in the Tower and executed.

Faithful servant of God and King

King Henry's appointment of More as his Lord Chancellor was a popular move, but it put More in a dilemma. He must give total loyalty to his king but More's conviction that he 'should first look unto God and after God unto the king,' meant that conscience won. He did not believe that the king's marriage to Catherine of Aragon was invalid nor would he accept Henry as head of the church in England.

Some forty years after More's death Thomas Stapleton wrote his biography, in which he describes More's last days: 'After receiving sentence of death and being led back to the Tower on July 1 1535, Thomas More prepared himself for approaching death. He was in no way cast down or anxious in mind: he was not only quite resigned, but even cheerful and merry…

'When the day arrived that was to bring More death … he was led out of prison. His beard was long and disordered, his face was pale and thin from the rigours of his confinement. He held in his hand a red cross and raised his eyes to heaven. His robe was of the very poorest and coarsest … Through the avarice or wickedness of the gaoler, he who had held such high office, went out clad in his servant's gown, made of the basest material that we call frieze'.

Prayer

Good Lord, give me grace to spend my life, that when the day of my death shall come, though I may feel pain in my body, I may feel comfort in soul; and with faithful hope of thy mercy, in due love towards thee, and charity towards the world, I may through thy grace part hence into thy glory. – Sir Thomas More 1478-1535

2 July

On 2 July 1865, **William Booth** preached in London's East End. Booth and his wife Catherine had left the Methodist Connexion, in order to follow a life of travelling evangelism, like their hero, John Wesley.

Mission to the heathen at home

'As I passed the flaming gin-palaces tonight, I seemed to hear a voice sounding in my ears, "Where can you go and find heathen such as these?" I feel I ought, at every cost, to stop and preach to these East End multitudes'. In these words William explained to his wife Catherine his call to focus his work on the hungry, drunken, diseased and crime-plagued masses of Victorian London's East End.

When William resigned as a Methodist minister to be a travelling evangelist it meant that he also relinquished his income. But Catherine wrote confidently: 'Does the securing of our bread and cheese make that right which would otherwise be wrong, when God has promised to feed and clothe us? I think not. And I am willing to trust him'.

Now Booth had discovered the particular field for his evangelism. In 1878, the Christian Mission (as it had been called at first) was renamed the Salvation Army. At a time when Britain was prepared to fight for territorial conquests, the Salvation Army was dedicated to fighting the forces of evil and winning men and women for Christ. Members and new converts alike were fired by the idea and enthusiastically prepared to follow their leader into spiritual battle.

'I have found my destiny. I must take the gospel to the people of the East End.' – William Booth 1829-1912

A newspaper reported **William Booth**'s preaching in London's East End, noting that 'Four professed to find peace in believing and two backsliders were restored'.

Soldiers in the King's Army

'In three Colts lane in an old wool shed,
We frighten the living and the dead,
  Sing glory, hallelujah!
And while the rats were running round,
The boys and girls salvation found'.

The children from London's East End sang their song lustily as they went with their leader, William Booth, on a never-to-be-forgotten outing to Epping Forest. In his early days when he had been sent to work in a pawnbroker's shop in Nottingham, Booth had seen the terrible effects of poverty. He determined to meet the material needs of the Londoners he came to help, not just try to save their souls. 'What is the use of preaching the gospel to men whose whole attention is concentrated upon a desperate struggle to keep alive?' he asked. 'He cannot hear you any more than a man whose head is under water can listen to a sermon'.

As well as a rat-ridden wool shed, Booth used a dancing academy, a skittle alley, a hay-loft, a public house and a music-hall as premises for preaching. He declared war on 'pinching poverty, rags and misery'. A battle was on and the Salvation Army was there to fight it. Under Booth's generalship the meetings in the wool shed grew into an international movement combating poverty, suffering and sin.

'Every cab-horse in London is given food, shelter and work. People ought to be looked after just as well as cab-horses are cared for.'
– William Booth 1829-1912

4 July

Thomas Barnado was born on 4 July 1845. Barnado was a medical student in London, training in order to go to China as a missionary. But he still found time to work among children, teaching in one of the so-called 'ragged schools'. One of the boys he met was Jim Jarvis. Barnado told the story of that eventful meeting many times, but it was first told in a magazine. The article was entitled 'How it all Happened'. What 'happened' was the setting up of Dr Barnado's Homes. The charity he began is still carrying out its caring mission in many different ways today.

How it all happened

It was half past nine and time for the children to go home. One small straggler lingered.

'Come on my lad,' Dr Barnado encouraged, 'time you were off. Your mother will be worrying'.

'I haven't got a mother. Please let me stay here!'

'Where do you live?'

'Don't live nowhere.'

'Well, where did you sleep last night?'

'Down in Whitechapel, sir, in one of them carts that's filled with hay. A chap there told me to come to your school and perhaps you'd let me sleep by your fire tonight'.

The night was cold, the wind keen, and the boy looked ill.

'Are there anymore like you?' Barnado asked.

'Oh, yes, sir, heaps of them – more than I could count'.

Dr Barnado took Jim back to his lodgings, gave him coffee and heard his story. An orphan, he had run away from a lighterman he called Swearing Dick, who ill-treated him. When Jim's tale was over Barnado, in turn, told him the story of Jesus. When he came to the crucifixion, Jim exclaimed, 'Oh sir, that was worse than Swearing Dick give me!'

At midnight they set out to find the 'heaps' more boys that slept rough. He did not know it, but Thomas Barnado's life-work was beginning.

William Thomas Stead, journalist and reformer, was born on 5 July 1849. Stead began his journalistic career on the *Darlington Northern Echo* and rose to be editor of *The Pall Mall Gazette*. He used his pen to publicise social wrongs. He met his death in 1912 in the Titanic disaster.

'A painful subject'

Florence Booth of the Salvation Army was outraged when she found young girls forced onto the London streets by greedy pimps. She and her husband Bramwell (son of William Booth) made every effort both to raise the age of consent and to make it an offence to procure young people for immoral purposes. Florence sought support from the great and the good, even writing to Queen Victoria who sympathised with her on 'the painful subject' but did nothing to help. But they found a champion in the journalist William Stead. Bramwell reported that when he told him of the plight of young girls forced into prostitution, Stead angrily banged his fist on the table and uttered the one word 'Damn!' But, 'some earnest prayer, a cup of coffee and he was braced for further efforts', Bramwell added.

Stead printed articles to publicise the shameful traffic in young girls for prostitution, in Britain and abroad. *The Times* complained that he was blackening the name of England before the world. So Stead decided to demonstrate how easy it was to buy a young girl, then send her overseas. To cover himself, he wrote to the Archbishop of Canterbury and the Roman Catholic Cardinal to tell them of his plans beforehand. Then he bought a young girl from her drunken mother and sent her to the safety of the Salvation Army in Switzerland. But in spite of safeguards the scheme backfired. A rival newspaper misrepresented the transaction and accused Stead of acting illegally. He was sentenced to three months in prison.

But his bold action was not wholly in vain. Thousands signed a petition, taken by the Salvation Army to Parliament, which resulted in the age of consent being raised to sixteen.

---

6 July

Kindness – to the executioner

'When he arrived at the place of execution and was about to mount the scaffold, he stretched out his hand for assistance, saying, "I pray you see me safe up, and for my coming down let me shift for myself." On the scaffold he wished to speak to the people, but was forbidden to do so by the Sheriff. He contented himself therefore with saying: "I call you to witness, brothers, that I die the faithful servant of God and the King and in the faith of the Catholic Church." After that, kneeling down, he recited aloud the fiftieth psalm: "Have mercy on me, O God."

'After saying the psalm and finishing his prayers he rose briskly and when, according to custom, the executioner begged his pardon, he kissed him with great love, gave him a golden angel-noble and said to him: "Thou wilt give me today a greater benefit than any mortal man can be able to give me. Pluck up thy spirits, man, and be not afraid to do thine office."

'Even before, he had asked his daughter and other friends to do whatever acts of kindness they could to his executioner. Then the executioner wished to bind his eyes, but he said, "I will cover them myself." He covered his face with a linen cloth he had brought with him and joyfully and calmly laid his head on the block. It was at once struck off, and his soul sped to heaven.'

(From *Life of Sir Thomas More* by Thomas Stapleton)

Baroness Cox was born in July (6th) 1937 into an upper middle-class family, the daughter of an eminent surgeon. She followed in their Christian faith. She became a nurse and married a neuro-surgeon. She brought up a young family while studying and and gained first class honours in sociology. She was created a peeress by Margaret Thatcher and became a Deputy Speaker in the House of Lords. She is an outstanding human rights campaigner, investigating for herself the plight of those who cannot speak up for themselves.

In 1991 Caroline Cox was asked to lead an international delegation to Armenia. Long-standing tension between the Armenians and the Azeris had flared up. Armenians had been forcibly removed from the disputed land of Nagorno Karabakh and the country subjected to incessant attack.

'International drugs runner'

Caroline Cox was to go to Karabakh many more times after that first official visit, when she had witnessed the conditions in hospital where surgery was performed without anaesthetics and surgical instruments sterilised over wood-burning stoves. The authorities gave her a list of the most-needed drugs and she obtained a Home Office licence to buy and export them. British Airways transported the crates free to Paris but there she and her companion had to risk walking nonchalantly along the 'nothing to declare' channel in order to get their precious cargo through. For the last stages of their journey they went by military helicopter, joining up with a medical team. But when visibility deteriorated, they were off-loaded in a snow-covered forest in Azeri territory. Their only option was to walk, keeping clear of roads and Azeri snipers. It was twelve kilometres to the nearest village and Caroline, fit and used to exercise herself, was concerned about some of the elderly medical staff.

When they came across a farmer with tractor and trailer, he carried their precious cargo and some of the team. Caroline battled on through the thick snow and when night fell, they helped each other slither and slide through the darkness. At last they arrived at the Armenian village and were received with welcoming fires and hot drinks to warm them through. Later, a stone was set up to commemorate the life-saving walk, which the locals called the Cox Way. Next day, the little party set off for the hospital and within twelve days of witnessing their desperate need, Caroline Cox had delivered the life-saving drugs.

8 July

In 1994 **Baroness Cox** was invited to Burma (Myanmar) by Dr Martin Panter, an English doctor working among ethnic minorities, to investigate the plight of the Karen people, driven out of their homeland of Burma.

'My heart will not fear'

Dr Panter and a team of eye specialists had planned a visit to the Karenni, when he was warned that a major Burmese air and military attack was planned in the same area at exactly that time. Dr Panter recognised the danger, especially for his children – aged 13, 9 and 3 – who were with him. The team met to pray and Dr Panter read from *Psalm 27*: *'When my enemies and my foes attack me, they will stumble and fall. Though an army besiege me, my heart will not fear; though war break out against me, even then will I be confident.'* They decided to go ahead. No attack took place and they completed their mission successfully.

On his next visit to Burma he heard what had really happened. The air strike *had* been timed to begin that day, when the morning mist dispersed – as it did each day without fail. But on that morning, as the planes circled above, huge clouds billowed up from the river, obscuring the target completely. They circled around until their fuel was spent, but the clouds persisted and they were forced to return to base while the military withdrew.

On one visit, Baroness Cox, Dr Panter and the team slogged up a mountain to visit Karen soldiers. Once at the top, they had to cross the ridge, in full view of Burmese snipers. Caroline Cox refused to listen to Dr Panter's warning and turn back. 'They are expecting to see us,' she replied simply and strode ahead. The soldiers were overjoyed. 'We thought we had been forgotten,' one said.

On their way back, Caroline heard a bell ringing through the jungle. Soon they came upon a wooden church among the trees, full of worshippers. Then she saw the bell. It had been made from the sawn-off top of a Burmese bomb. 'Instead of swords into ploughshares,' she commented, 'it was bombs into bells.'

(Source: *Baroness Cox – A Voice for the Voiceless* by Andrew Boyd)

On 9 July 1643, **George Fox** set out from home and family to find a faith to live by. George Fox was born in July 1624. The exact day is not known, nor are the details of his sisters and brothers, because a sexton's wife, at the church of Fenny Drayton in Warwickshire, cut out the pages of the baptismal records some time during the eighteenth century – to make covers for her preserves!

'Strike again!'

George Fox, founder of the Quakers, often faced imprisonment and abuse. One day he was dragged out of church, whipped by constables, then turned over to the crowd, who were armed with clubs and sticks. They beat him till he lay unconscious. Fox described the scene:

'I lay a little still, and the power of the Lord sprang through me, that I stood up again and stretched out my arms amongst them all and said with a loud voice, "Strike again!" There was a mason, a rude fellow, gave me a blow with all his might just atop of my hand with his walking-rule staff. And my hand and my arm was so numbed and bruised that I could not draw it unto me again. Then the people cried out, "He hath spoiled his hand for ever having any use of it more." The skin was struck off my hand and a little blood came, and I looked at it in the love of God, and I was in the love of God to them all that had persecuted me.

'And after a while the Lord's power sprang through me again, that in a minute I recovered my hand and arm and it was as well as it was before, and I had never another blow afterwards.'

'I saw also that there was an ocean of darkness and death, but an infinite ocean of light and love which flowed over the ocean of darkness. In that also I saw the infinite love of God; and I had great openings.' – George Fox 1624-1691

10 July

Dr Toyohiko Kagawa was born on 10 July 1888. Kagawa became a Christian after reading the Gospels and being drawn to the person of Christ. He prayed: "O God, make me like Christ.' He lived and worked as an evangelist in the filth and squalor of the slums in Shinkawa. He knew that the slums would remain as long as Japanese labourers were paid such low wages and forbidden to negotiate with employers. So he organised trade unions among the dockworkers.

'Let there be peace!'

Every second counted. Kagawa ran as fast as he could. He *must* reach the bridge that led to the shipyard before the mob of workers got there. He was weak from tuberculosis and repeated bouts of pneumonia, and each step seemed to be tearing him apart. His heart was pounding, but still he ran – panting, heaving, gasping for breath. He reached the bridge and heard the oncoming hum of angry marchers increasing to a roar.

Kagawa had agreed to lead the workers in a peaceful demonstration, and as a result had been arrested and put in prison for two weeks. Meanwhile, communist hotheads had roused the workers to march on the shipyard to break up machinery and damage cargoes. Kagawa heard of the march only just in time.

He leaned on the bridge for support, knowing that he had neither strength nor authority to command the workers. He prayed: 'O God, let there be peace!' The first angry men drew near and Kagawa held up his hand. They stopped and he began to speak, urging them to go peacefully home so that negotiations could begin.

Moved by the entreaty of the man they loved and honoured, the rioters left their communist leaders and turned quietly back. As a result, talks began with the employers and trade unions were recognised and accepted by management.

'Unions are necessary, but labour problems can only be solved by a change of heart in the labourer himself.' – Kagawa

On 11 July 1924 **Eric Liddell** won the 400-metre gold medal at the Olympics in Paris. It was in 1981 that the film, *Chariots of Fire*, won four Oscars and Best Film of the Year Award. Even if the film has been forgotten the music has not. The film told the story of Eric Liddell, a Christian who refused to represent the UK in the 100-metre sprint, because the heats were to be run on a Sunday. At the last minute he trained for the 400 metres and actually won it. A Scottish evening paper reported the race in dramatic terms:

Chock full of fight!

'It was Liddell that first caught the eye as they came round the first bend. The Scot set up a terrific pace. He ran as if he were wild with inspiration, like some demon. As he flew along to the accompaniment of a roar, the experts wondered whether Liddell would crack, such was the pace he set...

'"Liddell!" was shrieked; "Imbach!" was thundered by the Swiss; "Taylor!" was shouted ; "Butler!" "Fitch!" in turn were yelled.

'Liddell, yards ahead, came round the bend for the straight and as he did so, pulled the harder at himself for Fitch was getting nearer ... It was the last fifty metres that meant the making or breaking of Liddell. Just for a second it was feared that he would kill himself by the terrible speed he had got up, but to the joy of the British camp, he remained chock full of fight. Imbach, perhaps some fifty yards from the tape, fell. It was then Liddell or Fitch. The Scotsman had so surely got all his teeth into the race that the American could not hold and Liddell got home first ... by a remarkable finish.'

(From the *Edinburgh Evening News,* July 1924)

12 July

Kathy Staff was born on 12 July 1928. She is best known for her role as Nora Batty in BBC Television's *Last of the Summer Wine*. She always wanted to act, and after a gruelling apprenticeship in repertory, became a professional actor in 1949. Later, television provided an ideal opportunity for her talents as a character actor. She delighted viewers in *Coronation Street*, *Crossroads* and many comedy sketches as well as starring in films and an annual pantomime.

Wrinkles and all

'I find praise a bit embarrassing. I never think of myself as "famous". I just feel the same as I've always felt.' Kathy refuses to put on airs and it is her refreshing honesty and genuineness that are so endearing. She grew up in a tightly-knit Northern community and has never forgotten her roots. She and her extended family are still members of the church where she grew up.

Last of the Summer Wine has many funny moments off the air as well as on it. In one episode Nora was riding home on an old-fashioned boneshaker when Compo jumped out at her. She had to pelt him with vegetables from her bicycle basket before falling off. Kathy decided that to make the scene credible she must not fake the fall but do it for real. Once would have been fine, but she had to repeat the scene three times, ending up decidedly the worse for wear.

Kathy's Christian faith has been the rock solid basis of her life. She writes: I couldn't cope with my life without faith… Without God's strength I couldn't do what I do'. For Kathy, family comes first. 'Not like Nora Batty. You can take the rollers out and the apron and wrinkled stockings off, and she's just a heap on the floor. Being a Mum is the role you play twenty four hours a day.' She thinks the epitaph she would like best might be: 'She was a good Christian mum'.

(Source: *My Life, Wrinkles and All* by Kathy Staff)

Eric Liddell went as a missionary to China and in 1943 was interned in Japan with other British, American and so-called 'enemy nationals'. He died there of a brain tumour, exhausted too by his tireless and cheerful service to all in the camp.

Sunday observance

The thin, bronzed man in the multi-coloured shirt carefully collected each hockey stick from the teenage players and examined them for wear. There'd be no new ones – they were lucky to have even these in the camp. Eric bound them up carefully with strips torn from his own precious sheets.

When they were first interned with their families the teenagers had been hopelessly bored. With no privacy and nothing to occupy their time, they had wandered aimlessly around the camp perimeter at night with no outlet for their energies. So Eric Liddell organised hockey, rounders and baseball as well as chess and indoor activities. There was never any trouble with teenage high spirits after that. Except once. Eric, true to the principles that had made him famous in the 1924 Olympic Games, refused to organize games on Sundays. The young people jibbed at this rule and decided to arrange their own hockey match. It ended in a disastrous free-for-all. Eric said nothing but the next Sunday he went with them and refereed their match. He put their genuine need for exercise and the well-being of relationships throughout the camp above his own treasured observance of Sunday for the sole worship of God.

14 July

In July 1940, **C S Lewis** conceived the idea for Screwtape. C S Lewis wrote an enormous number of letters, many of which have been preserved; after his death some were edited and published by his brother in 1966. Not only did Lewis write to close friends but also replied with great courtesy and patience to a host of unknown correspondents who wrote to him for theological and personal advice.

'An idea for a book'

To his brother 20 July 1940

'After the service was over – one could wish these things came more seasonably – I was struck by an idea for a book which I think might be both useful and entertaining. It would be called "As one Devil to another" and would consist of letters from an elderly retired devil to a young devil who has just started work on his first "patient". The idea would be to give all the psychology of temptation from the other point of view. For example ... '

It was autumn 1942 by the time *The Screwtape Letters* (as it was finally called) was published; it was enormously successful and for the first time in his life Lewis had plenty of money coming in. He had always been hard up and his brother Warnie describes the way in which he cheerfully lavished cheques on all kinds of good causes and individuals – deserving or not. In the end his solicitor stepped in and arranged matters so that two thirds of his royalties went into a charitable trust from which cheques could be paid to those he wished to help.

Warnie remembers his brother's generosity and large-heartedness shown in so many ways. 'He met a tramp while walking on Shotover – a tramp who turned the conversation to the subject of poetry, quoting Fitzgerald with gusto. Jack went home, armed himself with bottles of beer and a verse anthology, trudged up to the top of the hill again, gave book and beer to the tramp, and bade him a cordial farewell.'

(From *Letters of C S Lewis* edited by W H Lewis)

15 July is **St Swithun**'s Day.

Is it going to rain?

St Swithun's Day, if thou dost rain,
For forty days it will remain;
St Swithun's Day, if thou be fair,
For forty days 'twill rain na'mair.

That old rhyme is probably forgotten now, but in the centuries before frequent broadcast forecasts, folklore provided rhymes and sayings to predict the weather to come. Of course they did not always get it right – any more than present-day meteorologists do.

St Swithun was Bishop of Winchester in the ninth century. He cared for his people, built and repaired churches and even built a bridge across the river. Because he loved the countryside so much, he asked that his body should be buried outside the church. He wanted sun and rain to fall on his grave and worshippers to walk across it.

His request was carried out and in the next hundred years weather and worshippers caused all signs of Swithun's grave to disappear altogether. Then, one day, his remains were accidentally found. The monks were shocked and hurried to bring his body inside the church and to bury it with due honour. Legend has it that the saint disapproved and that is why rain that falls on his feast day continues to fall for forty days and nights – in his memory.

16 July

On 16 July 1918, Nicholas II, last Tsar of Russia, was murdered. His daughter-in-law, *Grand Duchess of Russia,* was put to death the next day.

'We heard singing!'

On 9 July 1998 the Duke of Edinburgh took his place in Westminster Abbey for a very special service. Ten modern Christian martyrs were being honoured as the Archbishop of Canterbury, Dr Carey, unveiled new statues of them placed in empty niches on the west front of the Abbey. The Duke was attending because his great aunt – Grand Duchess Elizabeth – was among the honoured ten.

Elizabeth was born in 1864 and lived in England for some time. She blossomed into a great beauty and was married to the Tsar's fifth son, Grand Duke Sergei Alexandrovich. When he was assassinated in 1909 Elizabeth founded a home in Moscow for prayer and acts of charity and in 1909 she was one of the seventeen new 'sisters of love and mercy.'

One of Elizabeth's assassins, a Bolshevik called Ryabov, described what happened on that terrible day. A group of prisoners was led to a mineshaft; Elizabeth was the first of them. Ryabov recalled the scene: 'After throwing her down the shaft we heard her struggling for some time. Then I threw in a grenade. After a short while we heard talking and a terrible groan. I threw another grenade. And what do you think – we heard singing!' He went on to say that they ran out of grenades so they filled the shaft with dry brushwood and set it on fire. But, he added, 'Their hymns rose through the smoke for some time.'

The hymn-writer, **Isaac Watts**, was born on 17 July 1674 in Southampton, the son of an elder in the local Independent Church. He was a clever boy but because he was not a member of the Church of England, he was not allowed to study at Oxford or Cambridge. Instead he trained at a Dissenting academy and became a minister in London.

'Write something better!'

We probably take hymns pretty much for granted but they have not always been a regular part of church services. In earlier centuries metrical psalms were intoned to dull and monotonous tunes. The story is told that young Isaac Watts, as a teenager, complained bitterly about the kind of things that were sung in the church where his father was an elder. His father retorted: 'Then write something better.' So Isaac Watts did exactly that. Even though many of his hymns are based on Bible passages, Watts created them anew, composing over 450 hymns – inspiring verses that could be set to interesting tunes. Three hundred years later many of them still reflect the emotions and responses of ordinary men and women.

One of Watts' hymns – 'Our God, our help in ages past,' was written in 1714, shortly before the death of Queen Anne, when people were desperately worried about the succession to the throne. It has remained a theme song for times of national emergency. Many older people remember singing it in church on the Sunday that World War II broke out. Watts chose as his title for the hymn: 'Man frail, and God eternal' – a comforting reminder in times of trouble.

18 July

Nelson Mandela was born on 18 July 1918. He was brought up in the countryside, in a tiny village in Transkei. His father named him Rolihlahla, which literally means 'pulling the branch of a tree' but could better be translated as 'troublemaker.' He recognises that he has lived up to his name; he has raised storms and had to weather many himself.

President in the making

Nelson Mandela was born into the royal family of the Thembu tribe and his father was adviser to the king. But when Mandela was still very young, his father refused to answer a summons to appear before the local magistrate. He believed his duty was to answer to his king alone. For this 'offence' he was deposed without further inquiry and deprived of his status as well as his land, property and wealth. Nelson recognises that he probably inherited his father's sense of fairness as well as his stubbornness in matters of principle.

Nelson – the name he was given at school by an English teacher – led a happy carefree boyhood, joining in the games and sports and fights enjoyed by boys everywhere. One day he was riding a high-spirited donkey, who bucked and shied and finally bolted with him into a thorn bush. He emerged scratched and humiliated. 'I learned,' he wrote years later, 'that to humiliate another person is to make him suffer an unnecessarily cruel fate. Even as a boy, I defeated my opponents without dishonouring them.'

When he was nine, his father died and his uncle, the Chief, sent for him and became his guardian. He began to attend church, because Christian faith was an important part of life at court. Revd. Matyolo, the Methodist minister, attracted him not only by his preaching but by his whole way of life.

Later, at college, he came to know the principal, the Reverend Harris. Although he was a just and stern headmaster, off duty he was gentle and tolerant. He had an influence on Mandela, who writes: 'As an example of a man unselfishly devoted to a good cause, he was an important model to me.'

(Source: *Long Walk to Freedom* by Nelson Mandela)

After many twists and turns **Nelson Mandela** qualified as a lawyer and became deeply involved in the struggle for black rights. He was arrested and tried and at 44 he was imprisoned on Robben Island for 27 years. Later he was to become South Africa's first black President.

'My life in your hands'

When Mandela and his fellow-prisoners arrived on Robben Island they were met by loud-mouthed, hectoring guards. Life on this remote outpost was hard for warders as well as prisoners. Mandela courteously but firmly refused to kowtow to the guards' threats and soon became spokesperson for the whole group of political prisoners…

Mandela's damp cell was three paces long and six feet wide. Three flimsy worn blankets and matting for a bed provided the only warmth and comfort. By day the prisoners worked in the quarries.

Two of Mandela's fellow prisoners suggested that he should write his memoirs and somehow smuggle them out for publication. He wrote by night, and snatched sleep by day. But where to hide the five hundred page manuscript? Eventually, they put the rolled-up pages into old cocoa tins and buried them. A few weeks later Mandela was horrified to see men digging foundations for a wall near the spot where the papers were buried. Two tins were rescued but not the one Mandela had secreted under a pipe. When they saw that the pipe had been removed they knew that the manuscript had been discovered. Mandela was confronted with the papers, but insisted that the authorities must furnish proof that he was the author. In spite of absence of proof, Mandela was punished. For four years his study privileges were taken away. But a smuggled copy of the manuscript later formed the basis of Mandela's autobiography, *Long Walk to Freedom*.

In Mandela's first speech on his release he said: 'Friends, comrades and fellow South Africans… your tireless and heroic sacrifices have made it possible for me to be here today. I therefore place the remaining years of my life in your hands.'

20 July

Catherine Bramwell-Booth, granddaughter of William Booth, was born on 20 July 1883. The eldest daughter of Bramwell and Florence Booth, she grew up to follow in her parents' and grandparents' footsteps. She became a Commissioner in the Salvation Army and attracted considerable media attention when she celebrated her 100th birthday.

All you need is love

Catherine described her Victorian childhood as idyllic. The oldest of Bramwell and Florence's seven children, she can remember the freedom and spontaneity they enjoyed. 'We had marvellous times. We were never scolded or smacked. The great power was our love for our parents and our desire to please them.'

Florence tried hard to obey her mother-in-law's advice about the need to master a small child's will, but her own method of child-rearing was to rule by love. Unlike most Victorians, she did not impose a rigid framework but encouraged fun and adventure. Once, on a summer morning, she shooed the children out into the garden to pick an apple and finish their breakfast out of doors.

Florence let her children know that they were deeply loved. When a new baby was born she would call the children to admire the baby then tell them: 'Because I love the new baby does not mean that I love any of you any less. There is always more love to give; the more love we give, the more we have to give.'

Catherine's life in the Salvation Army was tough. But love was always her answer too. On her hundredth birthday she said: 'Love is the secret of life. Someone who hasn't loved another better than they love themselves hasn't begun to live. That *is* life, and I have been rich in people to love.'

(Source: *Catherine Bramwell-Booth* by Mary Batchelor)

Monday 21 July 1997 was the first day of the hearing of the appeal against **Sheila Bowler**'s murder conviction. The efforts of 'The Friends of Sheila Bowler', of television's *Trial and Error* team and of the national press at last succeeded. Sheila Bowler's second appeal was heard and after four and a half years in prison, she was acquitted of murder.

'We all of us think she's innocent'

Onlookers and jury may have read Sheila wrongly, but inmates and officers in prison learned to know her better. One said: 'We all of us think she's innocent. She's a lovely lady'. Another said: 'We all hope Sheila walks free on Monday, but we really don't want her to go – she's so kind to everyone.'

When Sheila first arrived at Holloway prison to begin her sentence she was horrified by the filth – cockroaches abounded – the unspeakable food and the noise. There were no curtains or carpets to muffle the sounds of constantly slamming doors, jangling keys, barked orders, blared tannoy announcements and the shouts and yells of prisoners.

Shut off from her clean, ordered world in Rye, Sheila courageously began to impose order on her life in prison. She joined the chapel choir, listened to Radio 4 – when she could afford batteries – and went to classes whenever available. She did any job she was given with meticulous efficiency. But she was plagued by migraine, mood swings and depression. Yet the chaplain noted: 'I am hopeful that her strong faith in God will sustain her in the coming days'.

Sheila was also learning unexpected lessons in prison: 'Holloway was the saddest place I'd ever come across,' she wrote; and later: 'I could weep at the sad spectacle they [prisoners] presented in chapel. No way should they be locked up as they are: it only magnifies their deep sense of guilt and inadequacy.' The brusque, efficient, middle-class, church-going woman was learning gentleness and mercy.

(Source: Newspaper cuttings and *Anybody's Nightmare* by Angela and Tim Devlin)

22 July

22 July is the Feast Day of **St Mary Magdalene**. The Western church identified Mary Magdalene with the prostitute who anointed Jesus' feet (*Luke 7:35-50*) and also with Mary of Bethany (*Luke 10:38-42* and *John 12:1-7*), but Luke tells us only that Mary Magdalene was a close follower and helper of Jesus and that seven demons had been cast out of her.

'Apostle to the apostles'

What were the demons that Jesus had cast out? Were they demons of despair, of depression, of addiction or of brokenness and loss? Whatever it was that had kept Mary from living a full and liberated life, Jesus set her free. No wonder she worshipped and served him with wholehearted loyalty and love. But now her Master was dead and his body gone.

She stood in the garden where his body had been, tears blinding her eyes. But she could make out the figure of a man standing close by. Perhaps he could tell her what she longed to know. As if in answer to her thoughts he said,

'Why are you crying? Who are you looking for?'

'I'm looking for the body of my dearest Friend and Master,' she burst out. ' We buried him here on Friday and now his body has gone from the tomb. Perhaps you are the gardener and you moved him?'

For a moment she thought he wasn't going to answer. Then he said, 'Mary!' and she knew his voice.

'My Master!' she cried, rushing forward to grasp him. She should have realized that he would conquer death and rise again to life. He was alive now for ever.

'Go and tell my disciples that I am alive,' he said. So Mary became 'the apostle to the apostles'.

(Source: *John 20*)

Susanna Wesley, mother of John and Charles, died on 23 July 1742.
Susanna, wife of the Reverend Samuel Wesley, had nineteen
children, the best known being the preacher, John and hymn-writer,
Charles. On 24 July 1732, she wrote to her son, John, telling him
some of her practices in bringing up children.

Cry softly!

'Dear Son,

'According to your desire, I have collected the
principal rules I observed in educating my family;
which I now send you.

'When turned a year old (and some before), they
were taught to fear the rod and to cry softly; by
which means they escaped abundance of correction;
and that most odious noise of the crying of children
was rarely heard in the house.

'It had been observed that cowardice and fear of
punishment often led children into lying till they get
a custom of it which they cannot leave. To prevent
this, a law was made that whoever was charged with
a fault of which they were guilty, if they would
confess it and promise to amend, should not be
beaten.

'No child should ever be chid or beaten twice for
the same fault; and that if they amended, they
should never be upbraided with it afterwards.'

(From John Wesley's *Journal*)

Poor Susanna! Only too often her wise and enlightened third
rule was not observed. Samuel, their father, was hot-tempered
and if he was around when one of the children duly confessed,
he would set about them and give them a good hiding. But
as Susanna commented in another letter to one of her sons:
'Tis an unhappiness almost peculiar to our family, that your
father and I seldom think alike.'

John Newton, one time slave-trader, was born on 24 July 1725. John Newton had not always been the saintly and respected clergyman of his later years. And he never forgot it. When he was very old he said, 'My memory is nearly gone but I remember two things: that I am a great sinner and that Christ is a great Saviour.'

Amazing grace!

'Oh! I have reason to praise God for that storm: for the apprehension I had, first of sinking under the weight of all my sins into that ocean and into eternity. Then I began to think: I attempted to pray and my first half-formed prayers were answered.' That was how John Newton described the storm that changed his life, when he wrote about it later to his wife.

His life had been hard; his mother – a loving Christian woman – died when he was only six. At eleven, he joined his father's ship and later was press-ganged into the navy. He deserted ship because conditions were so bad, and was caught and severely punished. He became involved in the slave-trade, then jumped ship again and spent a year in Sierra Leone, sick and degraded, bullied and ill-treated by an African woman.

At last, a message arrived from England and he returned, experiencing the terrifying storm he described on his way back. That storm shocked Newton into facing up to his own wrongdoing and finding faith. The rough sailor, who had been the slave of every kind of evil, became the slave of Jesus Christ, and gave the rest of his life to preaching the good news that had set him free.

Amazing grace! How sweet the sound
That saved a wretch like me!
I once was lost, but now am found,
Was blind, but now I see.

25 July is **St Christopher**'s Feast Day. St Christopher, first called Reprobus, is the patron saint of travellers – and more recently of those who drive cars. He died in about 250. The story is told that he determined to serve only the greatest and most powerful prince in the world. He found his Master in Christ, and was told to serve him by carrying travellers across a fast-flowing river that had neither bridge nor ford.

The world on his shoulders

One night, the legend goes, Christopher was wakened from sleep by a child calling from the river-bank. When he went out to look he could see no one, but the call came twice more. The third time he searched and found the child.

'Please carry me across the river,' the child said and Christopher tossed him lightly onto his shoulders, for he was a tall, strong man. He set off readily, thinking that his burden would be easy to bear.

But the waters of the river swirled about him and rose higher and higher while the child on his shoulders grew heavier and heavier. He began to be afraid that he would never reach the far side. But he struggled on, weighed down by his heavy burden and tugged by the currents. At last he reached the shore and thankfully set the child down.

'I felt as though I had the whole world on my shoulders,' he said.

'Don't be surprised,' the child replied. 'You have not only carried the world on your shoulders but you have carried the one who made the world. I am Jesus Christ – the King you serve.'

So Reprobus was renamed Christopher, or the 'Christ-bearer'.

26 July

George Borrow died on 26 July 1881. Borrow worked for the Bible Society for many years. He later told them: 'I can't forget that I spent the happiest years of my life in its service. Long may it flourish in spite of enemies and evil times.' More than a hundred years later, it is still flourishing.

The word master

The story is told that when the Bible Society summoned George Borrow for interview, he walked the 112 miles from Norwich to London in twenty-seven hours, spending only 5½d (old money) on a pint of ale, half a pint of milk, a roll and two apples.

Borrow had an amazing flair for languages. He chose the title *Lavengro* for his autobiography. In the Romany language that means 'Word master'.

Someone was needed to superintend the printing of the New Testament in Manchu – the Chinese language spoken at court. It would not be possible to send anyone direct to China, for Russia was the only country represented at the Chinese court. So Borrow would have to go to Russia. 'Go home and learn Manchu,' the Bible Society told him. Borrow had successfully passed the examination in Arabic and the committee had been told that he could read the Bible in thirteen languages.

He was equal to the task. Borrow was twenty-nine years old, but his hair was already white. He was six feet three inches tall and an unusual person in every way. He went home from London, armed with the very few books available in Manchu. But he could not even get hold of a grammar and other books promised to him were hopelessly delayed. But Borrow was unfazed. 'I was determined not to be discouraged,' he wrote.

George Borrow.

To China via Russia

George Borrow tackled the task of learning Manchu at full speed. Not many weeks after his interview with the Bible Society in London, he wrote to tell them that he had mastered the difficult language and was ready to go to Russia. So Borrow set off for St Petersburg where Tsar Nicholas lived in splendour.

First, Borrow had to contact the Russian who had made a preliminary translation of the New Testament into Manchu. This man could speak no other European language, so Borrow had to discuss the work in Russian.

The next problem was to locate the special type needed to print Chinese characters. When Borrow found the cellar where the type had been stored, he discovered that it had burst out of its original container and tiny bits of metal had been trampled under mud and filth from a flood some years before. It was a painstaking task retrieving, cleaning and sorting all the pieces.

Next Borrow had to bargain for paper at the nearby mill – then teach the printers how to use this unfamiliar type. No wonder he replied rather tartly to the Bible Society's complaint that he did not write home very often!

It took Borrow two years to complete the task. He had edited the text and superintended the whole printing process. All that remained was to take the Testaments to the Chinese court. Then, to Borrow's deep disappointment, the Tsar refused to issue him with a visa. Someone else would go.

Borrow returned dutifully to London and was soon off on another expedition for the Bible Society – this time taking the Bible to Spain.

28 July

Helen Beatrix Potter was born on 28 July 1866. 'My brother and I were born in London, because my father was a lawyer there.' But Beatrix Potter's spiritual home was the Lake District where family holidays were spent. Later in life, she settled, married and farmed there.

Peter Rabbit and other animals

'Dear Noel,' Beatrix Potter wrote, 'I don't know what to write to you so I shall tell you a story about four little rabbits whose names were Flopsy, Mopsy, Cottontail and Peter.'

A good many of us could repeat from memory much of the rest of that letter-turned- book recounting Peter Rabbit's adventures. Noel was the eldest child of Beatrix's one time governess and she used often to visit them, taking her pet rabbit or mice in a basket for them to see. For Beatrix Potter's skill at drawing animals came from scrupulous observation. Many of the animals in her books she kept as pets, and took with her wherever she went.

When Beatrix decided to put the story in book form she sought the help and advice of Canon Hardwicke Rawnsley. He had become a family friend during the Potters' annual visits to the Lake District. Rawnsley was enthusiastic about Peter Rabbit but although he sent the manuscript to six publishers, all turned them down.

But Canon Rawnsley did not give up. He turned the original, brilliant prose into rhyming verses and sent story and illustrations to the publisher Frederick Warne. The firm decided to accept 'the bunny book', but fortunately, requested prose instead of Rawnsley's verses.

When Beatrix was sad and distressed about the death of her much-loved brother, she confided in Canon Rawnsley again, telling of her deep grief in a letter to him. He, in turn, co-opted her help in one at least of his myriad enterprises – the National Trust. Beatrix Potter became the Trust's biggest benefactor. In her will she left the Trust fifteen farms, money and land. Her own home at Sawrey, property of the Trust, is a place of pilgrimage for millions of her grateful admirers.

(Source: *Beatrix Potter, Artist, Storyteller and Countrywoman* by Judy Taylor)

William Wilberforce died on 29 July 1833. Wilberforce is best known for his long campaign, as a Christian and a Member of Parliament, to abolish the slave-trade. But he also campaigned against cruelty to animals, widespread in a horse-drawn age. In 1824 he was a founder member of the society now known as the Royal Society for the Prevention of Cruelty to Animals or the RSPCA.

'Stop beating that animal!'

A short, bent, elderly gentleman trudged laboriously up the hill. In the road alongside him, two tired horses struggled and strained to pull their heavy load of coals up the steep street. Suddenly one of the horses fell and lay still in the road, too exhausted to get up, worn out with years of overwork. Its owner, a large, strong-looking man, was furious. He swore loudly at the horse, kicked it savagely, then began beating it again and again to make it get up.

In an instant, the little old man had rushed across.

'Stop beating that animal!' he ordered, 'how dare you ill-treat your horse! He is too ill and too old to get up. He needs your care, not your curses.'

The carter looked up astonished, his face like a thunder-cloud. He glared at the man who had dared to interfere. His whip was still raised and it looked as though he might use it on this stranger instead of the horse. Then the other carter nudged him fiercely and whispered, 'Look who it is – it's Mr Wilberforce!'

The mention of that well-known and respected name had immediate effect. The angry carter dropped his arm and his look changed from fury to wonder and admiration.

30 July

The Prince and **Princess of Wales** were married in July (29) 1981. Diana Spencer was born in 1961, third daughter of Earl Spencer. Her grandmother was lady-in-waiting and close friend to the Queen Mother. Her mother left home when she was six and her parents later divorced. She was the first Englishwoman to marry an heir to the throne for 300 years.

'The Queen of hearts'

'I think the biggest disease this world suffers from in this day and age is the disease of people feeling unloved, and I know that I can give love for a minute, for half an hour; for a day, for a month, but I can give. I'm very happy to do that and I want to do that.'

That was Diana's self-appointed task and perhaps that is why she was so loved herself. Like Friday's child, she was loving and giving, in a world starved of love. And she was able to express her love in hugs and cuddles, whether she was visiting elderly people or children with cancer. Her compassion was genuine and spontaneous and was gratefully received by a hungry, lonely, unhappy public. 'I don't go by a rule book,' she said, 'because I lead from the heart, not the head. But someone's got to go out there and love people and show it.' She was one of the first to make physical contact by touching and taking the hand of those suffering from Aids.

Diana was also admired and respected for the good causes that she embraced. Not long before her death she took up the cause of those maimed by land-mines and campaigned to have the use of these deadly weapons banned. In 1997 not long before her death, she flew to Angola, one of the world's most heavily mined countries and risked political criticism by highlighting the suffering and maiming caused. Photographs of her, in protective clothing, helped to focus attention on what, as she said, had been a largely neglected issue.

The Queen summed up many people's emotions when she said, after her death, 'May we, each and everyone of us, thank God for someone who made many, many people happy.'

Ignatius Loyola died on 31 July 1556. Ignatius lived at about the same time as Martin Luther. He too saw the need for reform. The Pope granted members of the Society of Jesus permission to travel around caring and preaching, rather than being confined within walls.

Soldier to saint

Ignatius Loyola trained as a soldier for Spain and led a colourful and daredevil life, until he was wounded in an enemy attack.

He returned to the family home in Loyola to recover and asked his sister-in-law for some books to pass the time. He looked forward to reading tales of chivalry and romance but the castle contained only religious books and Loyola was given a *Life of Christ* and *Lives of the Saints*. He read and re-read them, fascinated above all by the person of Jesus. He realised that he must choose – between his old buccaneering lifestyle and service for Christ. He chose to follow Jesus and at once he began to tell others about him too.

He was not a priest, so he was imprisoned and threatened with flogging for daring to preach. He decided to train and began his studies. When he was qualified, he and a few companions banded together to form the Society of Jesus. They took vows of poverty, chastity, and obedience to God and the Pope. The Pope finally granted the new order permission to travel around wherever they were needed to help others and preach about Jesus. When Ignatius died, the Society of Jesus had grown from ten to one thousand members.

Prayer of St Ignatius of Loyola

Receive, Lord, all my liberty, my memory, my understanding and my whole will. You have given me all that I have, all that I am, and I surrender all to your divine will ... Give me only your love and your grace. With this I am rich enough and have no more to ask.

1 August

On 1 August 1834 slavery was abolished in the British Empire. **William Wilberforce** is the first name that comes to mind in the fight against slavery. He died in 1823, but witnessed the partial success of his campaign with the prohibiting of slave-trading by Britain in 1807. Many others were involved in the struggle, one of them J D Carr, the founder of the biscuit firm Carr's of Carlisle.

All people are equal

They looked a strange pair walking down the Carlisle street together. J D Carr was an exceptionally tall man, large and fair; his companion, Frederick Douglass – an escaped slave – was black. There were no black people in Carlisle so everyone stopped to stare at the seemingly ill-matched pair. But to J D, a devout Quaker, all people were equal and he did not even share the patronising tone of the local newspaper which commented that 'for a negro he has an intelligent and even pleasing face.' The alternative local paper was more outspoken in deploring attempts to end the slave trade. 'I do not believe one word of what saints say regarding the ill-treatment of negroes,' it fumed.

J D's wife shared his concern to abolish slavery worldwide – not just in the British Empire – and she gladly entertained several escaped slaves, like Douglass, in their home. Their five young children heard at first-hand the evils of slavery as they listened open-mouthed to their parents' visitors. Douglass addressed a public meeting on three nights and held his audience, many of them in tears, throughout a three hour lecture. Douglass was similarly impressed with his kind host and hostess. He reported that they were 'as anxious for the emancipation of slaves as any with whom I think I have ever met.'

(Source: *Rich Desserts and Captain's Thin* by Margaret Forster)

'We cannot be free men if this is, by our national choice, to be a land of slavery. Those who deny freedom to others, deserve it not for themselves.' – Abraham Lincoln 1809-1865

The **Mothers' Union** is a Christian organisation within the Anglican communion, which promotes the well-being of families worldwide through prayer and practical action.

'Lady mothers' and 'cottage mothers'

There were peacocks in the fine gardens for Mary to enjoy and twenty-two bedrooms in the house. Thomas Heywood was a wealthy banker who could afford to retire and buy this fine Herefordshire house when Mary – his youngest – was four. The family travelled on the continent in their private coach where Mary perfected her French, German and Italian. She also had her voice trained to professional standards. But the family put their Christian beliefs into practice too. Mary taught Sunday School, her mother visited the sick and everyone attended family prayers.

Not surprisingly Mary married a clergyman. George Sumner was the son of the Bishop of Winchester and the two met at a ball in Rome on her eighteenth birthday. The wedding was a splendid affair, with 600 tenants and employees royally entertained. Later the couple settled to life in Old Alresford in the Winchester diocese and had two daughters and one son. But Mary found motherhood awe-inspiring. She said, 'It struck me how much I needed special training for so great a work, and how little I knew. I felt that mothers had one of the greatest and most important professions in the world and yet there was none had so poor a training for its supreme duties.'

Mary recognised that all mothers faced these 'supreme duties' – her elegant, aristocratic neighbours as well as the agricultural labourers' wives. Class barriers need not divide mothers. She decided to invite 'lady mothers' and 'cottage mothers' as she described them, to meet together in her drawing-room. It was a revolutionary idea for that time, but she issued invitations for an afternoon in 1876, and amazingly, persuaded both groups of women to come. Before the afternoon was out she had enrolled the mothers in a new women's group. Every member promised to bring up their children in the Christian faith and 'form their characters in strength and beauty.' For the next nine years Mary Sumner concentrated on the task of helping to improve family life in their own parish.

---

3 August

On 3 August 1666, M. Beaufort first met **Brother Laurence** and heard his story. M. Beaufort later wrote down the conversations, together with some letters Brother Laurence had written, and they were published in a little book which has been a source of help and inspiration to Christians ever since.

Sermons in trees

When Nicholas Herman was a young man of eighteen, he was out walking in midwinter, when the snow was on the ground. Suddenly he stopped in his tracks, arrested by the sight of a huge tree, rising bare and gaunt, its branches cold and seemingly lifeless against the bleak horizon.

But as he gazed, the picture flashed into his mind of what that tree would look like when spring came. New growth and fresh young leaves would transform the bare trunk and apparent death would give way to luxuriant life.

With that inner vision came an overwhelming realisation of the power and purposes of God. His whole life was born anew. He no longer cared to continue with his job as a footman and soldier. He wanted to give himself wholly to God, who had made himself known to him through a parable of nature in that instant of revelation. He joined the barefooted Carmelite Order in Paris, and because he was no scholar, he spent the rest of his long life as a lay brother, serving others.

'If in this life we would enjoy the peace of paradise we must accustom ourselves to a familiar, humble, affectionate conversation with God.' – Brother Laurence

Brother Laurence.

God among the pots and barrels

Nicholas Herman was renamed Brother Laurence and allocated to work in the monastery kitchen. It was not the kind of work he naturally enjoyed, but he found a way to make it more pleasurable. His love for God was so great that every task was done out of love. Love for God could make a pleasure out of picking up a straw from the kitchen floor, he said. He learned to talk to God and recognise his presence all day long. The heat, the banging of pots and pans, the steam and the greasy dishes never ruffled him.

One day he was ordered to Burgundy to buy wine for the monastery. Brother Laurence's heart failed him. He had no head for business and because he was lame it would be difficult for him to move around on the boat, unless he rolled his way over the barrels. He told God his problem: 'I can't do this, Lord,' he prayed, 'unless you help me.'

The help that God gave was enough for the task and the mission to Burgundy was successfully accomplished. But even when he failed, Brother Laurence did not spend time bewailing the fact. He admitted that when he tried to do things on his own, failure was all that he could expect. 'Lord, I keep failing,' he would say, 'I can't stop myself. But you can stop me and hold me up.'

God's presence and God's love made the monastery kitchen a place like heaven.

'I engaged in a religious life only for the love of God. Whatever becomes of me ... I will always continue to act purely for the love of God.' – Brother Laurence

---

5 August

On 5 August 642, **Oswald**, 'most Christian king' of Northumbria,
died in battle. Oswald became king in 642, after a battle against the
pagans. Before the battle, Oswald set up a cross and prayed for
God's help against the heathen forces. The place where he prayed
was called Heavenfield and can still be visited in Northumberland.
The Venerable Bede tells many stories about Oswald in his
Ecclesiastical History. After Oswald's death, Bede tells us, so many
people came to take earth from the spot where he fell, so that the
'holy dust' might cure their ills, that they left a hole six foot deep!

Pieces of silver

One day King Oswald was sitting at supper in his castle at
Bamburgh, home of the kings of Northumbria, overlooking
the golden sands and the wild North Sea. Beside the king sat
his much-loved Bishop Aidan, who lived on nearby Lindisfarne
island. A large silver dish, set out with tempting meats
prepared in the royal kitchen, had just been set before the
king and his guests.

As the king was about to help himself from the laden
dish, a servant hurried into the room and bowed low to the
king. Oswald recognised him as the official he had put in
charge of caring for the poor.

'Your majesty,' the official said, 'the street is full of poor
and hungry people, begging help from the king.'

Without a moment's hesitation, the king lifted the huge
dish of food and handed it to the servant.

'Take this,' he ordered; 'first share out the food, then have
the dish cut into pieces so that all those in need may have a
piece of silver.'

Alfred Lord Tennyson was born on 6 August 1809.
Tennyson's life spans the Victorian age and like many of
his time he struggled to reconcile Christian faith with new
Biblical criticism and new scientific theories.

Last crossing

Tennyson was born in a Lincolnshire rectory, the fourth son of
the rector of Somersby. Critics at first dismissed his poetry as
too sentimental, but he later became Poet Laureate and was
enormously popular in his own lifetime. Queen Victoria herself
was a fan; after Prince Albert's death she found comfort in his
verses called *In Memoriam*, written to express Tennyson's grief
at the death of a young man called Arthur Hallam, who was
an undergraduate friend of his at Cambridge.

Tennyson lived for many years on the Isle of Wight, and it
was when he was crossing the strip of water from the mainland
to his home that he wrote his last poem. It pictures death as
coming into harbour and meeting the pilot who has been his
unseen guide through the voyage of life. Tennyson requested
that this poem should always be printed at the end of his
works.

Crossing the bar

Sunset and evening star
    And one clear call for me
And may there be no moaning of the bar,
    When I put out to sea.
Twilight and evening bell
    And after that the dark!
And may there be no sadness of farewell,
    When I embark;
For tho' from out our bourne of Time and Place
    The flood may bear me far,
I hope to see my Pilot face to face
    When I have crost the bar.

7 August

This week, in August 1774, **Ann Lee** and her disciples
disembarked in New York harbour.

The Shaking Quakers

It was a terrible storm. A plank came loose and the *Mariah*
sprang such a bad leak that crew and passengers together
manned the pumps. But the water was gaining and the ship
was steadily filling with water. It was then that Ann Lee told
the captain: 'Be of good cheer. Not a hair of our heads shall
perish. We shall all arrive safely in America. For I was just now
sitting by the mast and I saw a bright angel of God, through
whom I received the promise.'

While she was speaking a wave struck the ship with such
strength that the loose plank was forced back into place. So,
three months after they set sail from Liverpool, the little group
of Shakers came ashore and began their mission 'to preach
the everlasting Gospel to America.'

Ann had first been attracted to the preaching of George
Whitefield, then joined a splinter group of Quakers. This new
offshoot became known as the Shaking Quakers because
although they met in silent meditation they soon outdid the
Quakers with their 'mighty trembling ... mighty shaking.' Ann
had married a kindly Manchester blacksmith but then endured
four difficult births – followed by the deaths of all four children
in infancy. After the traumatic forceps delivery of the fourth
baby, Ann experienced months of terrible anguish and guilt;
she believed that her 'concupiscence' had been the cause of
her children's deaths. Finally she emerged, feeling as if she
had been new-born – into a spiritual kingdom. From then on
she regarded 'cohabitation of the sexes' as the chief sin and
she also denounced all worldliness. The Shakers were fiercely
persecuted and suspected of heresy and witchcraft. Ann was
thrown into prison, but her spiritual standing grew and she
became leader of the group.

Soon the Shakers had a vision of going to America and
after a joyful meeting where they danced till morning, it was
decided to set off for the country God had chosen for them.

(Source: *The People Called Shakers* by E D Andrews)

Izaak Walton was born on 8 or 9 August 1593. He wrote biographies of well-known clergymen of his time, such as John Donne and George Herbert, but is best known for his book about fishing – *The Compleat Angler*. It ran into five editions in his own lifetime. It is full of good advice about every aspect of fishing, but above all it is a celebration of fishing as the best of all recreations. John Donne and George Herbert were among his fishing companions.

The Compleat Angler

'He that hopes to be a good angler, must not only bring an inquiring, searching, observing wit, but he must bring a large measure of hope and patience, and a love and propensity to the art itself; but having once got and practised it, then doubt not but angling will prove to be so pleasant, that it will prove to be, like virtue, a reward in itself.

'We may say of angling, as Dr Boteler said of strawberries, "Doubtless God could have made a better berry, but doubtless God never did"; and if I might be judge, God never did make a more calm, innocent recreation than angling …

'When I would beget content … I will walk the meadows, by some gliding stream, and there contemplate … the various little living creatures that are not only created, but fed, man knows not how, by the goodness of the God of nature, and therefore trust in him. That is my purpose; so, let everything that hath breath praise the Lord: and let the blessing of St Peter's Master be with mine. And upon all that are lovers of virtue; and dare trust in his providence; and be quiet; and go a Angling.'

'Of recreation there is none
So free as fishing is alone.'

Izaak Walton 1593-1683

---

9 August

Since 1998, **Mary Sumner**, founder of the Mothers' Union, has been commemorated on 9 August. She died, around that date in 1921, aged 93.

Mother of them all

For nine years, following the first drawing-room meeting for mothers in their Alresford rectory, Mary worked hard to improve family life in her husband's parish. She even held a meeting for husbands and reminded them to treat their wives with love and courtesy.

In 1885 at a Church Congress, the Bishop of Newcastle looked at the sad, pale faces before him at a meeting of women, and decided to call on Mary Sumner to address them instead. After the first shock, Mary warmed to her subject and ended by suggesting that they could all go back to their parishes and start 'a mothers' union wherein all classes could unite in faith and prayer to try to do this work for God.'

The idea spread quickly, and Mary gained support from the Duchess of Albany, daughter-in-law of Queen Victoria; later the Queen herself became patron of the Mothers' Union. Branches of the Mothers' Union sprang up not only in Britain but overseas. In 1916 at the age of eighty-eight, Mary Sumner attended the opening of the first London headquarters of the Union, named after her.

The Mothers' Union may *sound* a little old-fashioned, but it is thoroughly contemporary in its approach to present-day problems in countries around the world. There is still emphasis on the spiritual life of members, in prayer, worship and fellowship. Every day there is a 'wave of prayer' in which members pray for fellow-members across the globe. All issues which affect the family are given high-profile support and practical ways are found of meeting different family needs. Literacy, third world debt, health issues and civil and legal rights are all tackled. Small as well as large needs are met in sensitive and imaginative ways. In the UK, for example, gowns are made for still-born babies. Mary Sumner would approve.

Jennifer Paterson, television cook, died on 10 August 1999, the Feast Day of St Laurence, patron saint of cooks. Jennifer Paterson found fame late in life as one of the so-called *'Two Fat Ladies'* in a television cooking partnership with Clarissa Dickson Wright. Their programmes were watched by millions and the Prince of Wales was one of their fans.

One fat lady

Crash followed crash as Jennifer Paterson sent all the crockery from the *Spectator* canteen flying from the top-floor window. She had been cook for the magazine canteen but after that shattering incident the editor sacked her and gave her a cookery column to write instead. Public acclaim came when she was teamed with the equally idiosyncratic Clarissa Dickson Wright in a double act television series. With Jennifer – complete with crash helmet – on her motor bike and Clarissa in the side-car, they would roar off to varied assignments, cooking for rugby players, army recruits, a biker gathering or a village fête as the case might be. Their spontaneous exuberance and repartee, as much as their fine dishes, kept their viewers highly entertained.

'I think the Prince has poisoned me,' Jennifer complained, after a party at Highgrove. But she must have known that it was the onset of the cancer that soon ended in her death. She insisted on finishing the current series of programmes from her hospital bed and kept her outrageous humour, wit and sense of the ridiculous to the end. She continued to entertain friends in her hospital room but could feign near unconsciousness if any unwanted callers arrived. She did not suffer fools gladly and could not bear pomposity or pretence.

Her funeral – at Brompton Oratory – was no mere formality. Behind her banter and irreverent exterior, she was a devout practising Catholic with a deep religious faith and a strong belief in prayer. She was not afraid to die, believing strongly that she was going to a better place. Her life and death are wholesome reminders that the Christian life is abundant and full-blooded and that God calls men and women of very different gifts and temperaments to follow his way.

11 August

On 11 August 1999 the last total *eclipse of the sun* in the second millennium was visible in Britain and Europe. The first recorded eclipse occurred in China in 2136 BCE. A total eclipse was probably first forecast by the Greek philosopher Thales nearly six hundred years before Christ.

'Something more out there?'

In late 1503 Christopher Columbus and his crew were stranded on Jamaica. They desperately needed food, but they had outstayed their welcome and the islanders refused to give them more. Columbus noted in his *Calendarium* that a lunar eclipse was due on 29 February. He told the islanders that the moon would be dark and red to show the gods' displeasure with them. Columbus disappeared while the eclipse lasted, pretending that he was consulting the gods. The islanders promised to give their visitors food so Columbus reappeared, just before the eclipse ended, assuring them that the gods were appeased.

Eclipses have always impressed human watchers with fear, curiosity or wonder. Millions watched the 1999 eclipse of the sun – in aircraft, on television or directly, with the use of special protective glasses. And their reactions were incredibly mixed. Some were enthralled by the scientific explanations, others with the effect in nature, others with their own reactions of fear or excitement, as the atmosphere grew strangely cold and the light gave way to dimness and shadow. Some laughed, some cried, others clapped and shouted and clutched one another in excitement and with a thrill of fear. One onlooker said: 'It was really weird, man! It makes you wonder if there is something more out there.'

> *'How clearly the sky reveals God's glory!*
> *How plainly it shows what he has done!'*
>
> (From *Psalm 19*, GNB)

William Blake died on 12 August 1827. Blake went to a school for promising young artists but was then apprenticed to an engraver, instead of attending the more expensive Royal Academy School. When he had learned his exacting craft, he not only reproduced others' drawings but created his own original and innovative engravings, often to portray Bible characters or to illustrate his own poems.

Visions by day

The happiest times for young William Blake were when the great doors of the Abbey were closed and he was left entirely alone to do his work. His master, James Basire, the engraver, had set him to draw the many monuments in Westminster Abbey so that engravings could be made from them for the Antiquarian Society. Blake would move quietly about the Abbey, often standing on top of a monument to get a better view of the recumbent figures below.

Sometimes the peace would be shattered by the shouts and cries of the young boys from nearby Westminster School, allowed out to play. They would dodge round the tombs playing hide-and-seek or tag and tease the life out of the young artist. Then they ran off again to their lessons leaving Blake in peace. In the stillness he sometimes saw visions – once of Christ and his apostles. Blake had seen his first vision when he was a child of eight – a crowd of shining angels in a tree in Peckham Rye. These visions were the stuff of which his poetry and engravings were made.

'When the sun rises do you see a round disk of fire somewhat like a guinea? O no no, I see an innumerable company of the heavenly host crying Holy Holy Holy is the Lord God Almighty.' – William Blake 1757-1827

13 August

Octavia Hill died on 13 August 1912. The National Trust was founded partly through her efforts. As a result, stately homes, beautiful gardens, moors, cliffs and open spaces are conserved for everyone including visitors and tourists to Britain to enjoy.

A little bit of paradise

Plaster had peeled from the damp, dirty walls, and on the stairs a strategically placed bucket caught the constant drip of rain coming from the hole in the ceiling. The banister had gone. Water for the whole house was stored in a large, dirty, leaking water-butt. But Octavia, aged seventeen, felt proud of her new possession in Paradise Place, London.

At last she had somewhere to lodge some of the drunken, quarrelling, homeless people she cared for. As a good landlord, she saw that passages were scrubbed, leaks repaired and the water-butt replaced. But she never interfered with them by well-meant kindness. Her tenants were free to lead their own lives. She treated them as she treated all her friends, with courtesy and respect.

Octavia believed that Paradise Place should provide more than a roof over the head. Her tenants also needed fresh air, gardens and open spaces. At last she discovered an old dumping ground, cleared the rubbish and made a garden. Here the children could play and their parents sit and watch.

It was through Octavia's meeting with Reverend Frederick Maurice – one of the founders of the Christian Socialist movement – when she was only fourteen, that she began to care about city-dwellers and the homeless. Her reforms and the founding of the National Trust have given everyone in Britain the chance to enjoy a little bit of paradise.

On 14 August 1885 the Royal Assent was given to the Criminal law Amendment Act, for which *Josephine Butler* had campaigned for so long. Josephine Butler campaigned for a cause which Victorians considered unfit for ladies to mention. She determined to abolish the law which gave a special group of non-uniformed police absolute powers to arrest any woman they might think was a prostitute and enforce a medical examination. Josephine abhorred the attitude of condemning 'fallen' women but excusing men's vice. She believed that men and women were equal before God.

Picking oakum

Mrs Butler's soft white fingers struggled unsuccessfully to disentangle the tarry rope fibres. The other oakum-pickers in the damp, stone-floor shed laughed at her efforts. To their surprise and delight this quiet, beautiful lady joined in their laughter.

The women wondered why she had come. They knew themselves to be despised – either so poor that the state was forced to support them, or condemned to this life because of petty crime. Yet instead of preaching at them or condemning them, she chose to work alongside them.

The spontaneous laughter broke the ice. Josephine Butler began to talk to them, telling them first of her own tragedy in the death of her little daughter. Then eagerly, they began to tell her of their troubles and she was deeply touched. These were no hardened criminals but women fallen on bad times, often through no fault of their own.

She began to visit them often, sometimes reading to them from the Bible and one day, naturally and spontaneously, she poured out her heart in prayer for them all as they knelt on the cold stone floor. Then she took Mary, a prostitute who was dying, back to her own home in the respectable quarter of Liverpool and nursed her with loving care. Mrs Butler's campaign for justice and mercy had begun.

Women are called to be a great power in the future – Josephine Butler 1828-1906

15 August

James Keir Hardie was born on 15 August 1856. He was the illegitimate son of Mary Keir, a Scottish farm servant. His stepfather, David Hardie, was a ship's carpenter and he himself was a miner till he was 23. He became a Scottish miner's representative, a journalist and a Labour MP. He was the founder of the Labour party which celebrated its centenary in 2000.

The man in the cloth cap

Even the police on duty at the House of Commons did not take Keir Hardie for an MP. 'Do you work here, mate?' one of them asked him. Hardie said that he did. 'Where, on the roof?' the policeman went on; 'No, on the floor,' Hardie replied.

Certainly, in his loud check suit and bright red tie, Hardie looked quite unlike his soberly-dressed fellow MPs. Instead of the customary top-hat he wore a Sherlock Holmes-type deer-stalker, which earned him the name of 'the man in the cloth cap'. Even his bushy red beard convinced his colleagues in the House that he must be a fiery revolutionary.

Keir Hardie certainly entered politics in order to champion the cause of the under-privileged and downtrodden. Almost penniless himself, he was determined that their cause should be led by self-confessed Labour Members, who themselves belonged to the working-class.

Hardie may have looked like a revolutionary but the House was to find that he had no plans for violent change or class war. Although his parents were atheists, Hardie found inspiration and comfort from the Bible. He was not an orthodox Christian, but he took as his ideals the teaching of Jesus Christ in the Sermon on the Mount. He wanted justice for the overworked and the underpaid – especially in the mines – and he insisted on bringing it about by peaceful means.

When war broke out in 1914 Hardie felt he had failed in all his efforts to establish peace and international understanding. But his life and work were not in vain. Today we accept the importance of many of the things he strove for – fair wages, women's rights and racial equality – and forget how much we owe to him.

In August 1945 the new Labour government began business in the House of Commons after coming to power in the July General Election. **George Thomas** took his seat for the first time as Labour member for Cardiff Central on 15 August. Two days later he made his maiden speech. Many years later, as Speaker of the House of Commons, he still remembered the thrill and pride of walking into the Palace of Westminster for the first time.

Fight for justice

The Member of Parliament for Cardiff Central listened patiently and kindly as the two elderly ladies poured out their tale of woe. It was about their home. The two sisters had lived all their lives in the same house, caring for their parents until their death. Under the system of leasehold, a house reverted to the ground landlord or owner, when the ninety-nine years of the lease expired.

The years were up and the sisters would be turned out of their family home and left with nowhere to live. They were also faced with a bill for £400 for repairs, which the landlord considered necessary to bring the property up to standard.

George Thomas took the case to the landlord himself, arguing that the sisters could not pay the money anyway, and warning him that the whole community would be up in arms against him if he evicted them. The landlord agreed to drop his claim and allow the ladies to pay rent and stay in the house.

This was not an isolated incident. George Thomas vowed to put an end to the iniquities of leasehold. Through his constant campaigning, the Leasehold Reform Bill was finally passed by parliament. Now all leasehold owners have the choice of buying their property freehold and at a fair price.

17 August

William Carey, translator, botanist, pioneer missionary, was
born on 17 August 1761.

The prayer God didn't answer

'Would you rather have a sixpence or a shilling?' the
ironmonger asked.

Young William Carey, delivering goods for his shoemaker
master just before Christmas, could not believe his ears. A
Christmas box of a few pence might have been expected, but
a whole shilling seemed too good to be true.

And it was! When William went to spend it he discovered
that it was a counterfeit coin. So he substituted the bad shilling
for a good one in his master's takings. Then he felt frightened
as well as guilty. The penalty at that time for stealing any sum
over a shilling was death. Anyone convicted of stealing less
than a shilling was sentenced to be transported to America or
the West Indies.

'I made this deliberate sin a matter of prayer as I passed
over the fields home,' Carey later wrote. 'I promised that if
God would but clearly get me over this, I would certainly for
the future leave off all evil practices. A gracious God did *not*
get me safe through!'

His master discovered the false coin and sent the other
apprentice back to the ironmonger with it. The whole story
came out. The tradesman had been playing a practical joke
on young Carey. Carey was forgiven but he was deeply
ashamed. When he was sixteen he joined with a group of
Christians whose faith was genuine and whose lives were
upright and honest.

Attempt great things for God: expect great things from God. –
William Carey 1761-1834

18 August

William Carey had begun his working life as a shoemaker but through his studies he became the village schoolmaster. And he had dreams of a quite different calling.

Geography without tears?

'His pupils saw sometimes a strange sight, their master moved to tears over a geography lesson, as pointing to continents, islands and peoples, he would cry, "And these are pagans, pagans!"'

Perhaps this extract from the biography of the young shoemaker turned teacher and preacher is a bit far-fetched. It was written by his great-grandson. Carey was not an emotional man, but he did have intense compassion and concern for people from other lands who had not heard the gospel. At this time there were no great missionary movements or societies. Carey hung a large map of the world on his wall; it was made up of sheets of paper pasted together. He filled in the names of the countries and wrote alongside all the information he could gather about the population, the people, their customs and religion.

Carey determined to go himself and preach the gospel in India. He set out, taking a reluctant wife, three small boys and a brand new baby, and faced the hazards of a five-month voyage at a time when France and England were at war. His efforts to survive lasted seven years without one single convert to the Christian faith. Meanwhile his wife had become dangerously mad and funds from England took many months to arrive. But Carey never gave up. In time, Carey saw God turn his vision into reality.

Postscript: Carey – self-taught – eventually became a distinguished college professor in India. He translated the whole Bible into Bengali and parts of it into as many as twenty-four different languages and dialects.

---

19 August

In August 1945 **World War II** ended when Japan surrendered to the Allies.

Restoration

For fifty years the silk scarf had been preying on James Johnston's mind. It was a square made of white silk, a flag with the Japanese rising sun on it, and some writing in a language Mr Johnston could not read.

He was a private in the British army in Burma, desperately trying to reach Rangoon before the monsoon broke. As they surged forward across a bridge, a Japanese soldier fell dead. Mr Johnston swiftly removed the silk scarf from his cap, hoping to exchange it for few dollars with an American soldier. But instead he took it home as a keepsake, wearing it round his neck when he rode his motorbike.

In 1995, fifty years on, he was a widower of eighty, but still had that scarf. He remembered vividly the day he took it and the face of the dead soldier who had owned it. More and more he felt that he ought to give it back to someone with a right to it. But he did not know the dead soldier's name or where he came from. So he took the scarf to a Japanese University branch near his home. They translated the writing on the scarf: 'Written to wish Tomira Yamamoto good fortune in his posting to Burma'. Friends and family had signed it and added the address of the town hall where he had worked.

Staff at the university contacted the Japanese town hall and discovered that Tomira's widow was still living – now eighty-eight. Mr Johnstone sent her the scarf with a letter of explanation. 'I was just very glad that his scarf has now gone to the person who should have it.'

And that might have been the end. But one day the door bell rang and two strangers stood on the doorstep. Yet, 'the young man on the doorstep looked for all the world like the soldier whose flag I took all those years ago', Mr Johnston said. It was the dead soldier's son, who, with his wife had flown over from Japan to thank Mr Johnston in person for returning their father's scarf. By the end of that day, more than a soldier's scarf had been restored.

(Reported in *The Times*)

William Booth, founder of the Salvation Army, died on
20 August 1912. William Booth's desire to preach the
gospel always went hand-in-hand with the will to change
scandalous social conditions. The Salvation Army has
continued to care for people's total needs – body and soul.

Lights in darkest England

The trade unions protested in vain and in vain the government
passed regulations to try to protect workers. The match
makers still suffered. It was bad enough that their wages were
pitifully low, but worse still, their work meant that they were
continually handling deadly phosphorus. When they ate, they
carried the poison from their hands to their mouths and the
phosphorus attacked their gums. The result was a painful
and disfiguring disease known as 'phossy jaw'. The irony was
that non-poisonous, safety matches had already been
invented, but hardly any of them were being manufactured.

William Booth decided to do more than protest. In 1891
he opened his own match factory in London's East End, making
non-poisonous matches *only*. He employed about a hundred
people, paying them well over the odds and providing
comfortable work space, with facilities for washing and making
tea.

Next, he organised a campaign to make sure that these
matches were sold – not the phosphorus ones. His matches
went on sale as 'Lights in Darkest England', and advertisements
were displayed listing all stockists. Other Christians joined the
campaign. The public was encouraged to buy them – even
from the pulpit of Westminster Abbey. The British Match
Consumers' League was formed and members promised to
buy and use safety matches only. Matches became safe for
those who made them and those who used them too.

*'While women weep as they do now, I'll fight; while men go to
prison, in and out, in and out, as they do now, I'll fight while there
is a drunkard left, while there is a poor lost girl upon the streets,
while there remains one dark soul without the light of God – I'll
fight! I'll fight to the very end! – William Booth 1829-1912*

21 August

On 21 August 1985 *Irina Ratushinskaya* – Russian poet and dissident – was sentenced to a further five months for 'simulating' concussion, after guards had beaten her up. When Irina Ratushinskaya was a student, her childhood friend, Igor, told her that he had come to believe in God. They both experienced God's 'invisible hand' on their shoulder, guiding and guarding them.

Wedding rings

When Igor and Irina planned to marry they wanted a church wedding as well as the compulsory civil ceremony. A friend put them in touch with a priest at the Russian Orthodox Church in Moscow.

They went to Moscow and prepared for the service. A friend lent Irina a suitable dress, and together they stood nervously before Father Alexander. But their fears vanished as they looked into his face. They made their confession then took communion together for the first time.

Just as the service was about to begin in earnest, there was another crisis. 'Where are the rings?' they were asked. But they had none, nor could they have afforded any. Without rings the priest could not marry them. Their peace and happiness was rudely shattered. The wedding, it seems, would have to be cancelled.

Then Irina heard a rustling and whispering among the little crowd of onlookers in the church – mostly older women, who had come in to watch a wedding. They soon realized the problem, and began slipping the rings off their own fingers. 'Take this, dearie,' one woman said to Irina, 'I'm a widow and don't need it,' and a gnarled hand offered her a thin gold band. Another gave a ring to Igor. But moved by the gestures of love, Father Alexander said, 'Never mind rings, I'll marry you without any!'

'Everyone in the church felt that He was there,' Irina wrote: Igor, Father Alexander, their friends and the elderly onlookers. Joy filled them all.

(Source: *In the Beginning* by Irina Ratushinskaya)

The *International Red Cross* was founded on 22 August 1864.

Memory of Solferino

Henry Dunant could not forget the horrors he had witnessed at the Battle of Solferino and the sufferings of the wounded. A few years later he wrote a book – *A Memory of Solferino* – and paid to have it printed. He wanted, as a Christian, to prevent the worst of the sufferings war brought so, in his book he put forward the new idea that people should be trained in peace-time to treat the wounded of both sides if and when war came. These helpers would be allowed anywhere on the field to do their work of mercy, recognised by the sign of the red cross.

In 1864 representatives from sixteen countries met in Geneva and drew up the original Geneva Convention, which gives protection to all those who care for the wounded in war. Today the International Red Cross works in peace as well as war, bringing relief to vulnerable people and victims of every kind of disaster world-wide. The work of the Red Cross and Red Crescent movement is carried out by 127 million volunteers from 70 different countries and is the largest independent humanitarian movement in the world.

Bobbie is one of those volunteers, an ordinary housewife living in a small town not far from London. As well as teaching First Aid in schools, she attends sports fixtures, concerts and plays to give help if anyone has an accident or is taken ill. She is ready to wash and dress elderly housebound invalids before going to her own job in the morning. She helps man the local Red Cross centre, where medical equipment may be borrowed, as well as attending lectures and courses to keep her own skills honed. She also helps in fund-raising. Feeding the hungry, helping victims of natural disaster, caring for refugees and those wounded in war, wholly depends on generous voluntary giving as well as on volunteer helpers.

---

23 August

Roy Castle, famous entertainer and 'record breaker' faced illness and death from cancer with great courage. Years before, as parents, Roy and Fiona had faced possible tragedy. On 23 August 1980 their son, Daniel, had a serious accident. Fiona comments: 'It sometimes takes a crisis to put life, and our priorities, into perspective.'

Danny Boy

Fiona and the children were holidaying on the Isle of Man during Roy's three week appearance at the Gaiety Theatre. One day, while the rest of the family were beachcombing, fifteen-year-old Daniel climbed the cliff and sat watching them far below him. Suddenly his sister Antonia looked up and screamed, 'Daniel!' The boy was lying on a rock some thirty feet below the place where he'd been sitting. He lay there, in a crumpled ball, blood oozing from his mouth and ears.

In hospital it was confirmed that Daniel had a fractured, skull, pelvis and wrist, and a perforated lung. If he survived he might be paralysed or suffer brain damage.

Roy dashed back across the island with only minutes to spare before he appeared before an audience that knew nothing of the family tragedy. 'During the request spot some holiday-makers asked me to play – would you believe it – *Danny Boy*,' Roy recalled later. 'It was difficult,' he admitted, 'but I think I did it the best ever.'

Next day, a pastor and elder from the Castles' home church, flew across. They prayed with Roy and Fiona at Daniel's bedside. He had been unconscious and delirious for almost thirty-six hours. 'You can imagine our joy when at the end of the prayer, Daniel said "Amen"' Roy recalled.

It was the start of Daniel's slow recovery. Looking back, Roy said, 'I just can't imagine what it would be like to go through that kind of experience without the strength that comes from being a Christian. The whole thing proved to be a wonderful witness to the power of God.'

Selina, Countess of Huntingdon, was born on 24 August 1707.
The Countess of Huntingdon lived at a time when privileged
people were allowed to appoint their own domestic chaplains.
In order to spread her evangelical faith, she built 84 small houses
all with a chapel – and chaplain – attached. After her death the
chapels became a small denomination, called the Countess of
Huntingdon's Connection, which has about twenty ministers
today.

'Our dear Selina'

The Countess of Huntingdon's handsome front door was
thrown open once again to receive a fresh party of callers. The
guests were ushered upstairs while their servants were taken
to the large kitchen, where there was a well-spread table. They
were given a hearty meal, with other servants whose
employers had come visiting, then they would be treated to a
sermon. And it *would* be a treat – for those invited to speak
were the Wesleys, George Whitefield and other compelling
preachers of the day.

Upstairs in the drawing-room, their masters and
mistresses were being received by the countess. She was a
remarkable woman in every way. She cared nothing for
fashion and dressed just as *she* pleased. But she did care about
passing on her faith. What better way than to use her London
home – 'upstairs' and 'downstairs' too? People of quality would
never have listened to John Wesley in the open air or in country
barns, where he preached his sermons to the masses, but they
were perfectly willing to come to 'our dear Selina's' drawing-
room and listen there to the gospel that could change their
lives too.

*'Oh, that my poor cold heart could catch a spark from others, and
be as a flame of fire in the Redeemer's service! Some few instances
of success, which God, in the riches of his mercy, has lately
favoured me with, have greatly comforted me during my season
of affliction; and I have felt the presence of God in my soul in a
very remarkable manner.'* – Selina, Countess of Huntingdon
1709-1791

25 August

On 25 August 1997 the first Lakeside Praise took place at the Lakeside shopping centre. **John Guest**, originator of Lakeside Praise, is priest-in-charge at Stanford-le-Hope, near to Lakeside, one of Europe's largest shopping centres.

Paying and praying

The Reverend John Guest had experienced the busy, frantic crowds at the Lakeside shopping centre but on a Sunday the atmosphere seemed different. There was a relaxed, holiday mood. As John mingled with the cheerful shoppers he could imagine the centre spinning and dancing with entertainers in a thorough-going festival.

He passed on his vision for a Christian celebration to the Reverend Jill Edwards, the chaplain at the Lakeside Centre, and together they asked the management for permission to hold such a festival on the last Sunday in August. John, himself a Christian clown, contacted other Christian performers and booked them for 31 August.

Then, out of the blue, the management cancelled the booking in favour of a better offer and suggested Bank Holiday Monday for the Christian Festival. John and Jill agreed to the change, even though some of their artistes had to cancel. But the event was a huge success. Even the rain outside brought more shoppers in.

The year was 1997 and on 31 August – the day originally planned for the Festival – they awoke to hear the terrible news of the death of Diana Princess of Wales. Had they kept to that day, no celebration would have been possible.

August Bank Holiday Monday is now the regular date for the Festival and at the 1999 Lakeside Praise the centre's own top floor chapel was opened. A Sunday service is held and the chapel is open for shoppers who want to talk or enjoy an oasis of quietness.

'Our aim is to present the Christian message in a low-key way, not to do a hard sell. We are saying that the church is interesting, cheerful and alive.' – John Guest

26 August

St Augustine's Feast Day is in August (see 28 August).
St Augustine is one of the Fathers of the Christian church.
He was born in 354. He used his learning and brilliant
mind to combat the heresies that beset the early church.
Sadly, he also encouraged a negative attitude to the body
and to sex. He founded a small community from which the
Augustinian Orders take their rule, and was afterwards
appointed Bishop of Hippo, in North Africa.

'Take up and read'

Augustine was beside himself. He could not bear even to stay
inside the house. In a frenzy of anguish and distress he rushed
out into the garden, throwing himself down under the shade
of a fig tree. Then he began to weep, pouring out his troubles
to God. He could not go on any longer, torn between the life
he was living and the beckoning of God towards a life of
holiness and devotion to Christ. After a while, as his sobs
subsided, he seemed to hear a voice saying, 'Take up and read,
take up and read.'

At first Augustine thought it was the voices of children
playing a game but when it persisted he went back to the
place in the garden where he had put down his Bible and
picked it up again. He determined to open it and take what
was written as a message from God. His eyes fell on verses
from St Paul's letter to the Romans: 'Let us conduct ourselves
properly as people who live in the light of day – no orgies or
drunkenness, nor immorality or indecency, no fighting or
jealousy. But take up the weapons of the Lord Jesus Christ
and stop paying attention to your sinful nature and satisfying
your desires.'

Augustine recognized that these words summed up God's
challenge to his way of life. 'I had no desire or need to read
further,' he wrote. 'As I finished the sentence it was as though
the light of peace had been poured into my heart, all the
shadows of doubt dispersed. Thus you have converted me to
you.' – From Augustine's *Confessions*

27 August

Bernhard Langer was born on 27 August 1957. He has been a professional golfer for over 25 years, winning over 50 tournaments around the world including the US Masters in 1985 and 1993. He has been a member of the Ryder Cup Team nine times and once ranked number one golfer in the world.

Coping with the 'yips'

For the uninitiated, 'yipping' is the term used in golfing circles for a jerky, uncontrolled putting stroke, that – as Bernhard Langer says – 'sends scores soaring'! And he knows from experience. When he was 18 and began playing the European Tour, he first developed the 'yips'. But he was a determined young man and by the time he was 22 he won the Cacheral Under 25s Championship by a record 17 strokes. No more yipping!

Bernhard's father was born in Czechoslovakia. He escaped from a Russian prisoner-of-war train bound for Siberia and settled in Bavaria. Bernhard always assumed he was a Christian as he came from a Christian family and went to church. He became a professional golfer at fifteen, having started off caddying at the tender age of seven.

By the time he was twenty-eight Bernhard had everything most people dream of – success, fame, a beautiful wife and plenty of money. But he was still unsatisfied. On a US tour he went to a Bible Study and was amazed by what he heard. What he needed, he heard, was a personal encounter with Jesus Christ, who could give him new life – not because he deserved it, but through Jesus' free gift. Bernhard accepted that gift and found the satisfaction he had craved for.

Now, Bernhard has a different perspective. Before, he says, his priorities were 'Golf, golf and more golf, then myself, and finally a little time with my wife. Now it's God first, family second and then my career.' He has found in Christianity, he says, a new way of living, with Jesus Christ as Saviour, Lord and Friend.

As well as praying in the morning and at night, Bernhard often finds time to praise and thank God during the free minutes between shots.

(Grateful thanks to *Christians in Sport*)

28 August is the Feast Day of **St Augustine of Hippo**, born in 354. In spite of his subsequent learning and his standing as one of the great Church Fathers, he was not, he admits, a very good pupil at school. An encouragement to present-day parents?

'A misspent boyhood?'

Augustine called his days at school 'a dog's life'. His parents insisted very firmly that he must obey his teachers and told him that if he wanted to get on in the world he had to go to school, but he had no idea why or how it would help him. So he was packed off to school, where he was whipped if he did not learn quickly enough. He sadly observes 'many others have followed that course since, making a track of multiplied misery and toil for the sons of Adam.'

In his confession to God he admits that it was not that he was really bad at remembering his lessons or that he had no natural ability; the fact of the matter was that he preferred sport. He complains that the masters who punished the boys for neglecting their studies for games were just as keen on sport as the boys were. (It all has a very modern ring.)

But Augustine humbly confesses to God that he was wrong in not obeying both his parents and his teachers. 'The lessons they tried to force me to learn,' he admits, 'would have helped me later on.'

Prayer

Lord, my King and my God: I am offering you everything useful I learned as a boy, and everything I now speak and write and read and compute ... I give thanks to you, my joy, my confidence, my God, thanks to you for your gifts – and will you please sustain them in me? For in this way you will keep me safe, and develop and mature that which you have given; and I shall be with you, who gave me life in the first place. – From the *Confessions* of St Augustine

---

29 August

The Reverend Dr William Archibald Spooner died on 29 August 1930. Dr Spooner was a clergyman and teacher; he became Dean then Warden of New College Oxford between 1876 and 1924. He taught and befriended several generations of Oxford students.

Spoonerisms

Dr Spooner's subjects were divinity, ancient history and philosophy. But he was no dry as dust academic; his lectures were lively and interesting. He also made it his business to know all his students by name and he and his wife always made them welcome to their home. Life had not been easy for William Spooner. He was an albino and suffered all his life from weak eyesight but he overcame his disabilities courageously and earned a reputation for kindness and hospitality. He was excellent on social occasions, known for his witty speeches. But today his name lives on for what are now called – in his honour – spoonerisms.

One morning in chapel Spooner announced the hymn as 'Kinquering Congs their title take', and a suppressed ripple of laughter ran round the congregation. This was not the first time that the much-loved doctor had made the same kind of mistake. He once told a recalcitrant student who was being sent down for his laziness: 'You have deliberately tasted two worms, and you can leave Oxford by the town drain.'

At least, that is what he is *supposed* to have said. Once he gained a reputation for such transposing of letters, with comical results, it was easy enough for students to invent other likely or unlikely examples and attribute them to him.

Dr Spooner was described by a contemporary as a good man, 'undisturbed by storms'.

30 August

John Bunyan, preacher and writer, died in August (31) 1688. Bunyan was the son of a tinker. He was twice sent to prison for preaching as a non-conformist, the first time for 12 years. It was then that he wrote *Grace Abounding*. In his second, six-month, imprisonment he wrote his best-known book, *The Pilgrim's Progress*.

Days to remember

When Bunyan was twenty-one he married a poor girl who brought with her two books that had belonged to her father – *A Plain Man's Pathway to Heaven* and *The Practice of Piety*. Perhaps they made an impression on Bunyan; he certainly began to experience deep despair and guilt but after months of distress he began to feel that God *did* love and accept him. He describes his spiritual pilgrimage in *Grace Abounding to the Chief of Sinners*.

'Now my heart filled full of comfort and hope and now I could believe that my sins should be forgiven me; I was now so taken with the love and mercy of God that I thought I could have spoken of his love and mercy to me even to the very crows that sat upon the ploughed lands before me, had they been capable to have understood me; wherefore I said in my soul with much gladness, "Surely I will not forget this forty years hence"; but alas! within less than forty days I began to question all still.'

Later he recorded: 'I remember that one day, as I was travelling into the country and musing on the wickedness and blasphemy of my heart, that scripture came into my mind, "He hath made peace through the blood of his cross". By which I was made to see, both again and again and again that day, that God and my soul were friends by this blood; yea, I saw that the justice of God and my sinful soul could embrace and kiss each other through this blood. This was a good day to me; I hope I shall not forget it.'

If we have not quiet in our minds, outward comfort will do no more for us than a golden slipper on a gouty foot. – John Bunyan 1628-1688

31 August

Diana, Princess of Wales, died in a car crash on 31 August 1997. The marriage of the Prince and Princess of Wales ended in divorce and Diana was in Paris with Dodi Fayed when a car crash killed them both.

'A world in mourning'

The news of Diana's death broke into the uneventfulness of a late summer Sunday morning like a brutal and paralysing blow. And after the stunned silence, the flood of tributes began from national and world leaders, giving place to an outburst of grief from a whole people in mourning for the princess who had won their hearts.

Crowds gathered outside her London home; thousands kept vigil and piled up flowers, made small shrines and lit candles – in London and in New York too. Crowds packed the streets to witness the funeral procession, strewing flowers onto the funeral car.

It was an unparalleled outburst of grief. Many people had experienced that warmth and kindness personally while others had observed it in her compassion towards the sick, the young and the old. She was loved too for being transparently human. She, like many others, had suffered from depression, from self-loathing, from betrayal in love. And if she was a saint she was also, reassuringly, a sinner – an acceptable icon for the nineties.

Diana's death, on the verge of new happiness, reminded young as well as old of the inescapability of death. It was a timely reminder to a society that pretends that death will not come to us – not in the midst of life.

> Oh God, give me of thy holiness,
> Oh God, give me of thy shielding,
> Oh God, give me of thy surrounding,
> And of thy peace in the knot of death.
>
> Oh give me of thy surrounding,
> And of thy peace at the hour of my death!
>
> (Death prayer from *The Celtic Vision*)

At the beginning of September 1997 **Mother Teresa** of Calcutta was nearing the end of her life. It was the time when the world was reeling from the sudden death of Diana, Princess of Wales, another icon of the time.

Love in action

Most visitors to India's great city avert their eyes from the suffering and misery of the poor and dying. Mother Teresa chose to live among them, sharing their poverty and bringing them the love of Christ.

Born of Albanian parents and brought up in Yugoslavia, Mother Teresa heard God's call to become a nun. She was sent to teach in the pleasant and congenial Loreto Convent School in Calcutta. One day, in the poor part of the city, she recognised that this was where she should be. She received what she described as her 'call within a call', to serve in the filth and pain of the Calcutta slums.

The authorities gave her the pilgrim hostel near the temple of the goddess Kali, for her order of the Missionaries of Charity. Mother Teresa adopted Indian citizenship and the nuns wore the sari as their habit. From their centre, they went out into the streets to bring in the dying, so that they could 'die within sight of a loving face'. She rescued people of all ages, some of whom recovered. But all were lovingly cared for, clean and at peace, perhaps for the first time in their lives. In all of them Mother Teresa saw and served Christ her Master and Lord.

Here I am, Lord – body, heart and soul. Grant that with your love I may be big enough to reach the world and small enough to be at one with you. – Meditation of Mother Teresa, used by her world-wide Missionaries of Charity

2 September

On 2 September 1666, the **Great Fire of London** broke out. The great fire started in a bakery in Pudding Lane and finally stopped at Pie Corner. So some people declared that the fire was an act of God to punish them for their vice and greed.

London's burning!

'On September 2, after midnight, London was set on fire and on September 3 the Exchange was burnt; and in three days almost all the city within the walls and much without them. The season had been exceedingly dry before and the wind in the east, where the fire began. The people having none to conduct them aright could do nothing to resist it, but stand and see their houses burn without remedy, the engines being presently out of order and useless. The streets were crowded with people and carts, to carry away what goods they could get out. And they that were most active and befriended (by their wealth) got carts, and saved much; and the rest lost almost all.

'Almost all the booksellers on St Paul's Churchyard brought their books into vaults under St Paul's Church, where it was thought almost impossible that fire should come. But the church itself being on fire, the exceeding weight of stones falling down did break into the vault and let in the fire, and they could not come near to save the books.

'At last some seamen taught them to blow up some of the next houses with gunpowder, which stopped the fire.

'It was a sight that might have given any man a lively sense of the vanity of this world, and all the wealth and glory of it, and of the future conflagration of all the world. To see all the flames mount up towards heaven, and proceed so furiously without restraint; to see the air as far as could be beheld so filled with smoke that the sun shined through it with a colour like blood; but the dolefullest sight of all was afterwards to see what a ruinous confused place the city was. No man that seest not such a thing can have a right apprehension of the dreadfulness of it.'

(From *The Autobiography of Richard Baxter*)

Thomas More (1478-1535) wrote this letter to his wife when part of his house and barns had been burned through a neighbour's carelessness.

'Be merry in God'

'Mistress Alice, in my most hearty wise I recommend me to you. And whereas I am informed by my son Heron of the loss of our barns by fire, with all the corn that was therein; albeit, saving God's pleasure, it is great pity of so much good corn lost, yet since it hath liked him to send us such a chance, we must and are bounden not only to be content but also to be glad of his visitation. He sent us all that we have lost, and since he hath by such a chance taken it away again, his pleasure be fulfilled. Let us never grieve thereat, but take it in good worth and heartily thank him as well for adversity as for prosperity. And peradventure we have more cause to thank him for our loss than for our winning. For his wisdom better seeth what is good for us than we do ourselves. Therefore I pray you be of good cheer, and take all the household with you to church and there thank God for that he has given us and for that he hath taken away from us and for that he hath left us.

'And thus as heartily fare you well, with all our children, as ye can wish.

'At Woodstock, the third day of September, by the hand of your loving husband,

'Thomas More, Knight.'

(Quoted in the *Life of Sir Thomas More* by Thomas Stapleton)

4 September

Mother Teresa died on 5 September 1997.

Mother Teresa's way of love

'We need to find God and he cannot be found in noise and restlessness. God is the friend of silence. See how nature – trees, flowers, grass – grow in silence; see the stars, the moon and sun, how they move in silence … the more we receive in silent prayer, the more we can give in our active life. We need silence to be able to touch souls. The essential thing is not what we say, but what God says to us and through us. All our words will be useless unless they come from within – words which do not give the light of Christ increase our darkness.'

'Be kind and merciful. Let no one ever come to you without coming away better and happier. Be the living expression of God's kindness; kindness in your face, kindness in your eyes, kindness in your smile, kindness in your warm greeting …To children, to the poor, to all who suffer and are lonely, give always a happy smile – Give them not only your care, but also your heart.

'Make sure that you let God's grace work in your souls by accepting whatever he gives you, and giving him whatever he takes from you.

'True holiness consists in doing God's will with a smile.'

'I have found the paradox that if I love until it hurts, then there is no hurt, but only more love.'

(From *Something Beautiful for God* by Malcolm Muggeridge, and other sources)

Jonas Hanway died on 5 September 1786. Hanway was a traveller and philanthropist. He journeyed through Russia and Persia and published an account of his travels. He befriended chimney sweeps, waifs and down-and-outs, and advocated milder punishment for prisoners. He was the first Englishman to carry an umbrella.

Hanways and parapluies

It was a beautiful object. The handle was of ebony delicately carved with leaves and flowers. The outside was pale green silk and the lining of stone-coloured satin. Jonas Hanway held his splendid umbrella high over his head as he strode through the streets of London in the rain. Small boys jeered and coachmen complained that he was ruining trade. No one who sheltered under an umbrella would want to hire their cabs. There were those who complained for religious reasons too. Hanway was defying the heavenly purpose of rain – to make us wet!

But Hanway went on his way unperturbed. One onlooker described him: 'When it rained a small parapluie defended his face and wig; he was the first man who ventured to walk the streets of London with an umbrella over his head; after carrying one near thirty years he saw them come into general use.' Not only were they used, but for some years they were known as 'hanways.'

But the small memorial tablet to Jonas Hanway in Westminster Abbey makes no mention of umbrellas. It tells of Hanway's real life-work, once he returned from being a merchant overseas in Russia and Portugal (where he first observed the 'umbrello'). He gave all his time and money to caring for those who had no champions.

The tablet reads: *'The helpless infant nurtured through his care. The friendless prostitute sheltered and reformed. The hopeless youth rescued from misery and ruin and trained to serve his country. In one common strain of gratitude they bear testimony to their benefactor's virtue.'*

6 September

Samuel Smiles, who lived from 1812 to 1904, was a Scottish doctor, writer and social reformer. He was also involved in early railways. He wrote a number of improving books but is best remembered for *Self-Help*, in which he recounts briefly the lives of men whose example should be followed. One of his subjects was Jonas Hanway.

'Never Despair!'

Samuel Smiles describes Jonas Hanway's early years. His father was killed in a dockyard accident and his mother struggled to send her children to school. When he was seventeen Jonas was sent to Lisbon to be apprenticed to a merchant, where he worked hard and well. Later he went to Russia to trade, then on to Persia with carriage-loads of English cloth to sell. Caught up in a local rising, he narrowly escaped with his life and according to Smiles, adopted his motto – *Never Despair!*

When he could afford to, he retired to England to 'do as much good to himself and others as he was able.' He founded the Marine Society – to train lads for the navy – and worked to improve the Foundling Hospital, and the notorious workhouses. He travelled on the continent, observing how to improve standards in his own country. He helped to protect chimney-sweepers' boys and raised money for victims of fires in Canada and Barbados. 'Whenever a philanthropic work was to be done in London, be sure that Jonas Hanway's hand was in it,' Smiles comments.

'When he found his powers failing,' Samuel Smiles concludes, 'he prepared for death with as much cheerfulness as he would have prepared himself for a journey into the country. He sent round and paid all his tradesmen, took leave of his friends, arranged his affairs ...and parted with life serenely and peacefully in his 74th year ... Such, in brief, was the beautiful life of Jonas Hanway, – as honest, energetic, hard-working, and true-hearted a man as ever lived.'

Stephen Hales was born on 7 September 1677. He is sometimes called the 'father of plant physiology'. He also wrote on the circulation of the blood and blood pressure, ventilation and electricity and invented machines for – among other things – distilling sea water and preserving meat.

Perpetual curate

Those were the days! Overworked, overstressed clergy today would not recognise the job description of their eighteenth century counterparts. Like his good friend, Gilbert White, Hales found that being perpetual curate at Teddington left him ample time for experimenting and discovering, inventing and writing. White wrote about him: 'His whole mind seemed replete with experiment, which of course gave tincture and turn to his conversation, often somewhat peculiar, but always interesting.'

Hales' discoveries and inventions sprang from his curiosity. He investigated tirelessly, but often without thinking about the subjects of his experiments. He did much of his early work on blood pressure by experimenting on horses. He strapped them to farm gates which were laid flat in a field, then opened one or more of their major arteries. He measured how high the blood spurted by putting tall glass tubes over the incisions. He wrote: ' The farther researches we make into the admirable scene of things, the more beauty and harmony we see in them; and the stronger and clearer conviction they give us, of the being, power and wisdom of the divine Architect.'

But others of his time – such as the poets William Blake, William Cowper and Alexander Pope – felt deep concern about the welfare of the animals involved. Pope wrote of Hales, who was a neighbour of his and a friend: 'He is a very good man, only I am sorry that he has his hands imbued with so much blood ... How do we know that we have a right to kill creatures we are so little above, as dogs, for our curiosity?'

8 September

Roy Castle's funeral took place on 8 September 1994. Roy, supported by his wife Fiona, faced cancer with great courage. He helped and encouraged other sufferers and raised funds towards a lung cancer research centre.

No self-pity!

Fiona Castle's book about Roy's illness and death and her experiences of bereavement is entitled: *No Flowers – Just Lots of Joy*. It was the message she gave, off the cuff, to press and television, immediately after Roy's death.

Because Roy was a public figure, Fiona had the added stress of being in the spotlight during the trauma of his illness, death and all that followed. Characteristically, she emphasises the other side of that coin – the comfort she received from the many letters and expressions of sympathy that arrived just because she was so well-known.

Fiona explains how important she believes it is to recognize the difference between grief and self-pity. She describes her feelings when she caught sight of someone who at first glance looked like Roy. Hope was dashed immediately as the realisation dawned that it was not and could not be Roy. Such an immediate sense of sadness and loss is natural and appropriate she believes.

But she describes another occasion when she was arriving at Heathrow alone. She caught sight of a young girl, searching the faces of the arrivals, until she caught sight of the man she was meeting and rushed into his arms. 'I felt myself bursting into uncontrollable tears,' Fiona writes. 'There was no one to meet me, I had lost that special relationship for ever.'

Almost immediately Fiona recognised that her reaction was not genuine grief but envy for a relationship she had lost. 'I was wallowing in self-pity,' she comments, 'and I gave myself a stern talking-to … Grief is natural, and a process we must undergo, but self-pity is unattractive and self-centred. It is important to distinguish between the two.'

William the Conqueror died on 9 September 1087.

The Bayeux Tapestry finale

At some time during its nine-hundred-year history, part of the Bayeux tapestry was torn off – perhaps by an irate or humiliated Englishman! Scholars can tell from consulting the Anglo-Saxon Chronicle for 1066 what would have been depicted on that missing eight-foot fragment. It would have recorded the climax of the struggle between Norman and English forces; the meeting of the victorious, rampaging Norman troops with the nobles of London at Berkhamsted; the handing over of authority to King William at the castle, when swords and city keys were offered to him. After recording that official act of submission, the tapestry would have shown William's triumphant progress to London, where he was crowned King of the English in Westminster Abbey on Christmas Day 1066.

In 1996 Jan Messent, an embroiderer with an interest in Anglo Saxon and early Medieval history, was commissioned by *Madeira Thread Ltd,* to embroider the missing panel. The firm provided materials as like the original as possible. Only natural vegetable dyes were used. The Bayeux tapestry is not, in fact, tapestry at all but embroidery in wool on linen.

The new panel, perfectly matching the style of the existing 'tapestry', shows a man fleeing the battlefield and hiding in a tree, then the mounted Norman army meeting the English nobles, followed by the coronation. Outside the church, less than enthusiastic crowds are waiting. The words, inscribed in Latin, translate: 'And here, at Berkhampstead, the nobles of London yield ... Here sits William, king of the English. Everyone rejoices.' Probably not!

The new section of the tapestry was first displayed in Normandy, in William's birthplace, later at Berkhamsted, where the formal submission took place. The ruins of the once proud castle still stand, its green mound covered with primroses and daffodils every spring. And every springtime, too, on Easter Day, the Christians in the town hold a dawn service to celebrate the resurrection of Jesus, a greater King and a more welcomed conqueror than William I.

---

10 September

In this week, in 1828, the great Russian author **Count Leo Tolstoy** was born. Tolstoy's novel, *War and Peace*, is thought by many to be the greatest novel ever written. At first a dissolute gentleman about town, Tolstoy joined the army and fought in the Crimean War. He married and had thirteen children and settled on his Volga estate. He believed firmly in non-resistance to evil and endeavoured to put the Sermon on the Mount literally into practice, living in poverty. He left home after domestic quarrels and died in the siding of a railway station.

Theory and practice

Tolstoy recollects an early attempt to write a list of 'daily tasks and duties which should last me all my life':

'I took some sheets of paper, and tried, first of all, to make a list of my tasks and duties for the coming year. The paper needed ruling, but as I could not find the ruler, I had to use a Latin dictionary instead. The result was that, when I had drawn the pen along the edge of the dictionary and removed the latter, I found that in place of a line, I had only made an oblong smudge on the paper, since the dictionary was not long enough to reach across it, and the pen had slipped round the soft, yielding corner of the book. Thereupon I took another piece of paper and by carefully manipulating the dictionary, contrived to rule what at least *resembled* lines ... I proceeded to write, "Rules of my Life" ... but the words came out in such a crooked and uneven scrawl that for long I sat debating the question, "Shall I write them again?" – for long, sat in agonised contemplation of the ragged handwriting and the disfigured title page. Why was it that all the beauty and clarity which my soul then contained came out so misshapenly on paper (as in life itself) just when I was wishing to apply those qualities to what I was thinking at the moment?'

(From *Childhood, Boyhood and Youth* by Leo Tolstoy)

Count Leo Tolstoy.

'My life suddenly changed'

Tolstoy wrote:

'Five years ago I came to believe in Christ's teaching and my life suddenly changed … It happened to me as it happens to a man who goes out on some business and on the way suddenly decides that the business is unnecessary and returns home. All that was on his right is now on his left and all that was on his left is now on his right; his former wish to get as far as possible from home has changed into a wish to be as near as possible to it. The direction of my life and my desires became different and good and evil changed places…

'I, like the thief on the cross, have believed Christ's teaching and been saved … I, like the thief, knew that I was unhappy and suffering … I, like the thief to the cross, was nailed by some force to that life of suffering and evil. And as, after the meaningless suffering and evils of life, the thief awaited the terrible darkness of death, so did I await the same thing.

'In all this I was exactly like the thief, but the difference was that the thief was already dying while I was still living. The thief might believe that his salvation lay there beyond the grave but I could not be satisfied with that because besides a life beyond the grave life still awaited me here. But I did not understand that life. It seemed to me terrible. And suddenly I heard the words of Christ and understood them, and life and death ceased to seem to me evil, and instead of despair I experienced happiness and the joy of life undisturbed by death.'

(From *What I Believe* by Leo Tolstoy)

12 September

In this week of September in 1855 Sebastopol finally fell to British, French and Turkish troops after an eleven-month siege in the Crimean War. **Mary Seacole**, a Jamaican woman with experience of 'doctoring' and a warm affection for the British, travelled at her own expense and on her own initiative to the Crimea, to nurse and care for British troops and to set up the 'British Hotel' to supply officers and men with food and everyday needs.

A homely woman's help

'I have never been long in any place before I have found my practical experience in the science of medicine useful … In the Crimea, where the doctors were so overworked and sickness so prevalent, I could not be long idle, for I never forgot that my intention in seeking the army was to help the kind-hearted doctors…

'But before very long I found myself surrounded with patients of my own and this for two simple reasons. In the first place the men (I am speaking of the "ranks" now) had a very serious objection to going into hospital for any but urgent reasons … In the second place, they could and did get at my store sick comforts and nourishing food, which the heads of the medical staff would sometimes find it difficult to procure. These reasons, with the additional one that I was very familiar with the diseases which they suffered most from and successful in their treatment (I say this in no spirit of vanity), were quite sufficient to account for the numbers who came daily to the *British Hotel* for medical treatment.'…

But Mary Seacole also cared for the officers:

'Don't you think, reader, if you were lying, with parched lips and fading appetite, thousands of miles from mother, wife, or sister, loathing the rough food by your side … don't you think that you would welcome the familiar figure of the stout lady whose bony horse has just pulled up at the door of your hut and whose panniers contain some cooling drink, a little broth, some homely cake or a dish of jelly or blancmange?'

(From *The Wonderful Adventures of Mary Seacole in Many Lands*)

Mary Seacole.

'Do the little things'

More extracts from Mary Seacole's *Wonderful Adventures in Many Lands:*

'Tell me, reader, can you fancy what the want of so simple a thing as a pocket handkerchief is? To put a case – have you ever gone out for the day without one, sat in a draught and caught a sneezing cold in the head? You say the question is an unnecessarily unpleasant one and yet what I am about to tell you is true and the sufferer is, I believe, still alive.

'An officer had ridden down one day to obtain refreshments (this was very early in the spring), some nice fowls had just been taken from the spit and I offered one to him. Paper was one of the most hardly obtained luxuries in the Crimea and I rarely had any to waste upon my customers, so I called out, "Give me your pocket handkerchief, my son, that I may wrap it up." You see, he could not be very particular out there. But he smiled very bitterly as he answered, "Pocket handkerchief, mother? By Jove, I wish I had one. I tore my last shirt into shreds a fortnight ago and there's not a bit of it left now."

'Shortly after, a hundred dozen pocket handkerchiefs came to my store and I sold them all to officers and men very speedily.'

When the war ended Mary Seacole visited the cemeteries before returning to England (poorer than when she arrived). 'To all the cemeteries where friends rested so calmly, sleeping well after a life's work nobly done, I went many times … Over some I planted shrubs and flowers, little lilac trees … and flowering evergreens which looked quite gay and pretty when I left and may in time become great trees … And from many graves I picked up pebbles and plucked simple wildflowers, or tufts of grass, as memorial for relatives at home.'

'Be joyful; keep the faith; do the little things.' – St David (patron saint of Wales)

---

14 September

John Howard, prison reformer, was born in September 1726.

'This extraordinary man...'

John Howard had seen, first in Bedford gaol, then in many other prisons throughout England and Wales, horrific and inhumane conditions. And not all the prisoners were even criminals. Some were religious dissenters, others respectable tradesmen who had fallen into debt. All were packed in pell-mell, at the mercy of their gaolers, forced to pay him for every necessity. Some gaolers would not release a prisoner discharged by the courts, unless money changed hands. Howard persuaded the House of Commons to pass acts to abolish discharge fees and to insist on proper health care for prisoners. But he complained that the acts were not 'strictly obeyed.'

Although travel was uncomfortable and dangerous, Howard covered nearly eighty thousand kilometres on horseback and spent £30,000 of his own money visiting other prisons and trying to bring about reform. He travelled in France, Germany, the Netherlands, Switzerland and Russia. He had adventures enough – captured by pirates and quelling a riot single-handed. Sometimes he visited a prison in disguise, where governments might have forbidden him entry. He wrote a book – *The State of Prisons in England and Wales* – and used every possible means to bring about reform at home and abroad. Ironically, he died of so-called 'gaol fever' when he was in the Ukraine studying how to prevent plague and contagious diseases. John Wesley aptly called him 'one of the greatest men in Europe'.

*This extraordinary man had the fortune
to be honoured while living
In the manner which his virtues deserved:
He received the thanks
Of both houses of the British and Irish Parliaments,
For his eminent services rendered to his country
and to mankind*
(Inscription on the statue of John Howard in St. Paul's Cathedral)

15 September

On 15 September 1917, Russia was proclaimed a republic. After tending Russian émigrés in France, **Mother Maria** aroused German anger by her defence of Jewish people. Her movement, Orthodox Action, was closed down and she was arrested.

Love in action

Mother Maria spent the last two years of her life at Ravensbrück concentration camp. The journey there, sealed in cattle trucks, took three days; three days without water or sanitation. Once there, the guards' brutalizing regime did all in its power to destroy any natural, human feelings that remained. But Mother Maria befriended the hopeless and organized discussions and Bible readings in order to encourage the prisoners and keep their hopes alive.

The high chimneys of the crematorium constantly belched out smoke and Maria calculated that at the current rate of deaths, no one could expect to live for more than five months. But those with a strong faith were able to accept death and in that way to embrace life too.

In time Mother Maria's health began to fail and she could barely stand. Meanwhile the camp authorities could see that the war would soon be lost and they tried urgently to destroy records and to get rid of inmates too, before the Allies should arrive and discover the camps. Roll calls, which took place night and day, were now used to select those appointed to die. On Good Friday, 30 March 1945, Maria was selected. Or was it that she took the place of another victim? No one is quite certain what happened, in the confusion of those last two days, but it seems likely that then, or the next day, she *did* volunteer, and like her Master, died in another's place. The vans left with their cargo of doomed prisoners and Mother Maria went to the gas chamber on 31 March.

Mother Maria wrote: *By the laws of spiritual life ... whoever gives, receives, whoever impoverishes himself, gains in wealth.'*

(Source: *Pearl of Great Price* by Father Sergei Hackel)

16 September

John Bertram Phillips was born on 16 September 1906.

Ring of truth

In this day of numerous modern translations of the Bible, J B Phillips is in danger of being forgotten, but his translation, first of the New Testament Epistles and then of the rest of the New Testament, was ground-breaking. It all began when Canon Phillips was vicar in Redhill in Surrey, in the mid nineteen-forties, working with the young people of his parish. They told him what difficulty they had in understanding the Epistles in the King James' Version which was the only one used. The words were archaic and seemed completely irrelevant to their own lives and experience.

Phillips set about a new translation for their benefit and when it was published it sold like hot cakes. There had been some previous renderings in more modern English but nothing like the pungent, direct version Phillips gave. He made no pretence to precise scholarship but he had the gift of capturing the voice of the original everyday Greek, and bringing it right home to his readers. Somewhat neglected now, Phillips' translation of such passages as *Romans 12* is still unparalleled in its strength and the punch it delivers.

Phillips himself wrote of the effect the translating had on his own life. The task had utterly confirmed his own faith. In his words, he discovered that the New Testament has the unmistakable 'ring of truth'.

'With eyes wide open to the mercies of God, I beg you ... as an act of intelligent worship, to give him your bodies as a living sacrifice ... Don't let the world squeeze you into its own mould, but let God remould your minds from within, so that you may prove that the plan of God for you is good, meets all his demands and moves towards the goal of true maturity.' – Romans 12, J B Phillips' translation

17 September is the Feast Day of **Hildegard of Bingen**, born in 1098.

A very remarkable woman!

She wrote books on the Gospels, on natural science, on the body and its ailments; she wrote lives of the saints, poems and hymns. She was an artist and composed music. She preached; she wrote down her visions and denounced wickedness in colourful and symbolic language. In lighter moments she invented a language of her own – a mixture of German and Latin with its own alphabet. She corresponded at length with four popes, two emperors, the king of England, St Bernard of Clairvaux – and many others. She was a very remarkable woman.

Hildegard was born in Germany, the tenth child of noble parents, and educated from the age of eight by an anchoress. She became a Benedictine nun and in 1136 the prioress. Since the age of three she had experienced visions: 'These visions which I saw I beheld neither in sleep nor dreaming nor in madness ... I saw them in full view and according to God's will, when I was wakeful and alert.'

Hildegard was certainly one of the most gifted women of her time. Recent interest in her stems from the fact that as a woman she exercised such influence in her world and she is hailed too for her concern with creation and the natural world. 'Viriditas' – greenness – is a favourite word she uses to describe the grace of God shining forth in all living things. She was not a feminist nor an ecologist in the modern sense, but someone with great insight into the wholeness of creation and the glorious redemption of the cosmos by God, the 'Living Light'.

In a letter to an over-busy abbess Hildegard wrote:
As the fruit of the earth is harmed by a freak rainstorm, and as from untilled earth sprout no true fruits, but useless weeds, so a person who toils more than her body can bear is rendered useless in her spirit by ill-judged toil and ill-judged abstinence.

(Source: *The Wisdom of Hildegard of Bingen* by Fiona Bowie)

18 September

Dag Hammarskjöld died on 18 September 1961. He had a brilliant career. He was born in Sweden in 1905 and was a member of the Swedish Cabinet before becoming Secretary General of the United Nations. He worked relentlessly at being an 'international civil servant.' He believed that his task was to serve others and he never spared himself. He was killed in a plane crash in 1961, while on a UN peace mission. There have been accusations of a bomb plot, with claims that various countries, including the UK, were implicated in his death. He was awarded the Nobel Peace Prize in 1961.

'The only true profile'

'Dear Leif

'Perhaps you may remember I once told you that ... I kept a diary which I wanted you to take charge of someday. Here it is. It was begun without a thought of anybody else reading it. But what with my later history and all that has been said and written about me, the situation has changed. These entries provide the only true "profile" that can be drawn. If you find them worth publishing, you have my permission to do so.'

Dag Hammarskjöld's diary is not a day-to-day record of events but an expression of his innermost, personal thoughts about life, death and God. He described them as 'signposts, pointing a path of which the traveller did not wish to speak while he was alive.'

Death is drawing nigh –
For all that has been – Thanks!
To all that shall be – Yes!

If even dying is to be made a social function, then, please, grant me the favour of sneaking out on tip-toe without disturbing the party.

Dag Hammarskjöld

George Cadbury was born on 19 September 1839.

Bitter chocolate

Business was bad. The two young brothers – George was only twenty-one – took over the firm from their ailing father and determined to pay off debts and improve trade. They sold tea, coffee and cocoa nibs, (described as 'a most nutritious beverage for breakfast'). They worked six days a week from eight in the morning till seven-thirty at night and George economised enough to live on ten shillings (fifty pence) a week.

But the public would not drink chocolate. It was too bitter! They experimented with all kinds of additives to disguise the bitterness of the cocoa butter, but the end result could at best be described by George as a 'comforting gruel'.

Then George heard that a Dutch chocolate manufacturer had invented a machine to press out the cocoa butter. 'I went off to Holland not knowing a word of Dutch,' he said, 'saw the manufacturer with whom I had to talk entirely by signs and a dictionary and bought the machine.'

As a result Cadbury's were able to put on the market the first pure cocoa essence that tasted sweet. That was in 1866 and business began to boom. They were soon manufacturing tablets of chocolate as well as the 'nutritious beverage' that had originally been their stock-in-trade.

But George Cadbury cared about more than business. Every Sunday – his one day off – he set off at 6.30 am to teach Class 14 in the newly-formed Adult School, taking a flower for each member of his class. He described this school as 'a sort of co-operative system of carrying on class where one is our Master, even Christ'. And in true Quaker style, all who came were treated as equals, even though many were down-and-outs. All denominations joined in. Reading and writing came first on the programme, and Bible study followed.

Later in life George Cadbury held twice-yearly reunions for past members of his class in his large house and garden. Almost 1,000 people would turn up, thankful for the start that George had given them in learning and living.

20 September

George Cadbury.

A village called Bournville

In the Cadbury factory, every day began with Bible reading and prayers for all. But the Cadbury brothers were not hypocrites by any means; their Christianity did not stop at fine words. In an age when many factory owners cared very little about their factory-hands' well-being, George took care to provide first-class facilities. When the premises became too small, he decided to build a factory in the country. The brothers bought a site a few miles out of Birmingham near the tiny stream of Bournbrook – which suggested the factory's new name of Bournville.

George loved open space. He provided football fields for the men and a playground and garden with a lily-pond for the women. Inside the building there were warm cloakrooms for drying off wet clothes and a warming cupboard so that employees could heat their own food.

The brothers kept closely in touch with conditions in the factory. 'Mr Richard and Mr George would go down on their knees and crawl under the tables to see if the water-pipes were hot enough,' one worker said.

But working out of town presented transport problems. George decided to buy the land around the factory and build a village for his workforce. There was to be no jerry-building and every house would have a spacious garden big enough to grow vegetables. Fruit trees were planted and the garden dug over before each new owner moved in. Trees were planted lavishly along the wide roads. Later on George built schools and a shopping area. An Anglican church and a Friends' Meeting House were near at hand so that the whole person was catered for.

Prayer of George Fox, founder of the Quaker movement

O Lord, baptise our hearts into a sense of the needs and conditions of all.

News came on 21 September 1586 of an arms convoy on its way to Zutphen in the Netherlands. Next day **Sir Philip Sidney** led the attack into battle. Philip Sidney, born at Penshurst Place in Kent in 1554, was a courtier, poet and soldier. He was so loved and admired that after his death 200 poems were written in memory of him. One, by his friend Sir Fulke Greville, described him as 'a spotless friend and a matchless man'.

'Love my memory; cherish my friends'

When Philip Sidney rode to battle at Zutphen, he was not wearing greaves – the piece of armour worn by soldiers to cover and protect their legs. He had taken them off, on impulse, out of consideration for a fellow soldier who was without his. A bullet hit him on his unprotected thigh.

Fulke Greville, poet and courtier, describes how, as he lay wounded and desperately thirsty from fever and the heat of the sun, he passed his water-bottle, with its meagre ration of water, to a soldier lying nearby. 'Thy necessity is yet greater than mine,' he said. A few weeks later Sidney died as a result of his wound.

> Leave me, O Love which reachest but to dust,
> And thou, my mind, aspire to higher things!
> Grow rich in that which never taketh rust:
> Whatever fades but fading pleasure brings.
>
> Then farewell, world! Thy uttermost I see:
> Eternal love, maintain thy life in me!
>
> Philip Sidney

22 September

Michael Faraday was born on 22 September 1791. Faraday is regarded as the greatest of all experimental scientists. He belonged to a small, strict Christian group called the Sandemanians. They believed fervently in the Bible and that faith in Christ alone was necessary for salvation; they also believed that money should be given away. Faraday and his wife lived simply, refusing honours and giving away any money he earned. He saw a display of God's truth and magnificence in the science he loved.

The making of a scientist

Schooldays had been fun for Michael Faraday because he enjoyed the chance to play marbles in the street rather than the chance to learn anything much beyond the three Rs. At thirteen he became an errand-boy, delivering goods, but he was later given the chance to be apprenticed to a bookseller and learn the book-binding trade.

Michael often glanced through the books he was given to bind, and one day he became engrossed in a large encyclopedia on electricity. It was then that his lifelong love of science began. He tried to get a job at the Royal Society and at last managed to become a laboratory assistant to Sir Humphrey Davy, who was its president. At first he had the job of rebinding Sir Humphrey's books, but soon his work became more scientific and he even travelled abroad with his boss, meeting many famous scientists of the day.

Soon Faraday began to research and make discoveries for himself in electricity, chemistry and metallurgy. He made the first electric motor, the first dynamo and the first transformer. He was also a brilliant lecturer and communicator, who could make science interesting to ordinary lay people. But even more than he loved his science, he loved Sarah Bernard, the woman he married, and most of all he loved God.

The Reverend Francis Kilvert died on 23 September 1879. Francis Kilvert (1840-72) was one of the six children of the Reverend Robert Kilvert. His diary – or what remains of it – was not published until sixty years after his death. It gives a delightful portrait of mid-Victorian life in Welsh border country. He also spent some years as his father's curate at Langley Burrell in Wiltshire. Kilvert was a gentle, compassionate man, deeply observant and admiring of the beauty of the countryside. He was susceptible to female beauty too. He died when he was only thirty-eight, just a month after his marriage.

Kilvert's diary

'Why do I keep this voluminous journal? I can hardly tell. Partly because life seems to me such a curious and wonderful thing that it almost seems a pity that even such a humble and unadventurous life as mine should pass altogether away without some such record as this, and partly too because I think the record may amuse and interest some who come after me.'

Langley Burrell *Thursday, 24 September*
'This afternoon I walked over to Kington St Michael by Langley Burrell Church ... It was a day of exceeding and almost unmatched beauty, one of those perfectly lovely afternoons that we seldom get but in September or October. A warm delicious calm and sweet peace brooded breathless over the mellow sunny autumn afternoon and the happy stillness was broken only by the voices of children blackberry gathering in an adjoining meadow and the sweet solitary singing of a robin...

'In spite of the warm afternoon sunshine the solitary cottages, low-lying on the brook, looked cold and damp, but the apples hung bright on the trees in the cottage gardens and a Virginia creeper burned like fire in crimson upon the wall, crimson among the green. When I returned home at night the ... moon was at the full. The night was sweet and quiet ... the stillness was broken only by the occasional pattering of an acorn or a chestnut through the leaves to the ground'.

(From *Kilvert's Diary*)

24 September

In September 1739 **George Whitefield** was on board ship sailing from England to Philadelphia. George Whitefield (1714-1770), a contemporary of John and Charles Wesley, was a powerful and outstanding preacher in America and Britain. At Oxford, where he met the Wesleys, he agonised over earning salvation. His conversion – after recognising that salvation is God's free gift of grace – brought him great joy and a desire to preach the gospel to others. But his Journal reveals that a sense of sin still sometimes plagued him.

Temptations of a minister

Saturday, September 22 (on board ship)
'Underwent inexpressible agonies of soul for two or three days, at the remembrance of my sins, and the bitter consequences of them. All the while I was assured God had forgiven me; but I could not forgive myself for sinning against so much light and love … at length, my Lord looked on me and with that look broke my rocky heart, and I wept most bitterly … Were I always to see myself such a sinner as I am, and as I did then, without seeing the Saviour of sinners, I should not be able to look up…

'Alas, how mistaken are they who go out of the world to avoid temptations. I never am so much tempted as when confined on shipboard; a mercy this from God to keep me in action. Luther says he never undertook fresh work but that he was either visited with a fit of sickness or some strong temptation. Prayer, meditation, and temptation are necessary accomplishments, in his account, for every minister. May I follow him, as he did Christ.'

Whitefield wrote his Journal for publication. He wanted it to bring glory to God; he also wanted the money it raised to go towards the orphanage he founded in Georgia.

In September 1740 *George Whitefield* preached in Boston, Massachusetts.

The 'Thunderstorm Sermon'

George Whitefield climbed into the pulpit then knelt in prayer. There was no sound as the expectant congregation waited in anticipation until at length Whitefield stood up to preach. The sun was fitful, streaming in one moment, the next blanketed in cloud. 'See that emblem of life?' Whitefield asked, 'where will you be when your lives are passed away like that dark cloud?'

Soon the sun vanished completely, the sky darkened; thunder rumbled. 'O what pleas can you make before the Judge of the whole earth?' Whitefield asked. Now the storm was almost overhead and the church in gloom. 'O sinner!' he pleaded, 'By all your hopes of happiness I beg you to repent. Let not the wrath of God be awakened! Let not the fires of eternity be kindled against you!' At that moment lightning forked above, illuminating the darkness. 'See there!' Whitefield exclaimed, 'It is a glance from the angry eye of Jehovah. Hark –' He lifted his hand in warning and at that moment an ear-splitting clap of thunder crashed right overhead.

'It was the voice of the Almighty,' Whitefield said, 'as he passed in anger.' Then he fell to his knees in prayer, his hands covering his face. Soon, the storm passed. The clouds broke, the sun came out and a rainbow was reflected in the windows. Whitefield slowly rose to his feet. 'Look upon the rainbow,' he said, 'and praise him who made it.'

Asked if he would object to the sermon being published, Whitefield replied, 'No, if you will print the lightning, thunder and rainbow.'

(Source: *George Whitefield* by John Pollock)

26 September

Wilson Carlile, founder of the Church Army, died on 26 September 1942.

Determination

Wilson Carlile lay still, the pain in his back too bad for him to move. But he could think – think back over twenty-six years of success followed by total failure. He had always been clever with money. At seven years old, he had been given a little book for accounts – along with his weekly pocket money – which his father audited each month. When he joined his grandfather's firm at fourteen he had a fair idea of money matters. He set himself a goal: he would make £20,000 by the age of twenty-five. By today's reckoning he aimed to be a multi-millionaire.

Although he was not strong – he had trouble with his spine – Wilson had determination and he reached his target. But when the great financial crash of Black Friday came, he lost nearly £30,000. The shock, after years of overwork, brought on his old back trouble. His life seemed in ruins.

While he lay helpless his forthright Christian aunt came to visit him. She told him plainly that he needed Jesus Christ as his Saviour. Wilson was angry at first, but as he read one of the books she had given him, a change came over him. He determined to commit his life to Jesus Christ and to pass on the good news of the gospel to others.

He was ordained but as a curate he was shocked to realize that the people in his pews were all wealthy and comfortably off. Meanwhile those who *really* needed him were outside tramping the streets or living in the wretched slums nearby. Carlile determined to bring help and relief to them. He rallied some helpers and founded the Church Army. It still exists today, a hundred or so years later, bringing help and hope to those most needing it.

George Muller was born on 27 September 1805.

God will provide!

The door bell rang and George Muller went to answer it. No visitor was standing on the step, but there *was* something there. He stared hard, then bent down and picked up a large fender – which would protect the children from an open fire – and also a dish. Muller thanked God for another answer to prayer, and added the objects to his growing collection. Fenders and dishes, as well as cups, plates, knives, forks, and yards of calico and sheeting continued to arrive at the home of Mr and Mrs Muller. And George Muller was not really surprised. After all, he had asked God for them.

Muller had been appalled by the shocking conditions in Victorian workhouses, the only destination for orphans with no money and no other family to care for them. He determined to open an orphanage where children would receive love and care and Christian teaching. But he had no money. One evening he read in his Bible, 'Open thy mouth wide and I will fill it.' He took God at his word. He would ask God for everything he needed for his orphans, without letting a soul know what was required. Then he would wait patiently for God to provide.

Muller had another reason for wanting to run his orphanage 'by faith'. He felt sad to see how many well-off Christians spent their lives worrying and fretting over how to make ends meet. If he could show that God supplied the needs of his orphans, he thought, perhaps they would be readier to trust God too.

From a small home for thirty girls, Muller's Homes grew large enough to provide for 2,000 children. Today in Bristol they are still up and running, with facilities to meet today's needs. They provide family care centres, day care, educational care and homes for the elderly.

28 September

Edith Pargeter, aka Ellis Peters, was born on 28 September 1913.

Brother Cadfael

In *A Morbid Taste for Bones,* Edith Pargeter, as Ellis Peters, first introduced her readers to Brother Cadfael, the brother in charge of the herbarium in the twelfth century Benedictine monastery at Shrewsbury. The border country with Wales, which is the setting for her stories, is the countryside their author loved and where she lived for most of her life. The books were hugely successful and before long, readers were waiting impatiently for the next Brother Cadfael story to appear. Ellis Peters wrote twenty in all, in chronological sequence, set in the stirring and eventful times of King Stephen and Matilda. She cared about historical accuracy and loved the research and insisted: 'You must respect documented fact – only when the authorities fight over details do I use my own judgement and make a mix with fiction.'

But the historical background of the Brother Cadfael mysteries never obtrudes. The setting and the characters are utterly believable. We could picture Cadfael's herb garden and the little hut where he brews his concoctions long before television brought them to our screens.

Brother Cadfael himself is no innocent religious. Before he became a monk, he fought in the Crusades. His experience and knowledge of human nature enable him to solve the mystery or crime at the centre of each book. Yet he *is* innocent in the sense of being essentially good – untouched by the evil he encounters.

Ellis Peters' Christian beliefs inclined her to be more interested in the good in her characters than the evil. Brother Cadfael is too conscious of his own failures to judge others harshly. When he is accused of championing the black sheep he replies: 'There are very few all black … most of us have a few mottles about us. As well, maybe, as it makes for a more tolerant judgement of the rest of God's creatures.'

Edith Pargeter's birthday is also the Feast Day of **St Wenceslas**. In 1947 Edith Pargeter first visited Czechoslovakia as part of an international summer school. It was the beginning of a love affair with the country and its people which continued – when the political situation allowed – until 1993. She learned the language in order to translate many of the works by Czech authors unknown in English. In 1968, during the country's brief freedom under Alexander Dubcek, she was presented with the Czechoslovak Society for International Relations Gold Medal and Ribbon and hailed as 'a great friend of our country, music and literature.'

Good King Wenceslas

Wenceslas was brought up by his Christian grandmother and became king of Bohemia in his own right when he was of age. He bravely told the ruling party: 'Till now I have been under your control. Today I throw it off and shall serve God with all my heart.'

He tried to get rid of the slave-trade which had its centre in Prague and reformed the legal system. But his enemies hated his justice and mercy and in 929, when he was 22, Wenceslas was assassinated. The country reverted to pagan rule but the king was revered as a saint and many tales were told of his goodness.

One described how he cut down trees on his royal estate and carried the wood to his poorest subjects under cover of darkness. When the incensed head forester reported the thefts to the king, he commanded, 'Don't stop the thief. Give him a sound beating and let him go on his way.' The mystified forester carried out orders and Wenceslas took his beating cheerfully.

In Victorian times, Dr John Neale, may have based his 'moral tale' for his children on this legend. He later turned it into the carol that everyone knows and sings at Christmas.

30 September

30 September is the Feast Day of **St Jerome** who died in Bethlehem in 420. Jerome was one of the greatest Biblical scholars; he translated or revised the whole Bible from the original Greek and Hebrew languages into Latin – the Vulgate version.

'Translate words into deeds'

The unthinkable had happened. Barbarians had sacked the immortal city of Rome and a trail of desolate refugees began to arrive in the Holy Land. Some were aristocrats – now beggars – who told terrible tales of famine and even cannibalism in the city where Jerome had once lived and worked.

'Now,' Jerome wrote, 'we have to translate the words of Scripture into deeds; instead of talking of holy things we must put them into action.' An old man by now, he entered into relief work for the flood of asylum seekers of his time.

Jerome was a man of contradictions, gentle and compassionate yet with a sharp and acid tongue for enemies or heretics. His companion, Paula, along with other disciples, followed him to the Holy Land. She paid for a religious house for men and one for women. A hospice for travellers and a school for children were founded too. When Paula died in 404 Jerome said, ' I have lost her who was my consolation.' But medieval artists thought it safer to depict Jerome with a lion for companion.

St Jerome in his study kept a great big cat,
It's always in his pictures with its feet upon the mat.
Did he give it milk to drink, in a little dish?
When it came to Fridays, did he give it fish?
If I lost my little cat, I'd be sad without it;
I should ask St Jeremy what to do about it;
I should ask St Jeremy just because of that,
For he's the only saint I know who kept a pussy cat.

(Anon. From *Verse and Worse,* Arnold Silcock)

Ashley Cooper, seventh Earl of Shaftesbury, died on 1 October 1885. Throughout a long parliamentary career, Shaftesbury was impelled by his love for Christ to relieve suffering and distress wherever he found it. He championed the cause of nearly every philanthropist of the age.

Bedlam!

'The unhappy patient was no longer treated as a human being. His body was immediately encased in a machine which left it no liberty of action. He was sometimes chained to a staple. He was frequently beaten and starved and at best kept in subjection by foul and menacing language.'

(From *Lunacy, Law and Conscience* by Kathleen Jones)

The 'unhappy patient' was none other than King George III of England, believed to be mad. But the King's illness led to public airing of a topic that had previously been hushed up. Young Ashley Cooper was invited to serve on a committee of inquiry about treatment of the mentally ill and was shocked by what he found. He went to see conditions for himself and found patients chained hand and foot to a straw-lined bedstead in a crowded room. They were left there naked, with only a blanket for cover, and taken out once a week to be cleaned down at an outside tub in icy water. The doctors admitted that no attempt was made to treat or cure the patients.

Ashley Cooper's maiden speech to Parliament was on the subject of mental illness and in spite of his strong feelings, nervousness made him speak so softly that he could hardly be heard. 'My first effort has been made for the advance of human happiness. May I improve hourly!' he wrote in his diary.

And he did. Many exhausting hours were spent in the next fifty-seven years of his life helping the cause of the mentally ill – the most neglected and helpless group of people in the community.

2 October

On 2 October 1909 the first rugby football match was played at
Twickenham. On 1 October 1999 the new Millennium Stadium
in Cardiff staged the opening game of the Rugby World Cup.
Jonah Lomu plays on the wing for the All Blacks New Zealand
rugby side.

'The dark destroyer'

Six foot five inches tall and weighing nineteen stone, Jonah
Lomu is probably the biggest and most exciting player ever
to hit the Rugby Union scene. In 1994, at nineteen, he was the
youngest player ever selected for an All Black team. But it was
in South Africa in 1995 that he revolutionised the game,
scoring seven tries in four games. On the eve of the final match
a fax for the New Zealand team read: 'Remember rugby is a
team game. All 14 of you make sure you pass it straight to
Jonah.'

Although Jonah's family lives in New Zealand, his parents
are Tongan, and Jonah spent five early years there. 'Tonga runs
deep in me, like still waters,' he says.

He grew up in a rough area of Auckland where gangs
flourished. His uncle and cousin were both murdered. Jonah
recalls an incident when a mugger caught sight of him sitting
on a pavement and came in for the kill. Slowly Jonah rose
from the ground until he reached his full height. The mugger
quickly changed his mind and ran off.

In 1997 he was off sick with a severe kidney disorder and
his rugby future was in doubt. He recovered but needed to
lose excess weight to resume his place in the team. He
succeeded, and Jonah gives the credit to God. His mother is a
devout Christian and he shares her faith. He says: 'My heart is
an open book before God; I talk to the Lord often, even before
games. I ask him to protect all the players.'

3 October

St Francis of Assisi died on 3 October 1226. His feast day is 4 October.

Search for a beggar

Young Francis Bernadone stood behind the little market booth in the Italian town of Assisi, selling bales of cloth for his father, who was a respected citizen and a member of the guild of cloth merchants in the town. While Francis was busy serving a merchant, a beggar came up, pulling at his sleeve and whining for money. Francis was too busy unrolling bale after bale of cloth for his wealthy customer to attend to the beggar. But when the purchase was completed, he turned to look for him; but the beggar had disappeared.

Francis leaped from the booth, leaving the precious bales of velvet and embroidered cloth unguarded, and began a chase – across the market-place and up and down every alley of the labyrinth of Assisi's little streets. At last he found the beggar, and loaded him with money.

As he turned to go back to the market, Francis made a vow before God that he would never in all his life refuse to help a poor man. And he never did. Later he gave up his own possessions and comfortable life-style to embrace Lady Poverty, as he called her, himself. He lived simply and joyfully with his little band of followers. One chronicler of the time wrote about him: 'It was as though Jesus Christ walked this earth once more.'

Before his death Francis prayed for the brothers:

> God the King of all
> bless you in heaven and on earth.
> May whatever you ask worthily
> Come to pass for you.

---

4 October

Miles Coverdale's Bible was published on 4 October 1535. Miles Coverdale lived from 1488 to 1568. He was ordained, joined the Augustinian Friars at Cambridge but was there converted to Protestantism. He lived abroad to escape persecution and his translation of the Bible was the first full version of the Bible to be printed in English.

Safety chains

Miles Coverdale was fortunate to have a friend in high places. Thomas Cromwell, Secretary of State to Henry VIII, was sympathetic towards Coverdale's scheme to provide a Bible in English at long last. Coverdale based the New Testament and Pentateuch (the first five books of the Old Testament) on Tyndale's translation of 1525, then set about translating the rest himself. Unlike Tyndale, he was not a Hebrew or Greek scholar, but he could write superb English.

Cromwell then commissioned Coverdale to produce another version, and although the printing of it was banned in Paris, press, paper and compositors were shipped to England and the work completed there. The king gave his blessing to this Bible and ordered a copy to be placed in every church. It was known as the Great Bible because of its size – large enough to be used at the lectern. It was also very expensive. Parish councils did not want their precious copies stolen, so they often bought a chain and fastened the Bible to the lectern.

Psalm 23 in Coverdale's Bible

The Lorde is my shepherde, I can want nothinge. He fedeth me in a grene pasture, and ledeth me to a fresh water. He quickeneth my soule and bringeth me forthe in the waye of rightuousnes for his names sake. Though I should walke now in the valley of the shadowe of death, yet I fear no euell, for thou art with me: thy staffe and thy shepehoke coforte me.

5 October

St Francis of Assisi died in October 1226.

'Francis, repair my church'

St Francis had prostrated himself before the image of Christ on the cross in the church of San Damiano when he heard a voice saying to him, 'Francis, repair my falling house.'

Francis took this command of Christ literally, and determined to start work at once on the fabric of the church. He had no money for materials, so he filched a bale of his father's fine cloth and sold it. Not surprisingly, his father did not see things Francis's way and promptly disinherited this son who was so unfitted to follow him in the business. Francis repaired the church building, but that was only the beginning of an impetuous young man's passion for Christ. Francis was to find a different, spiritual way of restoring Christ's church which has lasted to the present day.

In September 1997 an earthquake shattered the beauty of the thirteenth century Basilica of St Francis in Assisi. Medieval frescoes by Giotto and Cimabue came crashing to the floor in clouds of dust. But the work of restoration soon began. Some of the fragments of shattered frescoes were no larger than postage stamps but they were put together again by loving and skilful hands. Computer-imaging as well as more traditional means were used to repair them. On 28 November 1999 – barely two years later – the Basilica was reopened. Crowds arrived for the opening Mass, to the triumphant strains of the Hallelujah Chorus from Handel's *Messiah*.

Cardinal Sodano, who presided, drew the comparison with St Francis's restoration in response to Christ's command. But he also reminded the congregation that ten thousand people in Umbria – made homeless by the same earthquake – were facing a third Christmas in temporary shelters. The newspapers were even blunter. One headline ran: 'Giotto is safe, but the people are not'.

'Within our hearts we must prepare a home and dwelling place for God our Lord, the almighty Father, the Son and the Holy Spirit.'
– St Francis

6 October

On 6 October 1536, **William Tyndale** was strangled at the stake, and his body afterwards burnt.

God's smuggler – to England

About 100 years had passed since Wyclif and his followers had translated the Bible into English and copied it so laboriously by hand. In the intervening years printing had been 'discovered', having been invented by the Chinese in the eleventh century. There was scope now for producing many hundreds of copies in a fraction of the time.

William Tyndale was a scholar who shared Wyclif's ideal of bringing the Bible to ordinary people in their own language. He went back to the original Hebrew Old Testament and Greek New Testament to make his translation. But the church was still bitterly opposed to an English Bible and England grew too hot for Tyndale and his unpopular views.

He fled to the Continent to finish translating and oversee printing, but enemies were constantly tracking him down. On one occasion he snatched up the precious manuscript only just in time, when the place where he stored his papers was set on fire as the result of an informer.

Once the printing was done, the New Testaments had somehow to be shipped to England. All kinds of ingenious hiding-places were devised. Wine-casks were made with false bottoms; copies were cunningly concealed inside bales of cloth. Sympathetic merchants smuggled the Testaments along with their wares. Once in England, the Testaments spread throughout the country. It looked as if Tyndale's desire that 'a boy who drives the plough in England shall know more of the Bible than many priests', might yet be realised.

Archbishop Desmond Tutu was born on 7 October 1931, educated at a Bantu high school, then gained a teacher's diploma and BA. After teaching he trained for the Anglican ministry, gained a BD at London University and worked in England as a curate. He lectured at a theological seminary in South Africa and was university chaplain. In 1975 he was appointed Dean of Johannesburg, in 1976 Bishop of Losotho and from 1975-85 served as General Secretary of the South African Council of Churches. In 1985 he was made Bishop of Johannesburg and in 1986 the first black Archbishop of Cape Town. He has been awarded numerous honorary degrees and honours as well as the Nobel Peace Prize.

Where colour counted

Desmond Tutu was nine or ten years old as he walked with his mother along the street. A white man wearing a cassock and a large black hat passed them, and as he did so, he raised his hat in greeting to Mrs Tutu. The boy could not believe that a white man would raise his hat to a black working woman. But the English priest was Trevor Huddleston, a man who was a strong influence in South Africa and in Desmond Tutu's life.

His mother was uneducated, but his father was a gentle dignified headmaster of a Bantu school. Desmond hated to see him humiliated by a white policeman or addressed as 'boy' by a slip of a salesgirl. Because of racial discrimination he said: 'You come to believe what others have determined about you, filling you with self-disgust, self-contempt and self-hatred … and you need a lot of grace to have that demon of self-hatred exorcised.'

Desmond Tutu received that grace from God. With his irrepressible wit he reduced racism to an absurdity. Suppose, he suggested, that only those with large noses, not white skin, were allowed at certain universities. With *his* large nose he would qualify.

> *Goodness is stronger than evil;*
> *love is stronger than hate;*
> *light is stronger than darkness;*
> *life is stronger than death;*
> *victory is ours through him who loved us.*
> Desmond Tutu

8 October

8 October is the Feast Day of St Bridget, who died in Rome in 1373.
Margery Kempe stayed in Rome for Bridget's canonisation in 1415.
Margery Kempe, medieval mystic, made pilgrimages to the Holy Land,
Santiago and Rome. She always dressed in white and often caused
distress to her fellow pilgrims.

The gift of tears

Was she a born exhibitionist or a very holy woman? Opinion
was divided. One of Margery's spiritual gifts was
acknowledged to be tears. In her own words she was
frequently overcome by 'vehement sobbings and great
abundance of tears'. Her fellow pilgrims found it most trying,
especially when the crying burst out at meal times. At one
time they handed her over to the papal legate with the
complaint that 'she ate no meat, would not withhold from
loud weeping and spoke ever of holiness.' She was certainly
spoiling the holiday mood.

Even her husband, John Kempe, sometimes found her
displays of fervour embarrassing. On one occasion they were
in Canterbury and her weeping had upset both monks and
priests. John could bear it no longer. He pretended not to
know her and walked quickly and quietly away. Margery was
heckled and threatened all day and at evening she stood
trembling outside the city gates, while the crowds shouted
'Take her out and burn her!'

Margery had no idea where her husband had gone nor
where he was lodging, so she prayed desperately, 'Blessed
Lord, help me and have mercy on me.' At that two handsome
young men came up and talked to her and asked where she
was staying. She only knew that it was a German man's house,
she said, but they found the way and escorted her safely there,
where she found her husband waiting for her.

Margery Kempe visited the anchoress Julian of Norwich, who
told her: *'Set all your trust in God and do not fear the talk of the
world ... Patience is necessary for you, for in that you shall keep
your soul.'*

(Source: *The Book of Margery Kempe* translated by B A Windeatt)

The **Great Fire of Chicago** raged on 8 and 9 October 1871.

'My reputation and my Bible'

It all began in Mrs O'Leary's barn. Her cow kicked over a lantern – so the story goes – and the fire began. It had been a tinder-dry summer in Chicago and since all the buildings – houses, churches, stores and factories – were made of wood, fire was a constant hazard. In fact there had been more than six hundred fires during the previous year. But the fire this Sunday evening was something different. Mrs O'Leary's cow may have started it but human error made it worse. The watchman on duty signalled the alarm to the wrong place and by the time fire fighters reached De Koven Street the fire had spread out of control. It raged for twenty-nine hours and covered seventy-three miles of streets.

The loss was terrible. Up to three hundred people were killed and 100,000 made homeless. Theatres, banks, stores, churches, hotels and railroad depots as well as ships in the Chicago River were destroyed.

D L Moody, the well-known evangelist, was woken in the middle of the night in his Chicago home, to hear the terrifying roar of the fire sweeping towards their house. He and his family hurried to find shelter. (His wife managed to save 'some few articles of dress.') Their house and church were both burned. When a friend asked Moody if he had lost all he replied, 'All but my reputation and my Bible.'

Work began five weeks after the fire to put up a temporary church-cum-school. It was one storey high and seated 1,500 people and was completed in thirty days. More than a thousand children, many with parents, came to the first meeting.

Relief flowed into the city, help coming from rival cities and even from overseas. Five million dollars arrived in relief funds. Among other gifts, 7,000 books were donated and these formed the collection for the city's first free public library.

---

10 October

On 10 June 1972 *John Betjeman* became Poet Laureate. He was a man of many and varied interests. Cornwall, landscapes, the church of England, railways and people and above all poetry and architecture were among his abiding enthusiasms and he wrote of them all with wit and perception.

No puposeless accident

He was a journalist for *The Architectural Review* as well as numerous other newspapers and magazines, he broadcast talks during World War II, wrote short stories – these were some of the bread-and-butter jobs that supported John Betjeman the poet. And whatever he said or wrote – however dry the topic might threaten to be – turned out to be interesting, amusing and free from pretence or pompousness. There is an immediate response of delight and shared recognition. His writings ring true.

From a broadcast at Christmas 1947:
'I cannot believe that I am surrounded by a purposeless accident. On a clear night I look up at the stars and ... know that the Milky Way is the rest of this universe ... I am told that some little clusters seen beyond the edges of the Milky Way... are other whole universes in outer space. It is too much, though believable. And then on any day about now, I can turn over a piece of decaying wood in our garden and see myriapods, insects and bugs, startled out of sluggish winter torpor by my motion. Each is perfectly formed and adapted to its life. From the immensity of the stars to the perfection of an insect – I cannot believe that I am surrounded by a purposeless accident.

But can I believe this most fantastic story of all, that the Maker of the stars and the centipedes, became a Baby in Bethlehem not so long ago? ... Well it's asking a lot ... but if it is not true, why was I born? And if it is true, nothing else is of so much importance ... Beyond my reason, beyond my emotions, beyond my intellect, I know that this ... story is true.'

(From *John Betjeman, Coming Home – an Anthology of Prose* by Candida Lycett Green)

George Williams, founder of the YMCA, was born on 11 October 1821.

Help for apprentices

The London drapers' shops were eye-catching. Plate glass had transformed the windows, giving large, uninterrupted displays of fashion, and the new gas-lighting illuminated the ill-lit streets and made passers-by stop and stare in. And they could go in, because shops stayed open late and service was excellent.

Drapers prospered and everyone was happy – except the apprentices. Young George Williams, up to London from his father's farm in the country, discovered at first hand what conditions were like. Apprentices not only worked long hours, but there was little for them to do, in what free time they had, except gamble and drink. Drapers provided accommodation for their own lads and often they were shepherded straight from the shop to bed and from bed to the shop, with perhaps one evening off a week for courting. They were herded together in dormitories and had no sitting-room or library. If they were ill they were given the sack.

George Williams did well and in time he was able to buy his own draper's shop. He and other Christians in the trade used to enjoy meeting together to talk and pray and they wanted to help the apprentices to do the same. On 6 June 1844 a group of twelve or fourteen men, including Williams, met 'for the purpose of forming a society the object of which is to influence young men to spread the Redeemer's Kingdom among those by whom they are surrounded.' It was the beginning of the Young Men's Christian Association – the YMCA.

12 October

Mrs C F Alexander died on 12 October 1895. Cecil Frances Alexander was the author of some of the best-known children's hymns. She wrote them to help children understand and remember basic Christian beliefs.

Hymns for little children

The fire at the school in Strabane raged pitilessly. The rescuers could see no sign of any more pupils to be pulled from the flames. But later they discovered six dead children inside the building. It was a school for handicapped children who could neither hear nor speak. So they could not shout for help nor hear the voices of those trying to rescue them but hid under their beds.

Fanny Alexander was devastated. She and her sister Anne had set up this school, touched by the plight of children who would otherwise have no chance to learn. She had always been a studious and caring young woman and when she married William, a Church of Ireland minister, there was plenty of scope for her charitable deeds. In 1867 when William became bishop of Derry and later Primate of all Ireland, life became very much more formal for Fanny; she even entertained the Prince of Wales when he visited Ireland.

But she is likely to be remembered not as a bishop's wife nor for her many kind deeds but as the author of *All things bright and beautiful, There is a green hill far away* and *Once in Royal David's City*. On Christmas Eve, when the Service of Nine Lessons and Nine Carols from King's College Cambridge is broadcast, millions of listeners watch the processional and thrill as the bell-like tones of a boy's voice pierce the stillness with those opening words. Whether we know it or not, Mrs Alexander is commemorated every Christmas.

In October 1915,(12th), *Edith Cavell* was executed by firing squad.
Edith Cavell, born in 1865, trained as a nurse and became matron of
the Berkandael Medical Institute in Brussels, a Red Cross hospital
during World War I. In 1915 she was arrested, charged with helping
Allied soldiers escape to neutral Holland, court-martialled and
executed. The night before, she wrote a farewell letter to her nurses.

Last letter of Edith Cavell

'My Dear Nurses.

'To my sorrow I have not always been able to talk to you
each privately. You know that I had my share of
burdens...

'I told you that devotion would bring you true
happiness and the thought that, before God and in your
own eyes, you have done your duty well and with a
good heart, will sustain you in trouble and face to face
with death. There are two or three of you who will recall
the little talks we had together. Do not forget them. As I
had already gone so far along life's road, I was perhaps
able to see more clearly than you, and show you the
straight path.

'One word more. Never speak evil. May I tell you,
who love your country with all my heart, that this has
been the great fault here. During these last eight years I
have seen so many sorrows which could have been
avoided or lessened if a little word had not been
breathed here and there, perhaps without evil intention,
and thus destroyed the happiness or even the life of
someone. Nurses all need to think of this, and to
cultivate a loyalty and team spirit among themselves.

'If any of you has a grievance against me, I beg you
to forgive me; I have perhaps been unjust sometimes,
but I have loved you much more than you think.

'I send my good wishes for the happiness of all my
girls, as much for those who have left the School as for
those who are still there. Thank you for the kindness you
have always shown me.

Your matron,
Edith Cavell'

14 October

William Penn was born on 14 October 1644.

The 'holy experiment'

Penn had tried in vain. It was impossible for Quakers – the Society of Friends – to gain religious tolerance in England; perhaps they could make a fresh start in a new country. Some Quakers had already settled in America so Penn approached the king with a request to buy land there which belonged to the English crown.

King Charles's answer surprised even the hopeful Penn. He insisted on giving him the charter to the whole large territory known today as Pennsylvania. In return, Penn must pay 'two beaver skins to be delivered at our castle at Windsor on the first day of January every year', and one fifth of any gold or silver mined in the province. Penn would be free to build towns and harbours, make laws, and rent and sell the land. The only thing he might not do was to declare war; but as a devout Quaker Penn was also an ardent pacifist who would have no intention of starting hostilities.

Penn began to plan what he called his 'holy experiment'. At the centre of his new land he would have a splendid city. The streets would not run higgledy-piggledy in all directions, but be laid out in neat rectangles. Houses would not be huddled miserably close together. Each would have 'ground on each side for gardens or orchards or fields, that it may be a green country town, which will never be burnt and always wholesome'.

This town of his dreams was to be called 'Philadelphia' – from two Greek words, *philia* (love) and *adelphos* (brother). Not only should his city be pleasant to live in, but if he had his way, it would be a place of brotherly love.

'In the rush and noise of life, as you have intervals, step within yourselves and be still. Wait upon God and feel his good presence; this will carry you through your day's business.' – William Penn 1644-1718

St Teresa of Avila died on 15 October 1582.

Trial by water

Teresa was no ordinary saint. She was an incredible mix of extrovert and introvert, saintly mystic and common-sense manager. Along with a propensity for organising things – and people – she had a lively sense of humour, a love of talk and laughter but also a deep sensitivity to the spiritual world and an intimate knowledge of God. She enjoyed housework and cooking and used to say: 'God walks also among the pots and pans.'

Known as 'God's Gadabout', she travelled about a good deal in her work of overseeing existing convents and founding new ones. Roads were bad and treacherous at times. Near the end of her life she was journeying with a group of sisters in severe winter conditions. Melting snow had swollen the rivers and bridges were unsafe. At one point the only way to cross a stream was to wade through it. Teresa insisted on going first to test its safety. She told the sisters that if she did not make it, they were on no account to try to rescue her, but to go back and save their own lives. She crossed successfully and the sisters followed.

One well-known story about Teresa – whether true or not – relates to this adventure. When she complained to God about the hardships they had endured he answered, 'But that is how I treat my friends.' Teresa replied, 'Yes, Lord. That is why you have so few of them!'

Prayer of St Teresa

Let us make our way
together, Lord;
wherever you go
    I must go
And through whatever you pass
there too I will pass.

16 October

Dame Rose Macaulay died in October 1958. Emilie Rose Macaulay was born in 1881 to intellectual upper-middle-class parents. She had a happy, carefree childhood in Italy, went to Oxford, lived in London and travelled a great deal. She was a witty and amusing speaker and writer. She was created a Dame Commander of the British Empire in the year that she died.

The cost of adultery

In her last novel, *The Towers of Trebizond,* (which Rose Macaulay described as 'my story') her heroine describes delightfully and most amusingly her journey – with Aunt Dot, Aunt Dot's camel and the Reverend Chantry-Pigg – to Turkey and to fabled Trebizond. Laurie, like Rose Macaulay herself, has been in a long-term relationship with a married man. 'I thought how odd it was,' she broods, 'all that love and joy and peace that flooded over me when I thought about Vere, and how it all came from what was a deep meanness in our lives, for that is what adultery is, a meanness and a stealing, a taking away from someone what should be theirs, a great selfishness, and surrounded and guarded by lies in case it should be found out. And out of this meanness and this selfishness and this lying flow love and joy and peace, beyond anything that can be imagined. And this makes a discord in the mind, the happiness and the guilt and the remorse pulling in opposite ways so that the mind and soul are torn in two, and if it goes on for years and years the discord becomes permanent, so that it will never stop.'

When Father Chantry-Pigg tries to persuade Laurie to end the relationship which has cut her off from her Christian faith, he asks, 'Shall you come back … when you will have nothing to offer to God but a burnt out fire and a fag-end? Oh, he'll take it, he'll take anything we offer. It is you who will be impoverished for ever by so poor a gift. Offer now what will cost you a great deal and you will be enriched beyond anything you can imagine.'

The first radio play was broadcast in Britain on 17 October 1922.
FEBA is an international Christian mission communicating through
radio and programme follow-up. It broadcasts – mainly from
Seychelles – to more than 40 countries and in over 55 languages.

A new beginning

Peter Shanduki had been light-fingered since he was a
schoolboy at the mission school in Zimbabwe. When he
started work in a car workshop, he had soon stolen enough
car parts to run his own business at weekends. Far from being
ashamed, stealing, for him, was 'another way of fighting white
oppression,' he explained. 'It was only a sin if you stole from a
fellow African.'

One Sunday morning Peter was at home servicing a car
and listening to the radio when a Feba service came on air,
led by Revd Gift Mabhaudi. The preacher talked about
Zaccheus, the tax collector who encountered Jesus in the
Gospel story, who had grown rich through stealing. Peter
suddenly realized, 'That's exactly what I am doing.'

He went indoors and, weeping, confessed to his wife that
he was a thief. She persuaded him to phone Gift Mabhaudi.

Next morning Peter went to his workshop manager and
told him the whole sad story. 'I am a changed man,' he said,
'Jesus Christ has changed my life. I'll bring back all the tools I
stole from you.' He went to collect them in the garage truck.

When he returned with his load the manager was waiting
with all 48 members of staff. He asked Peter to repeat his story
and his promise not to steal again. Afterwards the manager
was so impressed that he allowed Peter to keep his job.

Peter told Gift: 'That Feba programme brought me an
awareness of my sin and how I could be forgiven. Your
programme brought me a new beginning!'

18 October

18 October is the Feast Day of St Luke, the patron saint of doctors. He was a physician as well as the author of *St Luke's Gospel* and the *Book of Acts*. **Sir James Simpson** (1811-70), Scottish obstetrician and Professor of Midwifery at Edinburgh, championed the use of anaesthetic in childbirth and hospital reform.

Ahead of the times

Dr James Simpson realized that enthusiasm and persuasive pamphlets were not always enough to change the thinking of doctors and politicians. But statistics might. He was appalled at the number of patients who died as a result of being in hospital. He reckoned that the Battle of Waterloo was a safer place than an operating theatre! He also felt sure that he knew the remedy for the high death-rate. So he set about producing facts and figures to prove his case. He carefully collected evidence from records kept by hospitals throughout Britain. They supported his theory.

Patients in small cottage hospitals were far more likely to recover than those in big city infirmaries. Only one in eighty people died in the small hospitals; one in thirty died in the big ones. Simpson believed that large hospitals, with as many as fifty or sixty beds in a ward, spread disease and infection. He wanted small hospitals, with every bed kept as a separate unit.

He believed that hospitals ought not to be massive or permanent buildings. He recommended easily-built units that could be demolished and replaced regularly without great expense. If lightweight metal was used instead of bricks and cement, the framework could be dismantled and put together again on a new site every few years. In an epidemic, a hospital could be put up in a matter of days.

Simpson prescribed light, space and an abundance of fresh air for every patient. A century and a half or more later, with prefabricated buildings easily available, we have yet to benefit from Simpson's scheme. We have still to cut the rate of infection as a result of being in hospital. Sir James Simpson is still ahead of the times.

The Truth and Reconciliation Commission of South Africa
presented their Report in October 1998.

'The truth hurts but silence kills'

How can a person – and a nation – deal with wrongs and injustices in the past in order to go forward united into the future? That was the question that faced South Africa once apartheid was ended. Archbishop Tutu, who chaired the Commission, suggested the options open and the course they chose.

Some wanted to follow the pattern of the Nuremburg trials, after World War II, but Tutu had witnessed the resentment and pain they caused the German people. He recognised too that in South Africa guilty and innocent would need to make a future living together.

Others – specially those responsible for crimes under apartheid – wanted to declare a blanket amnesty. But anger and resentment would have gone on simmering beneath the surface.

South Africa chose a third way, to try to uncover truth but also to bring about reconciliation. An amnesty would be granted to those guilty of crimes if they admitted to the truth. Some who had been grievously hurt found healing just by being allowed to tell their story. Many found the generosity to forgive. Some even recognised that in a strange way the guilty ones were also victims of the vicious system of apartheid in which they had been brought up.

God of justice, mercy and peace, we long to put behind us all the pain and division of apartheid together with all the violence which ravaged our community in its name ... We pray that all those people who have been injured in either body or spirit may receive healing through the work of this Commission ... We pray too for those who may be found to have committed these crimes against their fellow human beings, that they may come to repentance and confess their guilt to almighty God and that they too may become recipients of your divine mercy and forgiveness.
– From Archbishop Tutu's prayer before the first meeting of the Commission

(From *No Future Without Forgiveness* by Desmond Tutu)

---

20 October

Christopher Wren, mathematician, astronomer and architect, was born on 20 October 1632.

'Look around you'

The Great Fire of London broke out on 2 September 1666. Only five days later, Christopher Wren presented his plans for a new London. Charles II had announced that a new city would be built in which houses would no longer be made of timber, but of more fire-resistant brick and stone. But the splendid new London which Wren envisaged, with broad streets and open squares, a fine waterfront and promenade by the River Thames, was never to be built. Objections were quickly made by the merchants and tradespeople; it would not be in their interests to have the new proposed open spaces.

But Wren had more success with his plans for St Paul's Cathedral. Before the Great Fire, he had already been asked to undertake repairs and new design work for the cathedral, whose tall spire had been damaged in a small fire nearly 100 years before. Design after design was submitted and many building difficulties overcome before the Great Thanksgiving service was held in the new cathedral at the end of 1697. Regular services began a few days later.

Wren planned a cathedral where all the congregation could *hear* what was going on. At one time services were muttered in Latin behind screens but those days were over. Now everyone wanted to be involved in the worship of God and in listening to the sermons. The acoustics of the new cathedral must allow everything to be clearly heard.

Wren's epitaph, written up in the cathedral, was composed by his son: *Si monumentum requiris, circumspice:* 'If you would see his monument, look around you.'

On 21 October 1854 *Florence Nightingale* and her nurses were travelling to the Crimea.

Lady with the lantern

When Florence Nightingale was commissioned by the government to go out to the Crimean war-front to take charge of the nursing, she found conditions too horrible to imagine. Sewers were choked, water supplies were polluted and rats were everywhere. There were shortages of everything – including food. The wounded were crammed together in filthy conditions, and those not killed in battle often died from starvation or disease caught in hospital.

Florence worked without rest, ordering supplies, organizing administration and caring personally for the wounded. She was sometimes on her knees for eight hours at a time bandaging wounds. Whenever a soldier was seen to be dying, she stayed with him to the end, easing his pains. She estimated that she witnessed 2,000 deaths during one winter. Although she was disillusioned by the selfish and heartless attitudes of many army leaders and administrators, she was full of admiration for the men whose gentleness and courage shone through the awful conditions. 'Before she came there was cursing and swearing,' one soldier said, 'but after that it was holy as a church.'

At nights Florence Nightingale went round the ward. One nurse who went with her said, 'It seemed an endless walk and one not easily forgotten. As we passed along the silence was profound; very seldom did a moan or cry from those deeply suffering fall on our ears. Miss Nightingale carried her lantern which she would set down before she bent over any of her patients.'

And this is how a soldier writing home described Florence Nightingale's influence: 'What a comfort it was to see her pass even. She would speak to one and nod and smile to as many more; we lay there by hundreds; but we could kiss her shadow as it fell and lay our heads on our pillow again content.'

22 October

Thomas Sheraton, English furniture-maker, died on 22 October 1806.

The preacher and his pulpit

'The plan of this pulpit is a regular hexagon which to me is the most beautiful and compact of all ... Fix the whole [pulpit] firm so that it may not by shaking produce a disagreeable sensation to the preacher.'

Thomas Sheraton gave those directions to country cabinet-makers who might be asked to design a pulpit, in his *Cabinet Maker and Upholsterer's Drawing Book*. He probably knew from experience the 'disagreeable sensation' experienced by a preacher using an unsafe pulpit; as well as designing and making beautiful furniture, Sheraton spent his life preaching. He made no money at either of his callings. He was brought up in Stockton-on-Tees, but moved to London for a while, where he lived in a poor street above his shop. He was described as looking like 'a worn-out Methodist minister with threadbare black coat.'

Sheraton cared very little about his own comfort. His mind was full of the furniture he designed and made and of the Christian gospel he wanted to preach – in church or in the open air. He returned to Stockton, in the North East of England, to become assistant minister at a Baptist church and he died as poor as he had lived. His furniture and his books now cost a fortune, but Sheraton declared himself content with 'a wooden-bottom chair' and 'common food and raiment wherewith to pass through life in peace.'

'Wherever the bounds of beauty, truth and goodness are advanced, there the Kingdom comes' – Donald Coggan, formerly Archbishop of Canterbury

On 23 October 1946 the United Nations General Assembly met for the first time. **Dag Hammarskjöld** was Secretary General of the United Nations. He wrote down some of his private thoughts and feelings in a journal he called *Markings*.

Signposts – to humility

'He came with his little girl. She wore her best frock. You noticed what good care she took of it. Others noticed too – idly noticed that last year it had been the best frock on another little girl. In the morning sunshine it had been festive. Now most people had gone home. The balloon-sellers were counting the day's takings. Even the sun had followed their example and retired to rest behind a cloud. So the place looked rather bleak and deserted when he came with his little girl to taste the joy of Spring and warm himself in the freshly polished Easter sun.

'But she was happy. They both were. They had learned a humility of which you still have no conception. A humility which never makes comparisons, which never rejects what there is for the sake of something "else" or "more"…'

'To be humble is not to make comparisons. Secure in its reality, the self is neither better nor worse, bigger nor smaller, than anything else in the universe…'

'There is nobody from whom you cannot learn. Before God, who speaks through all men, you are always in the bottom class of the nursery school.'

Prayer

Hallowed be thy name,
    Not mine.
Thy kingdom come,
    Not mine.
Give us peace with thee,
Peace with men,
Peace with ourselves,
And free us from all fear.

(Extracts from *Markings* by Dag Hammarskjöld)

24 October

The Treaty of Westphalia, which ended the Thirty Years War, was signed on 24 October 1648.

Peace – after thirty years

The city of Eilenberg in Saxony was crammed to capacity. The safe walls surrounding it made it an ideal sanctuary for refugees escaping the horrors of war. But as a result of the overcrowding plague broke out and thousands died. The city superintendent had conveniently gone away for a while and the other clergy had themselves died from the plague. Martin Rinkart alone was left to cope as best he could.

Sometimes he had to conduct thirty or forty funerals in one day and a day came when he had to take his own wife's funeral when she too succumbed to the plague. Plague was followed by famine and people began to die from starvation. It was a grim and bitter time but Rinkart worked tirelessly to try to bring comfort and help to those in the city.

There was great joy and celebration when the war of thirty years ended and the Peace of Westphalia was signed. Some say that Rinkart's well-known hymn was written for that occasion – it was certainly sung then. Others say that it was sung at his wife's funeral. More probably it was sung as a grace after meals during the grim days of the Thirty Years War and was widely used to give thanks for peace. Catherine Winkworth's translation of the hymn into English is the best of many versions and is still sung as a powerful reminder of God's faithfulness in good times and bad.

> *Now thank we all our God*
> *With hearts and hands and voices,*
> *Who wondrous things has done,*
> *In whom his world rejoices;*
> *Who from our mothers' arms*
> *Has blessed us on our way*
> *With countless gifts of love*
> *And still is ours today.*

The Battle of Balaclava, a major battle in the Crimean War, was fought on 25 October, 1854. *Florence Nightingale* determined to make a career out of nursing the sick, and in the 1840s she travelled Europe to study methods of nursing. She became a national hero for her courage and devotion in nursing the wounded in the Crimean War. In 1860 she set up a nurses' training school in London.

Notes on nursing

'More interesting than a novel' was one reader's comment on Miss Nightingale's new book, *Notes on Nursing*. It was soon to be the favourite coffee-table book, seen everywhere, though not everyone agreed with the author's new-fangled ideas on soap-and-water hygiene. 'That about the skin and washing and hot water. I don't believe a word of it,' one young lady confided. 'I'm quite satisfied with my skin and I don't want it better than it is.'

Florence Nightingale certainly had some very definite opinions:

Patients' needs

Patients need a bunch of flowers – a view out of the window. A pet of some kind, even a bird in a cage. Freedom from irritating noises like the rustle of a nurse's dress. Someone to understand their many fears and worries, and to guess their needs, because they are shy of asking.

Invalids' food

Milk is the most nourishing food but invalids should not be kept short of vegetables. Tea may not be nourishing but 'nothing is a substitute to the English patient for his cup of tea.'

Serve food carefully. 'Do not give too much, do not leave any food by the patient's bed. Take care nothing is spilt in the saucer.'

Women's work

Women should neither strive to do something because it is usually a man's job nor hold back from a job because it is not considered women's work. 'You want to do the thing that is good whether it is suitable for women or not.'

26 October

Alfred King of Wessex is thought to have died on 26 October 900.
Alfred was born in about 848, fourth son of Aethelwulf, King of
Wessex. Alfred successfully defended his country against the Danes;
he was also a wise legislator, a scholar, writer and devout Christian.
He longed to spread learning throughout the land and is said to
have translated part of the Bible into English.

Alfred – the Great

Alfred never expected to become king, but when his father
and two older brothers died he began to take his part in
resisting the Danish marauders. In one year alone he fought
eleven battles.

On one occasion, after he had become king, he was
celebrating Christmas at Chippenham in Wiltshire, when the
Danes, whose fleet had slipped past unnoticed, attacked and
killed many people. The *Anglo-Saxon Chronicle* tells us that
Alfred, 'with a little band made his way by wood and swamp;
after Easter he made a fort at Athelney. From that fort he kept
fighting the foe.'

Alfred was not skulking in a peasant's hut (burning the
cakes!) afraid and defeated. He was busy planning his next
campaign against the enemy. At length the two sides met in
battle and Alfred was victorious.

Today the thought of compelling an enemy to convert
to the victor's faith is shocking and repellent. But the fact
remains that if Alfred had lost that battle the strong tide of
paganism would have swept again across Britain and the
Christian faith would have been driven underground.

Prayer of King Alfred

Lord God Almighty, shaper and ruler of all creatures, we pray
for your great mercy to guide us to your will, to make our minds
steadfast, to strengthen us against temptation, to put far from
us all unrighteousness.

Shield us against our foes, seen and unseen, teach us so
that we may inwardly love you before all things with a clean
mind and clean body, for you are our maker and redeemer,
our trust and our hope.

King Alfred c848-c900

On 27 October 1682 the ship carrying **William Penn** and his
Quaker emigrants arrived in America.

Arrival of the 'Welcome'

It had been a terrible voyage, lasting two months. Nearly a
third of the original passengers had died of smallpox, which
had broken out in the cramped and unhygienic conditions
on board. Storms and lack of fresh food made matters worse.
But at last the *Welcome* sailed up-river to the Dutch settlement
of New Castle. On shore, an advance welcoming party awaited
them. There were Dutch, Swedish, English – and Indians (so-
called then). A table and chair were carried into the clearing
and quills and ink-well provided. Then the documents giving
Penn rights over the land were duly signed. The settlers
promised allegiance to their new ruler.

But the rightful possessors of the land were the native
Americans and Penn never forgot it. Previous settlers had
taken the land from them by fraud or force. If the 'Indians'
retaliated, they had been killed. But Penn insisted on treating
them with complete fairness. Although the king had granted
him full rights to the land, he recognized their prior rights and
refused to take the territory from them. The land must be
bought, and on fair terms. He would not let his agents bargain
for a low price, nor, on the other hand, would he be taken in by
any cunning demand by the native Americans for inflated
payments.

The Americans never forgot Penn's fairness and legends
about him were passed down for generations. His love of
running made him popular with them too. At thirty-eight he
could still outrun some of their 'braves'. He visited them in
their homes, unarmed and unguarded, believing that his surest
defence was 'God's spirit within the Indians' hearts'.

*'Right is right, even if everyone is against it; and wrong is wrong,
even if everyone is for it.'* – William Penn 1644-1718

28 October

Ivan Turgenev, the Russian writer, was born on 28 October 1818. Turgenev had a favourite game that he played with his friends, called 'the portrait game.' He describes it: 'I would draw five or six profiles, whatever came into – I don't say my head – into my pen; and everybody would write underneath each profile what he thought of it. Some very amusing things resulted. I have saved all these sketches and shall use some of them for future stories'.

'A face like all men's faces'

'I saw myself a youth, almost a boy, in a low-pitched wooden church. The slim wax candles gleamed, spots of red, before the old pictures of the saints. There stood before me many people, all fair-haired peasant heads. From time to time they began swaying, falling, rising again, like the ripe ears of wheat when the wind in summer passes over them. All at once a man came up from behind and stood beside me. I did not turn towards him, but I felt that the man was Christ.

'Emotion, curiosity, awe overmastered me. I made an effort and looked at my neighbour. A face like everyone's, a face like all men's faces. The eyes looked a little upward, quietly and intently; the lips closed, not compressed; the upper lip as it were resting on the other; a small beard parted in two; the hands folded and still; and the clothes on him like everyone's.

'"What sort of Christ is this?" I thought. "Such an ordinary, ordinary man. It cannot be." I turned away but I had barely turned my eyes from the ordinary man when I felt again that it was really none other than Christ standing beside me. Suddenly my heart sank and I came to myself. Only then I realized that just such a face is the face of Christ – a face like all men's faces'.

IvanTurgenev 1818-1883

At the end of October 1971, **Malcolm Worsley** completed his seventh and last prison sentence. When Malcolm Worsley left school at 15 he was drinking heavily. National Service, marriage and fatherhood failed to prevent a repeated cycle of drinking, crime and imprisonment.

'God help me...!'

Malcolm drove the stolen vehicle off the road into a lay-by, laid his head against the steering wheel and wept. He was bruised all over, his shoulder dislocated and his jaw broken. He had discharged himself from hospital, against medical advice, and was making for his home city of Bradford, knowing that the police were after him. He had tried to double-cross the violent gang he had been working with and the whole operation had ended in deep trouble for him. The rain slashed against the windscreen and the tears coursed down his cheeks. 'God help me! I'm in a mess,' he blurted out.

Once in Bradford Malcolm still felt anxious. Some of his old gang lived there; so did his mother-in-law, Margaret. He visited her and 'borrowed' her four-year-old son for company. But when he knew that the police were close on his heels, he decided to return the child to safety. In desperation he called on a local vicar.

The Reverend Max Wigley listened to Malcom's story, and reluctantly agreed to help. But when plans went awry Malcolm gave himself up. In prison he read and reread the New Testament the vicar had given him. In desperation he tried to pray: 'Dear God, Max Wigley says if I ask, you will help. I don't know who or what you are so I'm speaking to the light bulb. I don't know if this will work but I'm going to try.'

One day, instead of praying to the light bulb he knew that he was talking to God who was real, and with him in his cell. Then, for the first time, he was deeply aware of the crimes he had committed. The people he had hurt flashed before his eyes. For days he was caught up in agonies of shame. At last he submitted to God, admitted to his wrongdoing and cast himself on God's mercy. It was then that he experienced pardon, deep peace and new life.

30 October

Malcolm Worsley was at the end of his sentence and preparing to re-enter the real world as a Christian.

Back to square one?

'This will probably be my last letter to you from here [prison]. … Thank you for showing me how to become a Christian, Max. It seems such a long time since I was asking to see you in the police cells at Bradford. So much has changed for me since then. It is with much joy that I look forward to seeing you again…'

Max Wigley, the vicar who had received that letter, was waiting to meet Malcolm as he walked out of prison. (But it was not to be the last time he went 'inside'). Malcolm went first to Lindley Lodge, a Christian community where he was warmly accepted and helped in many ways to grow in Christian faith and action. Malcolm was determined to give up alcohol completely, but the urge to drink often seized him. His new friends supported him and soon he was taking the initiative in evangelism and in giving practical help to homeless and rejected people. He married Jennifer and wherever they were living, they both became involved in support and care of the abused, the homeless and the inadequate. They often worked with local social and probation staff who advised Malcolm to apply for professional training himself. Against all expectations as an ex-convict, Malcolm was offered a place and a student grant. Trouble *did* flare up when he reported at Lancaster prison for his student placement. The prison officer recognized him and utterly refused to let him in.

Malcolm survived the knocks and proved an excellent probation officer, able to empathise with the prisoners from personal experience. Eventually he was asked by the Governor of Haverigg prison, where he had been 'inside' himself, to apply for a probation officer's post there. It was unheard of for an ex-prisoner to return to the same prison with this new identity, but Malcolm got the job. The prison officer, who remembered him from other days, found it hard to hand over the keys of the prison to an ex-convict. Reluctantly he did so, and by God's grace Malcolm came full circle.

(Source: *Out of Bounds* by Judith Wigley)

31 October

On 31 October 1521 **Martin Luther** nailed his 95 Theses to the door of the Castle Church at Wittenberg, Germany.

By faith alone!

Tomorrow would be All Saints' Day – the signal for the rush to buy the indulgences that the Emperor Frederick always sold on that day. Townsfolk had only to pay the entrance fee to the Castle Church and view the holy relics on display to obtain 1,443 years remission from purgatory and total absolution for all repented sin. It was more than Martin Luther could bear.

Soon after noon, he crossed from his Augustinian cloister to the church and nailed his printed placard to the door that served as a notice-board. The *Theses* set out his arguments against the use of indulgences and attacked the church's preoccupation with wealth. He offered to have a public discussion on the subject with anyone who volunteered.

In the past, Luther too had been burdened by guilt. No penances or visits to the confessional gave him relief. On a visit to Rome he had dashed from one sacred relic to another. He had climbed on his knees the sacred staircase said to have been brought from Pilate's Palace in Jerusalem. All in vain; his fear of God and his sense of guilt remained.

It was while he was studying St Paul's Epistle to the Romans in order to teach his students, that light began to dawn. 'The just', he read, 'shall live by faith.' By faith! As he preached and taught from *Romans* the truth began to sink in. He could not *buy* indulgence from punishment or cancel out his sin by penance and good works. God's forgiveness was *freely given* in response to faith. Luther wanted the world to share the freedom and release that he had found by being put right with God through trust in Christ. He also wanted to put an end to the practice of making money for the church by selling pardons and indulgences. So he nailed his *Theses* to the door. Before long, the church had something to say in reply.

1 November

Earthquake and fire

It was All Saints Day and the churches were packed with Lisbon's prosperous citizens. Suddenly the ground shook and the foundations moved as a huge earthquake struck. For nine minutes the shocks continued. Almost three quarters of the city's fine buildings collapsed. But worse was to follow. The river Tagus receded, its waters piled up, then with mighty force the water rolled back, flooding a huge area of the city. Fire broke out and raged for six days before it was finally put out. Altogether some ten thousand people died.

Over two and a half centuries later earthquakes are still devastating cities and countries with terrible results. But the resulting deaths are not wholly 'acts of God'. Most of the deaths occur where lax authorities and money-grabbing contractors have put up shoddily built apartments, in areas that are known to be at risk from earthquakes. It is the poorest people who live in these areas who bear the brunt of the disaster.

A psalm for life's earthquakes, natural disasters, or the shocks and upheaval of national and personal events:

God is our shelter and strength
 always ready to help in time of trouble.
So we will not be afraid, even if the earth is shaken
 and the mountains fall into the ocean depths;
even if the seas roar and rage
 and the hills are shaken by the violence.
The Lord Almighty is with us; the God of Jacob is
 our refuge.

(From *Psalm 46*, GNB)

2 November

On 2 November 1953, **Chad Varrah** first offered his phone number
to anyone in despair. Chad Varrah founded the Samaritans, the
confidential phone line for all who are in distress. There are now
some 180 branches in the UK.

The befrienders

'I am being pushed around from institution to foster-home.
No place to go; nothing to want to get up in the morning for.
So I figure, why should I live, you know? As hard and as clearly
as I'm trying to look – I can't see one thing to live for.'

That was how one fourteen-year-old girl expressed her
despair and plenty of teenagers, very many boys now as well
as girls, can understand and even share her feelings. Some
find the pressures at school or college too great and are
anxious about studies or exam results. Even when suicide is
intended as a cry for help rather than a genuine attempt to
end everything, the result is final. The pain they have suffered
and the anguish to their families and friends is intolerable.

Chad Varrah, a London clergyman, recognised that the
anxious and depressed need help; but there were no help-
lines then, as there are today. So he opened a counselling
service at his church and discovered that many waiting to see
him went away feeling better for a chat with one of the
receptionists in the office. So he decided to set up a telephone
centre manned by volunteers – not psychotherapists or clergy
– people trained to listen and befriend callers in complete
confidence.

Today there is a great need for help among young people
as well as in groups most prone to suicide: farmers, doctors
and lawyers. Those in prison or awaiting trial are also high risk
and Samaritans visit many of our largest prisons and detention
centres. Those at the end of their tether can pick up a phone
and there *is* someone who will listen.

3 November

On 3 November 1978 **Delia Smith** presented her first series of cookery programmes on BBC television.

It works!

Delia comes in for a lot of flack but her fans – and there are many of them – won't hear a word against her. After all, Delia's recipes *work!* She has been criticised for being too simple. But that is just what viewers in a convenience-food society need. Delia explains procedures and guides viewers every inch of the way so that they can make one of her dishes and succeed. She also gives tips that help the most experienced cooks.

The secret of her success, Delia says, is in the testing. She tests and memorises and perfects her recipes before showing *us* how it's done. In her day-to-day life Delia admits that she relies on the Bible to get things right: 'My faith is very much based on the Word. I test everything by Scripture.'

Delia's Sticky Teabread

'It's unbelievably simple to make – it's dark and sticky and gets much better with a few days ' keeping,' she says.

150 ml water	1 tsp. bicarbonate of soda
100g sultanas	175g plain flour
150g caster sugar	1 egg
100g butter	1 tsp. baking powder

Preheat the oven to Gas Mark 4/350 F.

First grease a 1lb. loaf tin and line it with greaseproof paper, also greased. Then take a thick-based saucepan and put into it the water, sugar, sultanas, butter and bicarbonate of soda. Place the pan on medium heat, stir the ingredients together and bring them up to the boil. Then boil them for ten minutes exactly – but don't go away, watch it like a hawk, because if the temperature isn't controlled it might boil over. When the ten minutes is up remove the pan from the heat and allow the mixture to cool. Then add the beaten egg and the baking powder and sifted flour. Give it a good mix than place the mixture in the prepared tin and bake it for about one and a half hours on the middle shelf.

(Kindly donated by Delia Smith from *Frugal Food*)

4 November

Delia Smith has been nicknamed 'St Delia', but we don't connect her with fasting, as we might other saints and ascetics. **St Francis** imposed rigorous disciplines on himself but responded to the needs of others with wisdom and compassion.

The hungry friar

It was the middle of the night and St Francis and the brothers were sleeping peacefully. Suddenly the silence was broken by a loud cry: 'I am dying! I am dying!' The brothers sat bolt upright, suddenly wide awake and Francis immediately had the lamp lit and hurried across to the stricken brother.

'What is the matter?' he asked him gently, 'why should you be dying?'

'I'm dying of hunger!' he replied. Without more ado Francis had a meal prepared and when it was ready he ate with his hungry brother, so that he would not feel embarrassed eating alone. He told the other brothers to share the meal too.

When they had finished eating Francis said: 'My dear Brothers, I tell you that everyone must consider his own nature. If one of you can sustain himself with less nourishment than another, I would not have the one who needs more food imitate him. He should have regard to his own nature and allow his body what it needs, so that it is in a fit state to serve his spirit. For God requires mercy and not sacrifice.'

(Story taken from *Friar's Tuck,* the 1998 cookery book of the Society of St Francis at Alnmouth, Northumberland.)

Let everything that breathes praise the Lord!
Praise the Lord, for he is good;
let all who read this praise the Lord!

(From prayers inscribed on a wooden tablet by St Francis himself)

5 November

5 November is Bonfire Night. **Ronald Lancaster**, clergyman and retired teacher, makes fireworks and designs prestigious displays. He sees his work as an art form that brings enormous pleasure and happiness to many people. Two million people watched the largest firework display in living memory which he masterminded in 1995. It marked the fiftieth anniversary of VJ Day and was set off from barges on the Thames. Fireworks heralded the arrival of the new millennium in many countries around the world. His son, Mark, now works with him.

Licensed to make fireworks

'The whole world is watching – don't let us down!' The man from the Foreign Office whispered the words urgently to Mark Lancaster. They were at Victoria harbour in Hong Kong and Mark was masterminding the firework display at the handing over of the colony to China.

The rain was pelting down as it had been for the past five days. Would the display be utterly ruined? Mark knew now the kind of emotions his father experienced at the countdown to any big display. But Kimbolton Fireworks – and Mark Lancaster in particular – did not let them down. In fact, 8% of the total *was* lost but there were so many fireworks and the display was so magnificent and abundant that no one noticed – except Mark.

The Chinese were probably the first to make fireworks and to use them in religious ceremonies some 2,000 years ago. In some Mediterranean countries fireworks are part of Christian celebrations. In Italy they are set off after special Masses to mark the patronal festivals of local saints. In Britain bonfires and fireworks probably go back much further than the Gunpowder Plot of 1605. Country people used to celebrate All Saints' Day on 1 November with bonfires, probably adapting and continuing a pagan practice of celebrating their new year, which fell on that day. Whatever the occasion, fireworks are a beautiful, splendid and exhilarating way to celebrate.

On 6 November 1883 the last survivor of the first generation of
Pitcairn Islanders died. After putting Captain Bligh adrift in a small
boat, the *Bounty* mutineers collected women and supplies from Tahiti
then landed and set up home in the remote island of Pitcairn.

The Bounty Bibles

No one from England was likely to find them and take them
back to face hanging; Pitcairn was not even marked on sailors'
charts. But the mutineers took every precaution, butchering
the dogs on board – who might have barked and attracted
attention – and keeping a watch on the highest point of the
island for any passing shipping.

All should have been perfect for the men and their
Tahitian wives, but the idyll ended only too soon. Drunkenness,
fighting and murder erupted. Children were born and when
only two of the original men survived, one of them, Edward
Young, resolved to teach the new generation different ways.
But he was dying and his companion, John Adams, could
neither read nor write.

Young used a Bible, rescued from the *Bounty* before it
was burned, to teach Adams to read. John Adams, 'short, pitted
with smallpox and very much tattooed', himself a murderer,
not only learned to read but found that the Bible changed his
life. When Young died, Adams took on the role of father to the
whole colony. He taught the Bible to the children and became
an example of goodness and loving care. Thanks to him, the
next generation grew up to be honest and God-fearing.

John Adams' prayer

(Composed on Pitcairn island for use on 'the Lord's Day')

Suffer me not, O Lord, to waste this day in sin or folly
But let me worship you with much delight.
Teach me to know more of thee and to serve thee
Better than I have ever done before
That I may be fitter to dwell in heaven
Where thy worship and service are everlasting. Amen

7 November

On 7 November 1998 **three Christians** crossed the border from North Korea to study the Bible at a secret location in China. North Korea has been described as 'the world's last aggressively atheistic state.' Christians are publicly executed. Yet many who become Christians outside their own country, choose to return at the risk of their lives. One said: 'I want to go back and tell my fellow countrymen that the government deceived us when they told us there is no God – I have experienced Jesus and I want to tell them that.'

'Give us a thousand Bibles!'

Lee is twenty-seven years old; he and his two Christian friends hide in a bunker four metres below ground, in order to be safe from arrest – and death – in North Korea. When they crossed the border to a secret Christian centre, Lee told the story of his return to his home country. He had just become a Christian and wanted to take a Bible with him in spite of the risks. He hid his Bible inside a diary and prayed that the police would not find it. But when the police confiscated the book they seemed interested only in the diary. Lee was merely imprisoned and tortured for ten days – a light sentence – but after his release he was no longer able to work. Despite the pain, he said, he had been able to tell others the Good News.

His wife was horrified. She could not believe her ears. 'You can't possibly have become a Christian!' she exclaimed. He told her about the Bible-in-the-diary and his miraculous escape with his life and she too became a Christian. Lee started an underground Christian fellowship of seven. But many Korean Christians have no Bible. Twenty underground church leaders appealed to the secret Christian centres in China: 'Give us a thousand Bibles! We are ministering to 20,000 Christians!'

(Adapted from report in *Keston Institute Frontier*)

8 November

John Milton died on 8 November 1674. John Milton, once considered one of England's greatest poet, seems to be largely forgotten now. His most famous work – *Paradise Lost* – tells the story of Adam and Eve's idyllic existence in the Garden of Eden and their fall from grace through the wiles of the serpent, Satan.

Poet and pamphleteer

As well as writing poetry, Milton wrote pamphlets on political and religious matters. In the days before newspapers, radio or television, this was the most effective way of spreading ideas. Controversy would rage as pamphleteers published their views in hot succession. One of Milton's best-known polemics was against censorship of books and is still quoted when the press is in danger:

Innocence untried is not virtue
'I cannot praise a fugitive and cloistered virtue, unexercised and unbreathed, that never sallies out and sees her adversary but slinks out of the race where that mortal garland is to be run for, not without dust and heat. Assuredly we bring not innocence into the world, we bring impurity much rather: that which purifies us is trial, and trial is by what is contrary.'

(From *Areopagiticus*, a pamphlet against the enforced licensing and censorship of books, 1644)

9 November

Albert ('Bertie') Prince of Wales, was born on 9 November 1841. Queen Victoria spent summer on the Isle of Wight. A letter she wrote in July 1858 gives one reason why: 'London is very unhealthy on account of the dreadful state of the Thames which smells so frightful that hardly anyone can live nearby.'

Rains and drains

'Pray for a dry summer,' begged the Reverend Charles Kingsley's parishioners. But he refused.

'Shall I presume ... to ask God to alter the tides of the ocean, the form of the continents, the pace at which the earth spins round, the force, the light and speed of sun and moon? For all this, and no less I shall ask, if I ask him to alter the skies, even for a single day.'

But Kingsley had another reason for his objection. He explained in his sermons that rain was vital to clear the drains, sewers and wells and keep drinking water pure. Then, if cholera struck, it stood less chance of spreading. Kingsley was certain that cholera could be checked if drains and sewers were improved. He had been horrified to see the filthy sewers in Bermondsey, London, which were actually used for drinking water.

As a short-term measure, Kingsley organised a water-cart to take clean water round the area. He lectured and wrote articles on sanitary reform. Prince Albert, Queen Victoria's husband, was a staunch ally. When their son, Bertie, fell ill with fever, Kingsley moved near Sandringham so that he could get daily bulletins and telegraph them home, to be posted on the church door.

When the prince recovered, Kingsley preached a sermon in which he told the congregation that within a few years 2,000 people had died of fever that could have been prevented. Kingsley hoped that the publicity given to the prince's illness might bring home the need for clean water and good drains.

Martin Luther was born on 10 November 1483. He became a monk and also lectured at Wittenburg University. He did everything possible to achieve personal salvation before discovering from the Bible that God forgives and 'justifies' on the basis of faith. His preaching and writings brought him into conflict with the church – which he much regretted. One of his great achievements was to translate the Bible into German.

'My Katie'

Luther was forty-two and released from his monastic vows when he married Katherina, herself a former nun. He certainly needed a homemaker for a wife. He admitted that he had never made his bed 'from one end of the year to the other, so that finally the bed clothes and straw decayed with sweat. I never noticed. I was working so hard I simply used to fall down on it at night and know no more till morning.

Katherina grew fruit in the little orchard, kept fish in the pond, reared pigs, hens and ducks and tried to keep the house clean and tidy. But her husband still littered the house with his papers. And he invited everyone to come to stay – students, orphans, refugees.

Katie, who was a skilled nurse, often had a house full of invalids when the plague was raging. She took in women friends to have their babies at her home. She tried in vain to stop the 'Herr Doctor' from giving all their possessions away and once, at least, she succeeded. Luther wrote to a friend: 'I am sending you a beaker for a wedding present. P.S. Sorry, Katie's hidden it.'

What Luther had to say about Katie:

My Katie is in all things so obliging and pleasing to me that I would not exchange my poverty for all the riches of Croesus.'

'I would not exchange Katie for all France and Venice, because God has given her to me – and other women have worse faults.'

11 November

In 1918 armistice was signed at the eleventh hour of the eleventh day of the eleventh month. Between the two world wars, a two minute silence was observed each year at 11 o'clock on 11 November. **Remembrance Day** is now observed on the Sunday nearest to that date, although it is becoming increasingly popular to observe the two minutes' silence on 11 November at 11 o'clock.

Pleader for peace

Wilfred Owen was killed just one week before peace was declared. As well as being a soldier he was a poet, recognised now as one of the greatest of the so-called war poets. He wrote to his mother: 'I came out to help these boys – directly by leading them, indirectly by watching their sufferings that I may speak of them as well as a pleader can. I have done the first.' But he has done the second too. His poetry still pleads against the horrors of war.

In hospital on the Somme he wrote: 'Already I have comprehended a light which will never filter into the dogma of any national church: namely that one of Christ's essential commands was: Passivity at any price! Suffer dishonour and disgrace, but never resort to arms. Be bullied, be outraged, be killed; but do not kill…

'Christ is literally in "no man's land". There men often hear his voice: Greater love hath no man than this, that a man lay down his life for his friend. Is it spoken in English only and French? I do not believe so. Thus you see how pure Christianity will not fit in with pure patriotism.'

My subject is War, and the pity of War.
The poetry is in the pity.

(Owen's preface to his collection of poems)

Richard Baxter was born on 12 November 1615. He was a Puritan clergyman and lived through momentous days in England's history: the Civil War, the restoration of the monarchy, the Great Plague and Great Fire of London. He wrote over 130 books, the best-known being *The Saints' Everlasting Rest*. In a largely intolerant age, he believed in 'loving all Christians of what sort soever, that may be truly called Christians.' He suffered brutal treatment at the hands of Judge Jeffreys for alleged sedition and spent 18 months in prison.

Escape

'At seventeen years of age, as I rode out on a great unruly horse for pleasure, which was wont on a sudden to get the bit in his teeth and set on running, as I was in a field of high ground, there being on the other side a quickset hedge a very deep narrow lane about a storey's height below me, suddenly the horse got the bridle as aforesaid and set on running, and in the midst of his running unexpectedly turned aside and leaped over the top of the hedge into that deep lane. I was somewhat before him at the ground and as the mire saved me from the hurt beneath, so it pleased God that the horse never touched me, but he light with two feet on one side of me and two on the other, though the place made it marvellous how his feet could fall beside me.'

(From *The Autobiography of Richard Baxter*)

Prayer

Lord, I have nothing to do in this world but to seek and serve you; I have nothing to do with a heart and its affections but to breathe after you; I have nothing to do with my tongue and pen but to speak to you and for you and to publish your glory and your will.
– Richard Baxter 1615-1691

13 November

George Carey, 103rd Archbishop of Canterbury, was born on 13 November 1935 in Bow, East London, the eldest of five children; his father was a hospital porter. He graduated from Kings College London, later gained a doctorate and lectured at theological college. He became Bishop of Bath and Wells in 1988 and Archbishop of Canterbury in 1991.

God's calling

George Carey had not long become a Christian when he was called up in the RAF to do his National Service. Before he left his vicar told him, 'You must say your prayers every night.' But that was easier said than done. The young man imagined the ribald comments that would follow if he said his prayers in the communal sleeping quarters. But with characteristic grit he decided to kneel down by his bed and let everyone know about his new-found faith. Surprisingly, his action did not lead to heckling and insults but to interested questions. He was able to share his Christian faith with his new colleagues.

Dr Carey did not have a very easy start, as most would judge it. Although he passed the 13-plus, his parents decided against moving him from the school where he was happily settled; he left there at fifteen. He got a job as an office boy with the London Electricity Board before going at eighteen to do his National Service. By the time he went back to the Electricity Board he had decided that he wanted to be ordained. He was not deflected when a young priest told him that he would never make it. He felt convinced that God was calling him.

Without any A levels, it was a long, hard haul to reach the qualifications needed while still doing a day-time job. But he succeeded and in 1962 he graduated with a degree in divinity. The rest, as they say, is history. In many ways he might seem an unlikely person to have become 'Most Reverend and Right Honourable Dr George Carey, Archbishop of Canterbury'. But like his Master his roots are among ordinary people and like Jesus Christ, he serves and obeys God's calling with humility and love.

On 14 November 1940 **Coventry Cathedral** was destroyed in
an air raid. The new cathedral was consecrated in 1962.

Reconciliation

'Horror beyond words!' ran the newspaper headline of 15
November 1940. *'Thousands lose homes ...Cathedral among
buildings hit.'* Like other acts of destruction, perpetrated by
both sides, the bombing of Coventry might have led to
bitterness and anger. But the cathedral provost was
determined that another spirit would characterise Coventry.
The very morning after its destruction, the decision was made,
as an act of faith and hope, to build a new cathedral.

The cathedral's stonemason noticed two charred timbers
that had fallen from the medieval roof and lay across each
other, in the form of a cross. He tied them together and set
them up in the ruins of the sanctuary. Provost Howard had
the words 'Father forgive' inscribed behind the charred cross.
A local priest made another cross by binding together three
of the huge medieval nails that littered the ruins. That too
was placed in the sanctuary, on a simple stone altar. The Cross
of Nails has become a symbol of reconciliation and similar
crosses have been sent to other centres of devastation and
tragedy. The Community of the Cross of Nails was formed to
bring about reconciliation and to give towards renewal in such
places as Dresden – bombed so terribly by the Allies.

The architect, Sir Basil Spence, spoke about his feelings
when he first stood among the ruins of the old cathedral: 'I
was deeply moved. I saw the old cathedral as standing clearly
for the Sacrifice, one side of the Christian Faith, and I knew my
task was to design a new one which would stand for the
Triumph of the Resurrection ... In these few moments the idea
of the design was planted. In essence it has never changed.'
So the superb new cathedral stands alongside the ruins of
the old. Provost John Petty wrote in 1989: 'To walk from "The
Ruins" of the old Cathedral into the new building is to remind
me of the Christian message ... it is to walk from Good Friday
to Easter; from death to life.'

15 November

Johannes Kepler died on 15 November 1630. Kepler was a German astronomer. 'Kepler's Laws', which he formulated, describe the movements of the planets in the solar system. He also did important work in the field of optics.

God waits 6,000 years

In 1594, when the brilliant young astronomer Johannes Kepler was given the Chair in Astronomy at Gratz, he was expected to plot the horoscopes of the great and mighty. What we now understand as the study of stars and planets for scientific purposes was then little more than the practice of astrology. Kepler obligingly set about his predictions, relying on common sense and shrewd judgement.

Meanwhile, he was settling down to his real lifework of studying sun, moon and stars, observing and measuring how the heavenly bodies behaved. His studies and the tables of measurement he devised – using 'newfangled logarithms' – laid the foundation for the whole science of astronomy.

But Kepler was not a cold scientific calculator. He was fired with enthusiasm to discover the truth in order to restore glory to God. He wrote: 'Eighteen months ago the first dawn rose for me; three months ago the bright day; and a few days ago the full sun of a most wonderful vision; now nothing can keep me back. I have stolen the golden vessels of the Egyptians to make out of them a holy tabernacle for God. I am writing this book for my contemporaries or – what does it matter – for posterity. Has not God waited six thousand years for someone to contemplate his work with understanding?'

'When the storms are raging there is nothing nobler for us to be done than to let down the anchor of our peaceful studies into the ground of eternity.' – Letter to his son-in-law from Johannes Kepler during the Thirty Years' War

This week in 1911, on 17 November, **Ernest Lough** was born.
He died on 22 February 2000.

'Master Lough'

The year was 1927 and young Ernest Lough hurried round to the Temple Church in London from his school, only a few hundred yards away. When he arrived his heart was thumping – not just from running but from knowing that he was soon to take part in an exciting new project. *His Master's Voice* – the gramophone company – was to make one of the first electric recordings for which he was to sing Mendelssohn's *O for the Wings of a Dove*. It was one of the first times, too, that a recording had been made in a church.

Ernest admitted later that he felt 'nervous and excited' but his choirmaster, the organist George Thalben Ball, remembers only how stoically the boy survived the three-hour recording session during which he had to sing the aria again and again.

The record sold like hot cakes and six months later had to be remade because the wax on the master copy had worn out. It sold 600,000 copies in five years and is still available, transferred first to an LP and now on CD. Total sales are estimated at five million.

So famous did his voice become that for the remaining years that Ernest Lough sang as a treble soloist, tickets had to be issued for all services at the church. But even when his voice broke, Lough stayed on and was a chorister until 1970. For many people he remained the boy with the cherubic face still featured on the record sleeve and years later elderly ladies were still sending bundles of comics and sweets for 'Master Lough'.

At the start of World War II Ernest Lough joined the Fire Service and was there on duty when the Temple church was bombed. He was there too and sang baritone solos at its re-dedication by Dr Geoffrey Fisher in 1958.

HMV's claim on the record sleeve is probably true. They proudly announced that it was: 'the finest record of a boy's voice ever made.'

17 November

17 November is the Feast Day of **St Hilda**. Hilda, great-niece of King Edwin of Northumbria, was born in 614. She founded a double monastery – for men and women – at Whitby in Yorkshire, where the ruins of the abbey can still be seen. The important Synod of Whitby took place there in 664.

Celebrating together

There was a strange state of affairs at the palace in Northumbria. Queen Eanfleda was observing Palm Sunday, which meant keeping a rigorous fast, while her husband, King Oswy, was celebrating Easter in the great hall, with lavish feasting.

The reason for the royal pair being at cross purposes was that Eanfleda had been brought up in Kent and instructed to observe the Christian calendar imposed by St Augustine and his missionaries from Rome. They had landed on the Kent coast and were preaching and teaching their way through England. But King Oswy, living in the north of England, had followed the earlier way of St Columba and the Celtic missionaries. He had learned from them to keep Easter according to a different method of reckoning.

A difference in dates may seem a trifling matter but it symbolised the clash between the Celtic and Roman branches of the Christian church in Britain. A synod or church council was called at Whitby, with King Oswy himself presiding. Colman, abbot of Lindisfarne, spoke first and put forward the case for the Celtic reckoning, assuring them that he had the apostle John on his side. Wilfred of Ripon then spoke for the Roman calculation and insisted that St Peter had held his views.

King Oswy decided that it was safer to agree with St Peter, who kept the keys of heaven. So the Roman dating was accepted and the church in Britain joined Rome and Europe instead of following the Celtic way.

Alone with none but thee, my God, I journey on my way.
What need I fear, when thou art near O king of night and day?
More safe am I within thy hand than if a host did round me
*   stand.*

St Columba 521-597

Gavin Peacock, footballer, was born on 18 November 1967.
Gavin has played in over 250 league games for QPR, Gillingham,
Bournemouth, Newcastle United and Chelsea. In 1993-94, when
Chelsea was the only team to beat Manchester United twice in
the league, 1-0 in both games, Gavin scored the goal each time.

Faith in the game

It was an orange leather football and it had been presented
to Gavin's father. He had played for Charlton for seventeen
years and the ball was presented to him after a testimonial
match in his honour. He kept it but promised Gavin that it
would be his when he scored his first goal for his primary
school team.

'I can still remember it,' Gavin says, 'it was Guy Fawkes
night and the ball came across and I think I must have been in
the six yard box, but I stuck my leg out and it went in off my
knee – but it was a goal! I was delighted. The ball was mine
and I practised with it in the garden. That was a big milestone
in my mind.'

Training to be a professional footballer was all Gavin ever
thought of doing. His father never pushed him into it but he
freely admits that his father's advice and comments on his
game have been a real help. His Christian faith has helped
him too, whichever way the game is going.

'My faith runs right through my life,' he says, 'whether in
football or in my marriage or my relationships with other
people, my faith has helped me.' He prays about transfers and
is quietly sure that God will go on showing him the right way
to go when football days are done.

Hint

Gavin is naturally right-footed and his father left-footed. But
his father drummed into him the importance of being 'two-
footed'. So he practised hard with both left and right and
reckons that way he got a lot more goals.

(Source: *Christians in Sport* and an interview with Stuart Weir)

19 November

On 19 November 1863 **Abraham Lincoln** delivered his speech at Gettysburg. President Lincoln was present at Gettysburg when a cemetery was dedicated for the 3,600 Union soldiers who had died there in one of the worst battles of the Civil War. This extract is part of his famous speech on that day.

Liberty

'Fourscore and seven years ago our fathers brought forth on this continent a new nation conceived in liberty and dedicated to the proposition that all men are created equal. Now we are engaged in a great civil war testing whether that nation … can long endure. We are met on a great battlefield of that war. We have come to dedicate a portion of that field as a final resting-place for those who here gave their lives that that nation might live. It is altogether fitting and proper that we should do this. But in a larger sense we cannot dedicate, we cannot consecrate, we cannot hallow this ground. The brave men, now living and dead, who struggled here have consecrated it far above our poor power to add or detract … It is for us the living rather to be dedicated here to the unfinished work which they who fought here have thus far so nobly advanced…

'We here highly resolve that these dead shall not have died in vain, that this nation under God shall have a new birth of freedom and that government of the people, by the people, for the people, shall not perish from the earth.'

'My great concern is not whether God is on our side; my great concern is to be on God's side.' – Abraham Lincoln 1809-1865

William Cowper, poet and hymn-writer, died on 20 November 1800.

Depths of despair

Nothing gave him pleasure any more. Country walks, which had always delighted Cowper, now seemed drab and unsatisfying. He could no longer enjoy the sight of trees or wild flowers or take delight in quiet evenings by the fire. Worst of all, Cowper's happiness and joy in God had gone. He still went to church and taught Sunday School, but he did it all automatically.

In an age when no one understood as much about the workings of the mind and emotions, or knew how to treat depression and mental illness, the kindly-meant help offered by friends only made him worse. One night, after a terrifying nightmare, his quiet despair turned into raving madness. His greatest horror was his conviction that God had rejected and abandoned him.

For two years his faithful friend, Mrs Unwin, nursed him as best she could. Although she did not understand the disease that caused his madness, she persevered in gentle, kind and firm treatment until the darkness lifted and Cowper's sanity returned.

Lines Written Under the Influence of Delirium

Man disavows, and Deity disowns me,
Hell might afford my miseries a shelter;
Therefore Hell keeps her ever-hungry mouths all
    Bolted against me…
Hatred and vengeance my eternal portion,
Scarce can endure delay of execution,
Wait with impatient readiness to seize my
    Soul in a moment.

21 November

On Sunday 21 November 1999 the BBC *Songs of Praise* programme announced the hymn **How Great Thou Art** as 'top of the pops'. *How Great Thou Art* was first popularised in US and UK through the Billy Graham evangelistic team and is now top favourite of the nation.

'We sang it ninety-nine times'

The thunder rolled and echoed around the mountains in a little Carpathian village. Stuart Hine, a missionary in Eastern Europe before World War II, was visiting the village and had to shelter for the night from the violence of the storm. As he lay still, listening to the crashing thunder, he remembered the opening words of a Russian hymn he had often sung in the Ukraine. He began to translate into his mother tongue the first verse of *How Great Thou Art*.

Sometime later, he was walking through woods and forests in the mountain country of Romania when he heard a group of young Christians burst out singing that same hymn, overflowing with worship and praise for the beauty of God's creation. It was then that Stuart translated into English the second verse: *'When through the woods and forest glades I wander.*

He translated the last verse – *'When Christ shall come…'* – after World War II. Refugees were streaming into the UK, grateful for freedom and safety but still longing for their own home country. Stuart Hine wrote of the joy of Christian people when Jesus comes again to take them to their true home.

This favourite hymn has a strange history, extending over seventy years. It was first written in Swedish, translated into German, then into Russian, where it was widely known. An early translation into English didn't catch on but Stuart Hine's translation was immediately popular. A copy was given to Beverley Shea, soloist in Billy Graham's team. Bev Shea admits that over a series of meetings in New York in 1957, 'the choir joined me in singing it ninety-nine times!'

Today is St Cecilia's day. Since the sixteenth century St Cecilia has been honoured as the patron saint of musicians. The hymn voted second favourite in the BBC *Songs of Praise* 1999 poll was **Dear Lord and Father of Mankind.**

These foolish ways

John Greenleaf Whittier's life more or less spanned the nineteenth century. He was an American Quaker, a writer and poet, son of a poor farmer, but descended from one of the Pilgrim Fathers. He was largely self-educated but became a journalist and also published his first poems and stories when he was twenty-four. He devoted himself to the cause of emancipation and the abolition of slavery. By a strange irony, there was something else that he deplored – and that was hymn-singing in church.

Dear Lord and Father of Mankind was never intended as a hymn but is extracted from a long poem by Whittier, written in 1872, called *The Brewing of Soma*. Soma is an intoxicating drink made from plants. Hindu worshippers in India used it to induce a kind of intoxicated frenzy. Whittier believed that hymn-singing in church was just such an artificial method of stirring up false emotion. In fact, 'forgive our foolish ways' refers to the practice of singing emotional, rousing hymns.

It seems ironic that in 1884 an English Congregational minister should have taken the last six verses of Whittier's poem and printed them as a hymn in his new hymnal. He also changed some of the wording slightly, but the poet's original words have since been restored.

Whatever Whittier's views on hymns and hymn-singing there is no doubt that his verses, beautifully matched to their tune, continue to instil some of the tranquillity and quietness of Quaker worship to thousands of people and congregations today.

(Source: *The Penguin Book of Hymns* by Ian Bradley)

23 November

The Reverend John Flynn was born in Australia on 23 November 1880. John Flynn was ordained in 1911 and was the first superintendent of the Australia Inland Mission. In 1939 he became Moderator-General of the Presbyterian Church of Australia. It was Flynn's vision that led to the establishment of the Flying Doctor Service, whose first flight in 1927 saved a miner's life.

Accident and Emergency

The nearest neighbours 200 miles away – that's the situation for people who live in the Australian outback – an area in central Australia that is as big as the whole of Europe. In the early part of the twentieth century, farmers felt afraid to settle there because of the risk of being sick or injured when medical help was so far away.

John Flynn was concerned to bring help to the sick who were living in the outback as well as to preach the gospel to them. Setting up hospitals would be no real answer and carrying a sick person hundreds of miles over bumpy roads could be fatal. Somehow the doctors must get to them.

Most forms of transport were too slow for emergencies. Aeroplanes were the only possible answer and they were very unreliable at that time. But World War I encouraged the development of aircraft and made flying safer. John Flynn's plan began to look possible. But there was still the problem of how an SOS could be sent to the doctor. Wireless sets existed but relied on heavy and expensive batteries that needed frequent recharging so it was not feasible to issue them to all ranches. Then Traeger, a friend of Flynn's, had the brilliant idea of a radio that needed no batteries but would run on electricity, generated by pedalling with both feet. If he or she worked hard, the user could produce enough pedal-power to send a Morse message. And it would be cheap, so a set could be installed at all cattle-stations and at least one person there taught Morse – and how to pedal!

The words inscribed on John Flynn's tombstone near Alice Springs read: *'He brought gladness and rejoicing to the wilderness and solitary places'.*

Grace Darling was born on 24 November 1815. From the age of ten, Grace lived on the Longstone Lighthouse off the Northumberland coast. Her father, the lighthouse keeper, was a man of deep Christian faith. He entertained the family by playing his violin – hymns on Sundays – and reading to them from the Bible, and from the works of Bunyan, Baxter, Cowper and Milton.

The lighthouse keeper's daughter

On the morning of 7 September 1838, Grace rose and dressed quickly in her tiny room. She was used to the roar of wind and the crash of waves, but the previous night's storm had brought disaster. The *Forfarshire,* bound for Dundee from Hull, had broken up on the rocks of the Farne Islands.

Most of the sixty-three people on board had drowned, but Grace could make out a few survivors huddled on the rocks. At once she offered to row with her father in their small boat to rescue them. Her father knew that they would scarcely have enough strength to reach the rock, let alone row a boat-load back. They would have to rely on the survivors to help.

They set off on their dangerous and exhausting mission. Grace was small and slight, but she was determined. They reached the rock and Mr Darling clambered ashore, while Grace kept the boat steady in the rough sea. Four men and one woman were helped aboard, and some of the men gladly took their turn at rowing on the return journey. Once safely at the lighthouse, Mr Darling and two volunteers went back to fetch the four still remaining on the rock. All the survivors were eventually brought safely to Longstone.

Grace became a public heroine overnight, but did not live many years to enjoy fame. She died of tuberculosis at the age of twenty-seven; a plaque on the wall of a little cottage in Bamburgh – not far from the castle that was once home to the kings of Northumbria – marks the room on the mainland where she died.

25 November

Dame Lilian Baylis, manager of the Old Vic, died on 25 November 1937. Lilian Baylis was one of a large family with musical and theatrical talents. They toured South Africa as a troupe but when she became ill, Lilian came back to England and lived with her aunt Emma Cons. Together they purchased the Victoria Theatre in Waterloo Road (now the Old Vic). Lilian became manager in 1898.

'Purified entertainment'

No one could call the Victoria Theatre plush. It was situated in a rundown slum area of London for a start and the theatre itself was exceedingly scruffy. It had been a place where people went to watch cheap melodrama and to get drunk. Rats and mice scurried across the sawdust-covered floor and the seats were benches covered in oilcloth. Facilities for audience, performers and staff were pitifully inadequate.

Emma was determined that alcohol should never be served. She had seen too much of the way drunken husbands treated their wives among the slums where she worked. Both women were determined too that the entertainment provided should be wholesome and free from any coarseness or profanity. In time, Shakespeare was performed and school matinees given for local children. The aim was to devote the Vic to 'the benefit and enjoyment of the people for ever.'

Lilian worked with all her might to make the theatre a success. She willingly did anything and everything that needed doing – which once included scrubbing the stage. She raised money by every possible means and economised wherever possible. But she attributed success to God's help. She prayed about everything and would sometimes address the audience and ask them to pray too. She mixed high church practice with a colloquial and common-sense relationship with God. She once said of the Old Vic that she wanted to 'place on record our conviction that we could not have carried our work through either last season or this season without the aid of prayer.'

(Source: *Stairway to Heaven* by Mary Batchelor)

William Cowper was born on 26 November 1731.

Poems and pets

Slowly and painfully William Cowper began to emerge from the black horror of madness. But he was so shattered that he could only sit, still and numbed, unable to know happiness or feel free from the memory of horror that still troubled his mind.

One day a neighbour called; he was holding in his arms a brown, large-eyed hare. 'I thought Mr Cowper might like it,' he said, and Mr Cowper did. Others in the village were so pleased that something had at last done their friend good that William was inundated with presents of hares. He politely refused all but three – Bess, Puss and Tiny. These became his joy and constant interest. He watched their individual ways, gathering food for them and making them hutches. He was on the road to recovery.

Epitaph on a Hare

Here lies, whom hound did ne'er pursue,
Nor swifter greyhound follow,
Whose foot ne'er tainted morning dew,
Nor ear heard huntsman's halloo;

Old Tiny, surliest of his kind,
Who, nursed with tender care,
And to domestic bounds confined,
Was still a wild Jack hare ...

I kept him for his humour's sake,
For oft he would beguile
My heart of thoughts that made it ache
And force me to a smile.

William Cowper 1731-1800

27 November

The Reverend Lawrence Jenco was born on 27 November 1934. He served as a Roman Catholic priest in the United States. For twenty-five years he worked with the poor and the physically and mentally handicapped. He then travelled overseas for the Catholic Relief Services, going to Beirut in 1985. His book, written in 1995, is called *Bound to Forgive – the pilgrimage to reconciliation of a Beirut hostage.*

Unconditional forgiveness

He was chained, naked, and in solitary confinement, to the wall of a tiny cell in Beirut. He believed that it was a mistake and that he had been kidnapped in error for someone else. Father Jenco had been on his way to the doctor when he was seized, only a few months after arriving in Beirut to take up his position as Director of Catholic Relief Services.

He was held for eighteen months, often moved from one hide-out to another, and later sharing a cell with fellow-hostages. One of these, fellow-American Terry Anderson, who had given up any religion, was converted to his childhood faith through being with Father Jenco. 'He added more to my life than any other man,' he later said.

One day, a young guard, who had formerly treated Jenco with brutal contempt, came into his cell. Although Jenco did not know it then, it was the day before his release. The guard said softly, 'Dear father, can you ever forgive me?' His hostage, chained and blindfolded replied, 'Do you remember those early days? I hated you. I must ask for *your* forgiveness.'

Father Jenco's prayer

God, give me a new heart and a new spirit. You have asked me to love unconditionally. May I forgive as you have asked me to forgive, unconditionally. Then you will be my God and I will be your son.

(Acknowledgements to John Cusick who wrote the obituary in *The Independent* of 10 August 1996)

William Blake, artist and poet, was born on 28 November 1757.

Compassion

He died at the age of sixty-nine 'in a most glorious manner. He said he was going to that country he had all his life wished to see and expressed himself happy, hoping for salvation through Jesus Christ. In truth, he died as a saint.'

In spite of this gratifying account of the death-bed scene – recorded by an eighteen-year-old writer – William Blake was by no means an orthodox or conventional Christian. But he hated hypocrisy and showed genuine anger at the outrages committed against human beings and animals, especially when the perpetrators went piously to church. He bitterly opposed the brutal treatment of the little chimney-sweeps of London.

One day he witnessed a husband beating up his wife in the street and another time he saw a boy whose leg had been hobbled to a log as punishment. On both occasions he was so incensed that he physically attacked the offenders.

Blake was also loud in his condemnation of any who misused or ill-treated any of God's creatures. Many of his poems express his sentiments:

Prayer

Saviour, pour upon me thy spirit of meekness and love, annihilate the selfhood in me, be thou all my life. Guide thou my hand, which trembles exceedingly, upon the rock of ages. – William Blake 1757-1827

29 November

C S Lewis, scholar, story-teller and writer of Christian apologetics, was born on 29 November 1898. He died on 22 November 1963. Clive Staples Lewis, known to friends and family as 'Jack', was Irish-born. He taught medieval and Renaissance English literature at Oxford and Cambridge universities. His late, brief marriage to Joy Davidman has been portrayed on stage and screen in *Shadowlands*.

Surprised by joy

All his life C S Lewis experienced moments of intense and sudden joy, which came to him unexpectedly, out of the blue. His first memory of the experience was on reading Beatrix Potter's *Squirrel Nutkin* as a small child. Later, Norse myths brought the same stab of pleasure. He tried to analyse the emotion and track it down through reading and philosophy. But the more he tried to make the joy happen or even inquire into its causes, the less he knew of the genuine experience.

Lewis did not want to become a Christian, although several of his friends among *The Inklings* literary group were believers. Yet the truth of God's existence kept hammering home, and at last he admitted that God was God, describing himself as 'the most reluctant convert in all England'.

His belief in Jesus came later. 'I was driven to Whipsnade one sunny morning,' he writes. 'When we set out, I did not believe that Jesus Christ is the Son of God and when we reached the zoo I did. Yet I had not exactly spent the journey in thought. Nor in great emotion. "Emotional" is perhaps the last word we can apply to some of the most important events. It was more like when a man, after a long sleep, still lying motionless in bed, becomes aware that he is now awake.'

Lewis called the book that describes his spiritual journey *Surprised by Joy*. He recognised that the moments of joy that he had known from earliest years were in fact pointers or signposts to the perfect joy to be experienced in the presence of God.

John Bunyan, preacher and writer, was baptised on 30 November 1628. Bunyan was arrested for preaching as a Nonconformist and imprisoned several times. He was in prison when he wrote *Pilgrim's Progress*, the story of Christian's journey to the Celestial city. He sets out weighed down by the burden of his sin.

'The man that there was put to shame for me'

'Now I saw in my dream, that the highway up which Christian was to go, was fenced on either side with a Wall, and that Wall is called Salvation. Up this way, then, did burdened Christian run, but not without great difficulty, because of the load on his back.

'He ran thus, till he came at a place somewhat ascending; and upon that place stood a Cross, and a little below in the bottom, a sepulchre. So I saw in my dream, that just as Christian came up with the Cross, his burden loosed from off his shoulders, and fell from off his back; and began to tumble, and so continued to do till it came to the mouth of the sepulchre, where it fell in, and I saw it no more.

'Then was Christian glad and lightsome, and said with a merry heart, "He hath given me rest by his sorrow, and life, by his death." Then he stood still a while to look and wonder; for it was very surprising to him that the sight of the Cross should thus ease him of his burden. He looked therefore, and looked again, even till the springs that were in his head sent the waters down his cheeks…

'Then Christian gave three leaps for joy, and went on singing,

Thus far did I come loaden with my sin,
Nor could aught ease the grief that I was in,
Till I came hither. What a place is this!
Must here be the beginning of my bliss?
Must here the burden fall from off my back?
Must here the strings that bound it to me, crack?
Blest Cross! Blest Sepulchre! Blessed rather be
The man that there was put to shame for me.'

(From *Pilgrim's Progress* by John Bunyan 1628-88)

1 December

Edmund Campion was executed at Tyburn on 1 December 1581. Campion was educated at Christ's Hospital and St John's College Oxford, where he welcomed Elizabeth I on her visit there. Although he became a deacon in the Church of England, his conscience was uneasy. He fled abroad, became a Jesuit priest in Prague, and returned to England on the first Jesuit mission. He was arrested, taken to the Tower of London, tortured repeatedly and executed as a traitor.

'Your Queen and mine'

No one could have been a more loyal subject of the Queen, yet Campion had to enter his own country disguised as a jewel-merchant. He made his way to Stonor Park, a large house where the Roman Catholic owners worshipped secretly. He was smuggled in, dressed, innocently enough, as a workman, and hidden away in a tiny attic, four feet high. Here he could minister to the small groups of staunch Roman Catholics.

But it was not in Campion's nature to deceive or to lie low. He believed fiercely that true loyalty and patriotism lay in a return to Rome and papal supremacy. He eagerly wrote down the reasons for his belief. A printing press was somehow smuggled into Stonor Park and the persuasive *Ten Reasons* was printed. Four hundred copies were audaciously left on the benches of St Mary's Church in Oxford. There was an immediate hue and cry. Protestants refused to believe that any Jesuit could be a loyal patriot. He must be a spy and political traitor.

Someone gave the game away. Stonor Park was raided, the printing press discovered and Campion arrested in London. Repeated torture on the rack failed to make him give up his faith or admit to treachery. 'If our religion do make traitors, we are worthy to be condemned,' he told the Queen, 'but otherwise we are and have been as true subjects as ever the Queen had.'

On the scaffold Campion maintained his love and loyalty. 'I beseech you to have patience and suffer me to speak for my conscience. I pray for Elizabeth – your Queen and mine.'

John Brown and four of his sons were hanged at Charleston, USA, on 2 December 1859. John Brown was a direct descendant of Peter Brown, who had sailed from England in the *Mayflower*. John and his sons bent all their energies to helping slaves, organising escape routes for them to Canada. The song, *John Brown's Body*, was written not long after his death.

'His soul goes marching on'

It was the day of his execution. 'I, John Brown,' he wrote, 'am now quite certain that the crime of this guilty land will never be purged away but with blood.' He handed the letter to his guards and set out on his last journey – to the gallows. The story goes that on his way he stopped to kiss a black child. He remained firm to the end in his belief that slavery degrades humanity and contradicts the plain teaching of the Bible.

One day, he was leading a party of thirty slaves to freedom, when he was attacked by a band of men. He overpowered them and forced their leader to conduct the slaves to safety himself – on foot, because he had put a black woman and child on the leader's horse.

But John Brown's fearless tactics and ambitious plans led to arrest. He had planned to free all slaves in the state of Virginia and began by attacking the armoury at Harper's Ferry, but there he and four of his sons were arrested. At his court martial, he boasted of the slaves he had helped to safety and claimed, as he took the oath and kissed the Bible, that 'it teaches that in all things whatsoever I would that man should do to me I should do even to them.' His body may 'lie mouldering in the grave,' but for all who share his beliefs and have taken up the fight against injustice and human exploitation, 'his soul goes marching on.'

3 December

Robert Louis Stevenson died on 3 December 1894. Stevenson was born in Edinburgh but illness dogged him all his life and he travelled extensively for his health. His marriage to a divorcee, Fanny Osbourne, ten years older than he, was extremely happy and accompanied by her son, Lloyd Osbourne, they finally settled in Samoa, where Stevenson died at the age of 44. He is best known for his books *Treasure Island*, *Kidnapped* and *Dr Jekyll and Mr Hyde*.

Family prayers

Every evening, after meals and work were over, the Samoan war conch would sound on the back veranda of the Stevenson's Samoan home. It was a call not to war but to prayer. According to Samoan custom Stevenson held prayers for all their household. A little book of his prayers was published after his death, with an introduction by his widow.

One night, she tells her readers, 'the chief himself brought the service to a sudden check. As the singing stopped he rose abruptly and left the room. I hastened after him, fearing some sudden illness. "What is it?" I asked. "It is this," was the reply; "I am not yet fit to say, 'Forgive us our trespasses as we forgive those who trespass against us.'" He had just heard of the treacherous conduct of one in whom he had every reason to trust.

Prayer

Lord, behold our family here assembled. We thank thee for this place in which we dwell; for the love which unites us; for the peace accorded us this day ... Purge out of every heart the lurking grudge. Give us grace and strength to forbear and to persevere. –
Robert Louis Stevenson

4 December is the Feast Day of **St Osmund**. St Osmund died in 1099 –
just over a thousand years ago. He was nephew and chaplain to William
the Conqueror and became his Chancellor. He helped to compose the
Doomsday Book. He was later appointed Bishop of Salisbury.

Justice with mercy

In 1066 a chronicler in England wrote: 'Noble maidens were
exposed to the insults of low-born soldiers and lamented their
dishonouring by the scum of the earth.' The Bayeux tapestry
shows homes being ransacked and burned while their owners
stood by helpless. Ethnic cleansing and brutal mistreatment
of a conquered people group have been perpetrated
throughout history.

While many Normans who were given high office
dispossessed and bullied the English underdogs, Osmund set
an example by seeking peace and reconciliation with the
embittered people. When he was made Bishop of Salisbury
in 1087, he welcomed English clergy and appointed more of
them than in any other cathedral. As one of the conquering
Normans, he could have treated the English tradition with
contempt, but instead he used the same Latin form of the
liturgy that the English used and in every way tried to heal
the wounds between the two races and bring about peace
and agreement. He even adopted a past English bishop as his
patron.

Osmund brought peace and built community, showed
magnanimity to the weaker folk, treated their traditions and
heroes with respect and welcomed them as fellow workers.
There is a Latin inscription in Salisbury Cathedral which fits
him well: 'They weep today in Salisbury for he is dead who
was the sword of justice and father of Salisbury's Church. While
he lived he cherished the unfortunate and did not fear the
pride of the great.'

(Source: Article by Canon June Osborne, 1999)

5 December

5 December is the Feast Day of **St Birinus**. He died in about 650.
St Birinus came to England from Rome and stayed as a
missionary among the people of Wessex. In about 650 he
established a Saxon Minster on the site of what is now the Priory
Church at Christchurch in Dorset.

The unknown carpenter

Visitors to the Priory Church in Christchurch can gaze up at a
beam, high in an archway, which is known as the Miraculous
Beam.

Tradition has it that Flambard – a Norman bishop –
planned to build his new priory on St Catherine's Hill, about
two miles from where the present priory stands. But although
workmen trudged up the hill every day, carrying precious
building materials, next morning everything had vanished.
Later the materials were found stacked on the site where the
Priory now stands.

At last they decided that some divine purpose was at
work; they would build the Priory on the site chosen for them.
So they began to build, and as they worked they noticed
another workman, who shared their labours but never drew
pay or shared their meals.

At last, the church was nearly finished. Only the key beam
that would hold up the roof was needed. The workmen
measured and cut the timber, then tired but triumphant,
prepared to lift the beam into place. But to their bitter
disappointment, it was too short by several inches. Night was
falling, so disappointed and dispirited, they lowered the beam
to the ground and went home. Next morning they would have
to begin afresh.

But when next morning came, they discovered the beam
already in place, a perfect fit. Only the mysterious workman
was missing, never to be seen again.

'It was Christ, the carpenter!' they said in awed whispers.
'He was the unknown workman who helped us all the way
and made the beam fit!'

So the church became known as Christ's Church and the
place itself, once known as Twynam (the town 'between the
waters') became Christchurch, as it is today.

6 December

6 December is **St Nicholas'** s Day. St Nicholas has always been popular, the patron saint of children, sailors, merchants and pawnbrokers. He is reputed to have done many wonderful things, including bringing back to life three murdered children hidden in a brine tub. The only hard fact known about him is that he was Bishop of Myra, in Asia Minor, in the fourth century.

Believing in Santa Claus

St Nicholas has always been linked with giving presents. According to legend, Nicholas heard of the misfortune of three girls whose father had no money to give them dowries and so find them husbands. To save them from a life of prostitution, Nicholas determined to provide them with the money they needed. But so that no one would know about his generosity, he threw three bags of gold into their window at night.

So presents were given to children on St Nicholas's Day – and still are in some countries. But more often now, it is Christmas Day that is associated with present-giving, and St Nicholas has been transformed into Santa Claus. It was Dutch settlers in the United States who took with them the stories and customs associated with Sinte Klaas – the Dutch dialect form of his name.

In the sixteenth century, following the Reformation, saints went out of favour in Europe. But someone was needed to take the place of St Nicholas and give presents at Christmas, so in England a merry old character from early plays, known as Father Christmas, took over the part. By one means or another, present-giving characterises the season of God's gift in the coming of Jesus to our world.

Present-day letter to Santa Claus:
> Dear Santa Claus
> My name is Robert. I am six years old. I want a rifle, a pistol, a machine gun, bullets, a hand grenade, dynamite and tear gas. I am planning a surprise for my big brother.
> Your friend
> Robert.

7 December

In the first few days of December 1857, *George Muller* faced a problem. The central heating system in his orphanage in Bristol needed major repairs.

The wind of change

One thing was certain. They wouldn't get through the winter without doing something about the troublesome boiler. The brickwork must be dismantled, then the cause of the leak discovered and the damage repaired. It could take several days. Meanwhile, the children would be without any kind of heating. Muller decided that he must go ahead with the work – and trust God.

No sooner had he arranged for workmen to begin work the following Wednesday, than the north wind began to blow. Bitterly cold weather set in. He decided to ask God for two things. First, he prayed that the wind would change from north to south; second he asked God that the workmen would 'work with a will'.

All weekend the north wind blew. On Tuesday it was still blowing. By Wednesday morning it had veered round completely and blew softly from the south. An unexpectedly mild spell of weather took over as they let the huge boiler go out. The children scarcely noticed any drop in temperature.

The workmen arrived, the bricks were pulled out and to their great relief the cause of the trouble was quickly located. Repairs began. That evening Muller went to see the foreman. 'They will work late this evening,' he promised Muller in the men's hearing, 'and again tomorrow.' Then the plumber said, 'We would rather work all through tonight and get the work done.'

Muller wrote in his journal: 'I remembered the second part of my prayer, that God would give the men a mind to work. Thus it was: by the morning the repair was accomplished, the leak was stopped, though with great difficulty, and within about thirty hours the brickwork was up again and the fire in the boiler; and all the time the south wind blew so mildly that there was not the least need of a fire.'

8 December

Lesslie Newbigin was born on 8 December 1909. He died in January 1998. After graduating from Cambridge, Lesslie Newbigin worked on the staff of the Student Christian Movement, then went as a missionary to India, becoming Bishop of Madras in 1965. In the UK he lectured in theology and was Moderator of the General Assembly of the United Reformed Church. After retiring in 1983 he continued writing.

Christ and the Cross

Lesslie Newbigin went up to Cambridge an agnostic, but in his first year he was deeply impressed by a fellow student who was a Christian. Then, at nineteen, he spent his summer vacation in Wales, at a Quaker centre that provided recreation for unemployed miners. Lesslie saw at first hand the bleakness and hopelessness of the coal-mining community at that time. One night, as he lay in bed, overwhelmed with concern for these men, he had a vision. He saw the cross touching both heaven and earth, embracing the whole world and the whole of life. His conversion resulted from this experience and Jesus Christ and his cross remained central to his faith and his life.

Newbigin combined tolerance and sensitive understanding of others with an unshaken faith in the truth revealed in Christ. He was not an ivory tower theologian but a pastor and preacher who thought as he worked and spoke or wrote about theological questions only when he was specifically asked. He emphasised the need to make the Christian faith relevant to the culture in which it is preached, not to import a western-style faith with all its accretions. In his own western culture he helped the church to see the need to adapt the form in which the gospel is preached to new attitudes and values. But he still believed that it is not possible to arrive at the existence of God by human argument or discovery.

As Christians tell their story, he said, they must expect people to ask, 'Why should I believe your story?' The Christian must make the story as credible as possible, but beyond that he or she can only say, 'It is not my story or invitation, it is an invitation from the one who loved you and gave himself up for you.'

9 December

Jonathan Dodgson Carr, founder of Carr's Biscuits, was born on 9 December 1806. J D, as he was always known, was born into a Quaker family in Kendal. He was a very strong but gentle person, hard-working and peace-loving. His father was a wholesale grocer. Instead of entering his father's business, J D apprenticed himself to a baker then later set off for Carlisle to set up his own shop and factory.

'Be Just and Fear Not'

He was normally gentle and unruffled but some things made J D angry and he was very angry about the government's Corn Laws. Now just a fact of history and politics, in practice these laws kept the price of bread artificially high and cruelly prevented the poorest people from buying their staple diet.

J D was scrupulously honest and fair. He was also, as a Quaker, against violence of any kind. But he was determined to do all in his power to get the Corn Laws repealed. As well as leading the Carlisle branch of the Anti-Corn Law League, he took more positive action to make the iniquitous effects of the laws known. He put two sets of loaves in the window of his baker's shop – the shop that everyone passed. Both kinds of loaf were selling for the same price, but the very small ones had a notice in front saying 'taxed'. The large loaves were marked 'untaxed.'

Rather more daring for a sober-dressed Quaker, J D had a fancy waistcoat made. It was of rich brown velvet with a lighter design of wheat ears and a large embroidered FREE on it. Wearing this, he advertised the cause wherever he went.

In 1842 the figures for poverty in Carlisle were grim – 5,561 out of a population of 22,000 were at starvation point. J D organised a huge meeting of the Anti-Corn Law League, addressed by John Bright and Richard Cobden.

Success came not long after and J D's workforce threw a party for him in the packing room. The room was brightly decorated and over the chair set aside for J D Carr was a banner reading: Be Just and Fear Not.

(Source: *Rich Desserts and Captain's Thin* by Margaret Forster)

10 December

In this week in 1773, on 16 December, the **Boston Tea Party** took place. In 1773 the British parliament allowed the East India Company to sell tea in the colonies without paying taxes. This meant that they could undercut the American merchants. The colonists boycotted tea and finally boarded three East India Company ships in Boston harbour and threw overboard enough to make 24,000,000 cups of tea! The incident – known as the Boston Tea Party – sparked off events which finally led to the American War of Independence.

Tea and sympathy

According to legend, tea has been known in China since 2,700 BCE. It was widely available in England by the eighteenth century but opinion was divided then, as now, as to whether tea is good for us. In 1756 Jonas Hanway wrote an *Essay on Tea* in which he claimed: 'men seem to lose their stature and comeliness, women their beauty through the use of tea.' Dr Johnson was indignant and wrote a review defending tea vigorously. Boswell comments: 'I suppose no person ever enjoyed with more relish the infusion of that fragrant leaf than Johnson.' Hanway replied angrily to Johnson's review and Johnson wrote again – the only occasion, Boswell commented, when he 'condescended to oppose anything that was written against him.'

Johnson described himself in his review as: 'A hardened and shameless tea-drinker, who has for twenty years diluted his meals with only the infusion of this fascinating plant; whose kettle has scarcely time to cool; who with tea amuses the evening; with tea solaces the midnight, and with tea welcomes the morning.'

William Cowper shared Johnson's enjoyment of tea and company. He wrote *The Winter Evening*:

Now stir the fire and close the shutters fast,

Let fall the curtains, wheel the sofa round,

And, while the bubbling and loud-hissing urn

Throws up a steamy column, and the cups

That cheer, but not inebriate, wait on each,

So let us welcome peaceful evening in.

11 December

Alexander Solzhenitsyn, Russian writer and dissident, was born on 11 December 1918.

Telling the world

Solzhenitsyn was in a world of his own. He was writing in his little wooden shack in the country. It had no running water, gas or electricity and was often flooded by the river, swollen in winter. But in summer it was an ideal place for Solzhenitsyn to write undisturbed.

But on this September day in 1965 he *was* disturbed. A friend and staunch supporter of his arrived, ashen-faced, to tell him that the three copies of his new book had been seized by the authorities. When he returned home he found that other incriminating manuscripts had been found and taken.

Solzhenitsyn lay low at a friend's dacha. He wrote: 'I strolled for hours through dark cloisters of pine-trees ... with a heart empty of hope vainly trying to comprehend my situation and, more important, to discover some higher sense in the disaster that had befallen me.'

Solzhenitsyn was mortally afraid that his exposé of the camps would never reach the outside world and he felt desperately depressed. But he was smuggled into Estonia where he could hide and continue writing for a while. Then, back in Russia, he encountered Olga Carlisle in 1967. She was a Russian painter and journalist, married to an American and visiting Moscow. At the end of the evening Solzhenitsyn escorted her to her hotel, steadying her on the icy streets. Then he told her: 'I want you to see to the publication of *The First Circle* in the West.'

'I'll do my best,' she replied sombrely and she was as good as her word.

(Source: *Alexander Solzhenitsyn, a Century in his Life* by D M Thomas)

'If only there were evil people somewhere ... and it were necessary only to separate them from the rest of us and destroy them. But the line dividing good and evil cuts through the heart of every human being. And who is willing to destroy a piece of his own heart?' – Alexander Solzhenitsyn

Tomorrow, 13 December, is celebrated in Sweden as **St Lucy**'s Day.

Festival of light

In Sweden a pagan festival, held on what according to the old calendar was the darkest night of the year, was transformed long ago into the feast of St Lucy. The monks who brought the gospel to Sweden brought the story of St Lucia too. According to legend, Lucia was a Christian girl living during the persecution of the Roman Emperor Diocletian, who brought food to Christians hiding in the catacombs of Rome. She wore lights on her head to leave her hands free. She was said to have been denounced by her rejected suitor and finally killed with a sword-thrust to her throat.

In Sweden and in the United States where Swedish immigrants have brought the custom, St Lucy's Day begins in the morning. The girl in the family chosen to be Lucy, gets up early, dresses in a white gown with a red sash and arranges a crown of green leaves on her head, with white candles attached. (Electric candles are often used nowadays for safety.) Then she carries a tray of coffee and saffron buns to the rest of the family still in bed, and sings them a song about the coming of St Lucy.

Recipe for Pepparkakor biscuits

These Swedish ginger snaps can be hung on the Christmas tree.

400g sifted flour	230g butter or margarine
1 teaspoonful bicarbonate of soda	230g soft dark brown
1.5 teaspoons of ground ginger,	sugar
ground cloves and cinnamon	2 egg whites

Sift flour, spices and soda. Cream butter and sugar until fluffy, then beat in egg whites. Slowly work in dry ingredients. Wrap and chill for 12 hours. Roll out dough to .5 centimetre thick on lightly floured board. Cut into fancy shapes. Place on ungreased baking sheet, leaving space between. Cook in preheated oven (350 C, Gas Regulo 4) for 10-12 minutes, until brown round edge. Cool on wire rack. Icing, using egg white, may be piped in patterns on cooled biscuits.

13 December

Dr Samuel Johnson, writer and lexicographer, died on 13 December 1784.

'Quite composed'

There was no doubt about it, Samuel Johnson was afraid of death. In 1777, when Johnson was sixty-eight, James Boswell wrote: 'It appears from his *Prayers and Meditations,* that Johnson suffered much from a state of mind "unsettled and perplexed," and from that constitutional gloom, which, together with his extreme humility and anxiety with regard to his religious state, made him contemplate himself through too dark and unfavourable a medium. It may be said of him that he "saw God in clouds". Certain we may be of his injustice to himself in the following lamentable paragraph …"When I survey my past life, I discover nothing but a barren waste of time, with some disorders of body, and disturbances of the mind, very near to madness, which I hope He that made me will suffer to extenuate many faults, and excusing many deficiencies."'

But in 1784, just before Johnson's death, Boswell was assured that 'after being in much agitation, Johnson became quite composed, and continued so till his death.'

Before receiving communion in his apartment, he 'composed and fervently uttered this prayer':

Almighty and most merciful Father, I am now, as it seems, to commemorate for the last time, the death of thy Son Jesus Christ, our Saviour and Redeemer. Grant, O Lord, that my whole hope and confidence may be in his merits, and thy mercy … Have mercy upon me, and pardon the multitude of my offences. Bless my friends; have mercy upon all men. Support me, by thy Holy Spirit, in the days of weakness, and at the hour of death; and receive me, at my death, to everlasting happiness, for the sake of Jesus Christ. Amen

14 December

Prince Albert, Consort to Queen Victoria, died on 14 December 1861.
'I am only the husband,' Prince Albert told a friend, 'and not the master
of the house.' But Queen Victoria adored him and his influence was
great. She was only forty-two when he died; her grief, her mourning
and her withdrawal from public life lasted for years.

'No more than 'a feverish cold'?

'God have mercy on us! If anything serious should ever
happen to him, he will die.' The speaker was Stockmar, German
doctor and mentor to Prince Albert. He recognised signs of
illness on Albert's last visit to Coburg. The prince himself
seemed to have some premonition of the end. He was in an
accident, and had leaped from his coach when the horses
panicked and tore off. He told his daughter Vicky that his last
hour had come.

Albert's death was attributed to typhoid – or gastric fever
as it was euphemistically called – but some now think that he
had been suffering for some time from stomach cancer. The
doctors said that the Prince should be told that he had no
more than 'a feverish cold' but he told his daughter, ' I am
dying.'

During his last days and hours, Albert frequently repeated
the words of Toplady's hymn, *Rock of Ages*. He commented: 'If
in this hour I had only my worldly honours and dignity to
depend upon, I should be poor indeed.'

> Rock of Ages, cleft for me,
> Let me hide myself in thee.
> Let the water and the blood
> From thy riven side which flowed
> Be of sin the double cure,
> Cleanse me from its guilt and power.
>
> Not the labours of my hands
> Can fulfil thy law's demands;
> Could my zeal no respite know
> Could my tears for ever flow,
> All for sin could not atone
> Thou must save and thou alone

15 December

Remembering friends at Christmas

It the early years of Queen Victoria's reign children would have made their own 'Christmas piece' – a piece of paper with special heading and borders – on which they carefully inscribed, in best copper-plate writing, greetings to their family. But in the mid nineteenth century commercial Christmas cards began to appear.

Sir Henry Cole was an English designer, writer and civil servant with characteristic Victorian energy and creativeness. He planned and largely organized the Great Exhibition of 1851, under the patronage of Prince Albert. He was a resourceful assistant keeper at the Public Records Office, introduced the penny post and invented the adhesive stamp. Under the pseudonym 'Felix Summerley' he set up a firm for what he called 'art manufacture' and as well as publishing children's books, he published the first Christmas card in 1843. His artist friend, John Horsley, designed it and it sold for the princely sum of one shilling. Another card of about the same date is now preserved in the British Museum.

Christmas cards did not catch on until cheap postage and newly invented printing methods made them less expensive to buy and send. By the end of the nineteenth century they were being cheaply produced all over Europe. A printer in Boston also made cards with scenes of Jesus' birth.

Christmas cards with a wintry landscape and a stage-coach plunging through thick snow, is thought to be a reminder of an otherwise long forgotten winter. In 1836 there was a terrible snowstorm in England and mail-coaches were held up or caught in drifts. That winter lingered in folk memory and snow at Christmas is still regarded as a fit setting for the celebrations.

More and more people complain about the effort and expense of sending cards. But they link us with people we no longer see and might otherwise lose touch with altogether – friends and relatives to whom we still owe a debt of love and friendship. And 'charity cards' give us the opportunity too, to give to others in need at Christmas.

16 December

Jane Austen, novelist, was born on 16 December 1775. Emma Woodhouse, is 'clever, handsome and rich'. Through her own painful mistakes and misapprehensions, she grows up in the course of the novel.

Faithful wounds of a friend

During a picnic outing to Box Hill, handsome young Frank Churchill announces:

"'Ladies and gentlemen, ... Miss Woodhouse ... demands from each of you either one thing very clever ... or two things moderately clever or three things very dull indeed, and she engages to laugh heartily at them all."

"'Oh! Very well," exclaimed Miss Bates, "then I need not be uneasy. 'Three things very dull indeed.' That will just do for me, you know. I shall be sure to say three dull things as soon as I open my mouth, shan't I? – Do not you think I shall?"

'Emma could not resist.

"'Ah! ma'am, but there may be a difficulty. Pardon me – but you will be limited as to number – only three at once."

'Miss Bates ... did not immediately catch her meaning; but, when it burst on her a slight blush showed that it could pain her.'

Later, Mr Knightley has Emma on her own:

"'Emma ... how could you be so unfeeling to Miss Bates? ... I had not thought it possible."

'Emma recollected, blushed, was sorry, but tried to laugh it off ... "It was not so very bad. I daresay she did not understand me."

"'I assure you she did. She felt your full meaning ... Were she your equal in situation – but, Emma, consider how far this is from the case. She is poor; she has sunk from the comforts she was born to ... Her situation should secure your compassion ... It was badly done ... This is not pleasant to you, Emma – and it is far from pleasant to me; but I must, I will, – I will tell you truths while I can, satisfied with proving myself your friend by very faithful counsel."'

(From *Emma* by Jane Austen)

17 December

Thomas Guy died on 17 December 1724. He was born in 1644, the son of a lighterman and coal-dealer in Southwark, London. He was apprenticed to a bookseller before setting up in business himself. He dealt mainly in Bibles and at first imported most of them from Holland. Later, he obtained the right from Oxford University to print them himself. He made an immense fortune both from his business and his shrewd investments. He paid for the building of Guy's Hospital in London.

Poor little rich man

It was evening when Thomas Guy's visitor arrived. He came to the little shop where Guy could be seen any day eating a dry crust at mealtimes and working at all other hours. But his visitor knew that despite appearances Guy was a rich man. He told him that he had come to ask the secret of his success in making money. Guy did not take offence but suggested that they should talk in the dark to save the cost of candles.

Thomas Guy looked so badly off that once, as he stood looking over London Bridge he was mistaken for a down-and-out and offered money by a kind passer-by. Yet when he died he left huge amounts of money for the upkeep of almshouses and hospitals – and still there was £80,000 left to be shared among relatives and friends. Guy realised that the nearby St Thomas's hospital was badly overcrowded and had begun by paying to have three new wards added to it. But he knew that there was still too little help for the sick and poor around him, so he paid for a brand new hospital at a cost of £18,793 16s – an enormous sum at that time.

Thomas Guy had no wife or children so it was only his own creature comforts that he neglected. Some might consider he was mean, but others would judge him the most generous man of his time.

18 December

Dorothy Sayers, scholar, playwright and detective writer, died on 18 December 1957. She was the only child of older parents, her father a clergyman, scholar and teacher. As well as writing detective novels and Christian apologetics, she translated Dante's *Divine Comedy*.

Advertising truth

'If he can say as you can,
Guinness is good for you
How grand to be a Toucan
Just think what Toucan do!'

Large hoardings, emblazoned with a colourful toucan and a glass of Guinness accompanied Dorothy Sayers' verse, part of a series of witty advertisements that she wrote in the thirties. She worked at an advertising agency until she could afford to live by her writing. One of her best detective novels – *Murder Must Advertise* – is set in the advertising world she knew so well.

During World War II Dorothy Sayers gained popularity, and notoriety too, for the cycle of plays she wrote for radio – *The Man Born to be King*. Few people today would find them shocking, but church people brought up in the tradition of the King James' version of the Bible and stained-glass window representations of Jesus, were horrified by what they regarded as the 'blasphemy' of the play's colloquial English and the fact that an actor impersonated the voice of Jesus. But the plays brought the story of Jesus alive for the first time for many listeners.

'God was executed by people painfully like us, in a society very similar to our own. He was executed by a corrupt church, a timid politician and a fickle proletariat led by professional agitators. His executioners made vulgar jokes about him … and hanged him on the common gibbet – a bloody, dusty, sweaty and sordid business. If you show people that, they are shocked. So they should be. It is curious that people who are filled with horrified indignation when a cat kills a sparrow can hear the story of the killing of God told Sunday after Sunday and not experience any shock at all.'

(Dorothy Sayers' introduction to *The Man Born to be King*)

19 December

In the year 1652 **Christmas Day** in England was officially cancelled. 25 December has always been a day for celebration, perhaps to mark the darkness and death of the old year and to encourage the birth of light and the new year – or perhaps because people in the northern hemisphere need some kind of half-way merry-making in order to endure the entire winter. In Britain, early missionaries transformed the pagan rites of Yuletide by designating 25 December as the birthday of Jesus Christ.

Christmas is cancelled!

In 1652, during the Commonwealth, the Puritans ruled the country and they strongly disapproved of keeping any day special – except Sunday, 'the Lord's Day.' So they passed an act of parliament to cancel Christmas 1652, and to show that they meant it, they decided that parliament would sit just as on any other day of the year. Everything connected with Christmas was banned – from mince-pies to church attendance.

John Evelyn, the diarist, defied the ban and went to church with his wife. He records what happened. As they were receiving communion a party of musketeers broke in. They waited till the service was over, then arrested the worshippers. They soon let them go again, unsure how to punish people for going to church.

No one is likely to cancel Christmas again, but perhaps for many people the real Christmas *is* cancelled. A 1999 On Digital survey showed that many young people know more about characters on television than they do about the Nativity. Among under-30s, twenty-eight per cent could name the gifts of gold, frankincense and myrrh brought by the wise men to Jesus, while sixty-four per cent knew the name of the television detective who drives a red Jaguar. One in twenty wanted to go to church at Christmas, while one in four wanted to watch television.

I have often thought, said Sir Roger, it happens very well that Christmas should fall out in the middle of winter. – Joseph Addison 1672-1719

At this time airports, ferries, railway stations and motorways are crowded as travellers go away or come home for **Christmas**.

Emergency service

A major incident could happen at any time. A train could be derailed, a plane crash land, or there could be a pile-up on the motorway. We prefer not to imagine such catastrophes, but the emergency services must be constantly prepared.

In some areas, as well as the police, ambulance and fire services, a fourth emergency service is trained and waiting – a team of clergy and ministers of religion.

Father John Herve is an Anglican vicar with a parish on the outskirts of Birmingham. For some years he was an army padré, now he is the co-ordinator of the Birmingham Major Incident Team, which includes representatives of all the main Christian denominations, and of the Jewish, Muslim, Sikh and Hindu faiths. They can be mobilised from the police major incident room. Father John Herve organises regular training sessions, run by the army. All thirty of the team are issued with distinctive fluorescent tabards and are given advice: 'Wear suitable clothing for many hours in the open. Wear clerical collar and tabard if you have one. Take wellington boots and a torch, and suitable items like the Bible and oil.'

But the training is about more than practical advice. Father Herve, who has a post-graduate degree in pastoral studies, knows the need to respond to victims and their families in a sensitive and suitable way. People in shock or emotional distress must not be exploited, but cries for help must be heard and responded to. Ministers may be asked to pass on messages or listen to a person's regrets for past wrongs. They may hold a victim's hand or put up with being shouted at. They support and accompany casualties until they arrive at the hospital, when the hospital chaplains take over.

'I'm not trying to spread gloom and doom,' Father Herve says, 'but we're not talking about "if" but "when". We'll only get one shot and we'll have to be ready.'

21 December

Remembering young and old

There are many legends about Thomas' experiences, after the time of Jesus' life, death and resurrection. An ancient tradition tells how he took the gospel to India and for many centuries the Christians in Kerala have called themselves 'St Thomas Christians'.

St Thomas was made the patron saint of old people and of children. In bygone years both groups of people were allowed to go 'a-Thomasing' on 21 December, collecting money to buy their Christmas dinner.

One contemporary way of giving to people in need is through a Christingle service. No one is sure of the origins of this popular service for children and families which was revived by John Pensom, of the Church of England Children's Society, some thirty years ago. Christingle means Christ-Light and celebrates the coming of Christ, the Light, into our world. Gifts of money are presented, then Christingles are given to the children, and carols are sung by the light of the candles.

To make a Christingle

You need: *An orange (= the world); a candle(=Jesus, the light of the world); red band(= the blood of Christ, shed for the world); 4 cocktail sticks (= the four seasons); nuts and fruit (= the fruits of the earth)*

1. Make a hole for the candle in the top of the orange.
2. Fasten a band of red round the middle of the orange(flame-proof crêpe paper or tape from a cycle shop).
3. Place a square of aluminium foil, about 20cms square, round the bottom of the candle. This acts as a shield and catches grease.
4. Put the candle firmly in the hole in the orange, making sure it is kept upright.
5. Add four cocktail sticks (goose quills were once used) on which are put raisins, glacé cherries and nuts.

The American evangelist, **D L Moody**, died on 22 December 1899. Dwight Lyman Moody was only four when his father, a stonemason, died suddenly, leaving his mother with seven children; a month later twins were born to her. Young Moody was not a keen scholar, preferring 'fun and frolic'. When he was seventeen he left home and sought out his uncle in Boston.

'World-famed evangelist'

Moody's uncle was no easy touch. He had heard enough about his nephew's wild ways not to employ him right away in his boot and shoe store. He waited till the lad ran out of money, then offered him a job along with plenty of good advice and some strict instructions about his behaviour out of working hours. One condition was that the young man should attend Mount Vernon Church and Sunday School. Moody agreed – he was at his wits' end – and within three months had sold more boots and shoes than any other salesperson. He had also begun to go to the church. 'One day Mr Kimball, his teacher, called upon him at his place of business and, putting his hand kindly on his shoulder, asked him if he would not give his heart to Christ.' Soon after, Moody's Christian life began.

He moved to Chicago where he had the same outstanding success selling boots and shoes. But he was itching to 'sell' his faith and after some time he opened a mission in rented accommodation, which soon became too small for the numbers attending. When he was twenty-two Moody resigned from business to become an evangelist full-time, vowing to rely on God entirely for money.

In 1873 Moody felt strongly that he should preach again in Britain. He announced his plans and prepared for the journey although he had no money to pay the passage. He still refused to ask anyone but God. Hours before they were due to leave, a friend, who knew nothing of his dilemma, called to say good-bye and pressed 500 dollars into Moody's hand. The family travelled as planned and huge numbers in Britain were converted.

(From the obituary in *The Christian Herald* of 4 January 1900)

23 December

According to legend, it was **St Boniface**, missionary to the Saxons, who lit the first Christmas tree. Boniface, born in Devon and christened Wynfrith, is better remembered in Germany than in his homeland. He was forty when he set out on his missionary journey to the Saxons, never to return home. He tried to adapt the Christian faith to local culture but opposed idolatry and especially the worship of trees.

The first Christmas tree

The villagers of Bortharia had been suffering from storms and plague. They decided that they must try to appease the god Odin by offering him a human sacrifice. Led by their chief, they assembled in the forest clearing at midnight. The priest tied the boy – the chosen victim – to the sacred oak and prepared to slaughter him.

At that moment, the breathless silence was broken by a shout. The dark-clad figures of Christian monks loomed out of the darkness and their leader, Boniface, called out, 'Stop, in the name of Jesus Christ!'

The villagers were terrified. What new punishments would their god inflict on them for such blasphemy? But Boniface told them, 'If Odin is really god, he can defend himself and prove his power. Let the boy go!'

There was no sign from Odin– no thunderbolt hurled at the Christian monk. The boy was untied and Boniface began to tell the Bortharians the good news of God's love made known in Jesus.

Then he offered them a young fir tree in place of the oak, planting it and placing a candle on it. His companions added their candles and the fir tree shone out in the dark forest, a symbol of God's ever-burning love and of the light that has come into the world through Jesus, his Son.

The church is like a great ship pounded by the waves of life's various stresses. Our job is not to abandon the ship, but to keep it on its course. – St Boniface

The carol *Silent Night* was first sung on Christmas Eve 1818. Sadly, **Joseph Mohr**, who wrote the words, died in poverty and distress, never knowing that his carol had become famous, widely loved and sung in many countries in the world.

Silent night

It was Christmas Eve in the little Austrian village of Oberndorf and that night the church would be full for the customary midnight service. But there would be no music from the organ. The constant dampness from the river nearby had finally made it impossible for Franz Gruber, the organist, to squeeze a single note from it. But the assistant vicar, Joseph Mohr, decided to provide some item that would make the service special in spite of the lack of organ accompaniment. Sitting down, he quickly wrote a new carol, then sent it across to Gruber, so that he could compose a tune to fit the words. Together they would sing the new carol to the Christmas congregation, accompanied by a guitar.

The carol was greatly appreciated and there the story might have ended. Christmas came and went and an organ builder arrived to mend the organ. Either Herr Gruber showed him the carol or else he may have come cross the sheet of music in the course of his work. He played it over and took a great liking to it.

Wherever he went he played the carol and in time two strolling families of singers learned it and added it to their repertoire. One group travelled to the United States and played and sang it there. The other sang it before the King of Prussia.

Soon *Silent Night* became known far and wide. It was translated into many languages and today, almost two hundred years later, it will be sung again in churches, town centres, schools and homes in countries all over the world.

25 December

Christmas Day. In December 1999 the church of St Martins-in-the-Fields in London unveiled a sculpture in Trafalgar Square, to celebrate Christmas and the new millennium.

The Word made flesh

The small children from a school in Soho arrived in Trafalgar Square and began to undo the wrappings that shrouded the huge block of Portland stone. The onlookers saw first a tiny leg, then the whole form of a baby. It was life-size, but looked tiny against the plinth of stone on which it rested. It was new-born; the umbilical cord still buried deep in the surrounding block of stone. Its smooth lines contrasted with the roughened plinth, set at a slight slope so that the baby looked frighteningly vulnerable. The children were lifted up so that they could reach the sculpture and touch the smooth, gentle lines of the baby and see his small frown of puzzlement and the little fist held near his mouth.

Usually the clergy and people of St Martin's-in-the-Fields celebrate Christmas by placing a crib and manger scene in nearby Trafalgar Square, telling the Christmas story through the eyes of St Luke and St Matthew. But for Christmas 1999 and the millennium, they chose to depict the wonder of the incarnation through St John's account. Portland stone, of which the sculpture is made, has also been used for the church, the National Gallery and other buildings surrounding the Square. This stone is some 135 million years old, symbolising, in the sculpture, the eternal Word, the Son of God eternally existent. Set against that power and agelessness is the form of the fragile, helpless new born baby. The eternal God has taken on our humanity and come to earth not as a strong man or a glorious prince, but as a tiny, helpless baby.

Mike Chapman, the sculptor, said: 'I am not a churchgoing person, but when I was working on this piece I felt drawn in. If God really did become incarnate … that would be amazing.'

The Word became a human being and lived among us. – John 1

26 December

26 December is the Feast Day of **St Stephen**, the first Christian martyr.

'Forgive them!'

There was an angry muttering and growing indignation in the court-room. Then the voice of the prisoner, Stephen, rang out clearly:

'Look!' he cried, 'I can see the heavens open and there is Jesus Christ – standing at God's right hand!'

His accusers shouted out in horror. How dare he say such things about that impostor they had handed over to the Romans for crucifixion!

Those nearest to him seized Stephen and manhandled him out of the court and into the street. The rest followed and they half-carried their prisoner along with them until they were outside Jerusalem's sacred walls. Then they threw him down and the first eager councillor picked up a boulder and hurled it at the defenceless man. It caught him a glancing blow and he staggered, but kept his footing.

Cloaks were hurriedly loosened and stacked beside young Saul, leaving the men free for action. They picked up the boulders and stones strewn by the roadside and threw them full force at Stephen. Half-stunned, he sank to his knees, blood streaming down his face.

'Lord Jesus,' he cried out, 'receive my spirit!' then he sprawled full-length on the dusty ground. He spoke once more: 'Lord,' he prayed, 'forgive them this sin.'

It was all over. Their hatred and energy spent, the men turned away from their dead victim and picked up their cloaks. But one of them remembered hearing words like Stephen's only a few months before. He had been at Jesus' crucifixion and heard his dying words: 'Father, forgive them, they don't know what they are doing.' And Jesus was the one that Stephen claimed was now gloriously alive.

(Source: *Acts 6-7*)

27 December

Louis Pasteur was born in France on 27 December 1822. Until he was eighteen, Pasteur planned to be an artist. Then he turned to science, first physics and chemistry, then crystallography. He made startling discoveries in this field by the time he was twenty-five. He became a professor at Lille University, where he was expected to apply science to local industrial problems. Experiments in fermentation led to the discovery that living organisms are the cause of disease and decay. Pasteurisation of milk (partial sterilisation to destroy bacteria) was one result of his experiments. A deep faith in God lay behind Pasteur's whole life as a man and scientist.

Something nasty in the beet juice

Monsieur Bigo was a very worried man. He made his living in Lille by producing alcohol from beet juice. He was applying the yeast, as usual, to convert the juice to alcohol, but for some unknown reason the juice refused to be converted. He hurried along to the new professor for help.

Pasteur knew nothing at all about fermentation, but he went along to Monsieur Bigo's factory and took samples of the reluctant juice back to his laboratory to examine under the microscope. He discovered that in addition to the small globules of yeast, other small particles were present in the juice. He suspected that these particles were the cause of the trouble.

Up to this time scientists had believed that yeast was merely a catalyst – that is, a substance that by its presence somehow made fermentation occur spontaneously. Pasteur recognised that the yeast was in fact a living organism. Somehow, the foreign bodies – also living organisms – were inhibiting the fermentation process.

Pasteur proved his point to a sceptical scientific public by demonstrating that once air was excluded and scrupulously clean containers used, fermentation was successful. A happy Monsieur Bigo had only to exclude the foreign bodies and his beet juice would ferment once more and his business thrive.

Louis Pasteur said: 'There are two opposing laws – one, a law of blood and death, forces nations always to be ready for battle. The other, a law of peace, work and health, whose only aim is to deliver man from calamities. The one places a single life above all victories, the other sacrifices hundreds of thousands of lives to the ambition of a single individual.'

Mad dogs – and Joseph Meister

The year was 1940 and Joseph Meister, gatekeeper at the Pasteur Institute in Paris, was ordered by German invaders to open Louis Pasteur's burial crypt. Rather than obey, he committed suicide.

He had good cause to be fiercely loyal to Pasteur. Fifty-five years earlier, he had been bitten on his hands, legs and thighs by a mad dog. His case was hopeless; he would die a horrific and terrifying death, though it might be a few months before the first signs of hydrophobia appeared. There was only one person who might be able to save him – and he was not a doctor.

Louis Pasteur had been experimenting with his theory of inoculation against rabies, through giving repeated doses of vaccine taken from a rabid dog. So far he had experimented only on other animals, but always with success. He did not dare to risk his vaccine on a human being yet. But friends and relatives of Meister begged Pasteur to help him. He had been so severely bitten that he was certain to contract the disease, so there was nothing to lose.

After much mental anguish Pasteur agreed to inoculate Meister. Sixty hours after the accident he had the first, weak dose of vaccine. Twelve more followed, each stronger than the one before. At the end of the course, the patient showed no sign of the disease and returned home, healthy – and full of gratitude to Pasteur.

The case made history. Only fifteen months later, 2,490 people had received the life-saving anti-rabies vaccine.

29 December

Christina Rossetti, poet, died on 29 December 1894.

'Give me the lowest place'

'I'm so sorry, William, that I never gave you the paint box I promised you when you were a child. And I have to confess that once, when you told me not to see anyone, I had Charles to lunch.'

The words were spoken in a low voice as Christina lay, weak and dying, in the stuffy bedroom of her London house. When the windows were open, the sound of three different barrel organs competed in the square outside. She was very weak by now and even shook her head when her brother William suggested bringing her beloved cat, Muff, to sit on the bed.

Christina was not melancholy by nature but deeply passionate. She was also wholly committed to her Christian faith and believed it necessary but painful to repress her strong emotions and reject human love and success which might threaten Christian humility and self-control. Victorian concepts of religion and a woman's role made her strive always to try to take the lowest place.

But her poetry is not all grey and desolate, much of it is vibrant with life and joy. At Christmas we sing her beautiful carol, *In the bleak midwinter* and remember her too in the joyful *Love came down at Christmas*.

Open wide the windows of our spirits and fill us full of light; open wide the door of our hearts, that we may receive and entertain Thee with all our powers of adoration. Amen. – Christina Rossetti 1830-1894

Angela Burdett-Coutts died on 30 December 1904, aged 92.
Baroness Burdett-Coutts, one of the richest women in Victorian
England, had inherited the fortune of her grandfather, the founder
of Coutts bank. She was a kind and gentle woman, using her
wealth to set up and support many good causes. Charles Dickens
described her as a 'most excellent creature.'

'A most excellent creature'

Tourists to Edinburgh usually stop to look at Greyfriars Bobby,
the sculpture on Candlemaker Row of a faithful dog who
would not leave his master's grave. The sculpture was
commissioned by Angela Burdett-Coutts, who was a leading
light in the RSPCA.

Two years before, she had commissioned a bronze
likeness of her own much-loved terrier, Little Fan. At first the
sculpture was proudly exhibited at the Royal Academy, but
later disappeared completely. It was finally discovered in use
as a doorstop at Wright's butcher's shop in York. In the 1950s
it was presented to one of the assistants in Wright's as a token
of gratitude for her hard work and later fetched thousands of
pounds at auction.

Angela Burdett-Coutts set up a home for 'fallen women',
endowed churches, and built homes for the poor. In spite of
all Charles Dickens could say to dissuade her, she showed great
kindness to David Livingstone and his family, buying the most
modern microscope available to help the missionary explorer
in his work and showering his wife Mary with boxes and gifts
to take back to Africa.

Miss Burdett-Coutts was given a peerage in 1871 and the
next year she became the first woman to receive the freedom
of the City of London. When she married, at the age of sixty-
seven, her husband took *her* name.

'Life whether in man or beast is sacred.' – Angela Burdett-Coutts

31 December

Ring out the old ...

At the end of the last century and millennium, many people crowded round the television set, watching the face of Big Ben and joining in the countdown to midnight. Then, with awe-inspiring grandeur – and slightly off-key – the chimes of Big Ben boomed out, ushering out the old and welcoming the new.

It was 1859 when Big Ben was installed in St Stephen's Tower at the north end of the Houses of Parliament. The massive bell weighs more than thirteen tons and it took a wagon with a team of sixteen horses to transport it from Whitechapel, where it was cast. The bell – and later the clock too – was probably called Ben after Sir Benjamin Hall, Commissioner of Works at the time.

Ever since 1924, the chimes of Big Ben have been broadcast by the BBC as part of their daily time signal. Grandly and a little pompously, Big Ben reminds us of the passing of time every day, not only at the year's end.

> Ring out the old, ring in the new,
> Ring, happy bells, across the snow:
> The year is going, let him go;
> Ring out the false, ring in the true.
>
> Ring in the valiant man and free,
> The larger heart, the kindlier hand;
> Ring out the darkness of the land,
> Ring in the Christ that is to be.

(From *In Memoriam* by Alfred Lord Tennyson 1809-92)

'Where will God's way lead us now? But HE himself stands always at the end of the road' – Ludwig Steil, German pastor who was arrested and died in Dachau in 1945

Proper names and entries

Index

Index

Entries listed by century

Biblical characters indicated by ‡

Index

TILL THE FAT LADY SINGS

BOB JACKSON

An outrageous mixture of

Barchester and Ambridge!

St Agatha's is a welcoming, middle-of-the-road parish church in the centre of a town called Yawtown. The Revd Vincent Popplethwaite is a pretty unassuming sort of a vicar – he only wishes that everyone would stop considering clergy as a breed apart.

Bob Jackson has written a brilliantly satirical, at times risqué and yet affectionate novel which tells how the good people of St Agatha's confront and come to terms with some of the greater (and lesser) issues which insistently lap at the shores of today's church.

Meanwhile, beyond human agencies, there are signs that the Holy Spirit is accelerating his work – not to mention the Grim Reaper.

ISBN 1 897913 29 X

Highland Books   Price £4.99

Shut Up Sarah
Marion Field

Was she privileged? Sarah was born into the Taylorites, the most exclusive of those Brethren who look to J N Darby as founder. You may have seen them:

- Women with scarves who stick together
- Schoolchildren who never accept invitations
- Groups of men declaiming the Bible in a shopping street

This true story of a teenage daughter refusing to be browbeaten by either family or elders will be compulsive reading for mature teenagers struggling between loyalty and the need of change—as well as for any who want to understand how certain Brethren could have lost their way.

'I highly recommend this book ... This gifted writer in her second book has written a true story in a compelling fictional style.'
Jennifer Rees-Larcombe

ISBN 1-897913-28-1

Highland Books   Price £5.99

A Window To Heaven

Dr Diane M. Komp

What would you do as a hospital doctor when children facing death—or their parents—witness to you about faith? The official line is not to get involved, to stay 'professional'. But that was not Dr Komp's reaction …

'I have met people who claim they lost their faith over the agonising question, How can a loving God let innocent children die? Dr Komp is the first person I've met who found a personal faith while treating such dying children. Her story —and theirs— deserves our attention'.
Philip Yancey
Author of *Disappointment with God*

'Unforgettably inspiring'
Sandy Millar, Holy Trinity Brompton

'Out of harrowing experiences while looking after children with cancer, Diane Komp, a paediatric oncologist of international repute, draws conclusions about the human condition that should make us pause and think …
I read it with a lump in my throat.'
J.S. Malpas D.Phil., FRCP, FRCR, FFPM
St Bartholomew's Hospital, London
ISBN 1-897913-32-X
Highland Books   Price £3.99

THE STRENGTH OF A MAN

DAVID ROPER

This book is for men who are hungry for spiritual growth; it will strike a particular chord with those who find it natural to signal their masculinity either positively (all-male sports, perhaps) or by what they don't do (maybe ironing or dancing).

It contains 50 short (max. 4 pages!), sharply-observed jottings on a wide range of topics which men have always thought about — and usually prefer to keep to themselves.

The author, a former pastor, now leads a ministry which supports pastoral couples in America.

'David Roper knows and understands men. He is also well acquainted with the One whom he calls the manliest man of all'
Stuart Briscoe

'Translates God's word into everyday living'
Rod Redhead, Maranatha Ministries

ISBN 1 897913 34 6

Highland Books   Price £6.99

REBUILDING YOUR BROKEN WORLD

GORDON MACDONALD

'Broken worlds' are failures tinged with a measure of guilt. As the author says 'there are far more broken worlds out there than anyone realises or admits.' Platitudes about learning from our mistakes are not enough; we need spiritual power to answer and then to get free from the key questions: *'How could I?'* and *'Can I avoid doing it again?'*

THE BOOK THAT HELPED PRESIDENT CLINTON DEAL IN PRIVATE WITH THE LEWINSKY SCANDAL.

'One of the most significant books of all time'
George Verwer

ISBN 0 946616 49 3

Highland Books   Price £4.50